STORIES, VISIONS AND VALUES IN VOLUNTARY ORGANISATIONS

Corporate Social Responsibility Series

Series Editor:
Professor David Crowther, De Montfort University, UK

This series aims to provide high quality research books on all aspects of corporate social responsibility including: business ethics, corporate governance and accountability, globalization, civil protests, regulation, responsible marketing and social reporting.

The series is interdisciplinary in scope and global in application and is an essential forum for everyone with an interest in this area.

Also in the series

Whistleblowing and Organizational Social Responsibility:
A Global Assessment
Wim Vandekerckhove
ISBN 0 7546 4740 1

Repoliticizing Management: A Theory of Corporate Legitimacy
Conor Cradden
ISBN 0 7546 4497 9

Making Ecopreneurs: Developing Sustainable Entrepreneurship
Edited by Michael Schaper
ISBN 0 7546 4491 X

Corporate Social Responsibility in the Mining Industries
Natalia Yakovleva
ISBN 0 7546 4268 2

Ethical Boundaries of Capitalism
Edited by Daniel Daianu and Radu Vranceanu
ISBN 0 7546 4395 6

Human Values in Management
Edited by Ananda Das Gupta
ISBN 0 7546 4275 5

Nonprofit Trusteeship in Different Contexts
Rikki Abzug and Jeffrey S. Simonoff
ISBN 0 7546 3016 1

Stories, Visions and Values in Voluntary Organisations

CHRISTINA SCHWABENLAND
London Metropolitan University, UK

Routledge
Taylor & Francis Group

LONDON AND NEW YORK

First published in paperback 2024

First published 2006 by Ashgate Publishing

Published 2016 by Routledge
4 Park Square, Milton Park, Abingdon, Oxon OX14 4RN

and by Routledge
605 Third Avenue, New York, NY 10158

Routledge is an imprint of the Taylor & Francis Group, an informa business

British Library Cataloguing in Publication Data
Schwabenland, Christina
    Stories, visions and values in voluntary organisations. -
    (Corporate social responsibility series)
    1.Non-profit organizations - Great Britain 2.Non-profit
    organizations - India 3.Non-profit organizations - Great
    Britain - Management 4.Non-profit organizations - India -
    Management 5.Voluntarism - Cross-cultural studies 6.Social
    change - Cross-cultural studies 7.Great Britain - Social
    conditions - 1945- 8.India - Social conditions - 1947-
    I.Title
    361.7'63

Library of Congress Cataloging-in-Publication Data
Schwabenland, Christina.
    Stories, visions, and values in voluntary organisations / by Christina
    Schwabenland.
        p. cm. -- (Corporate social responsibility series)
    Includes index.
    ISBN-13: 978-0-7546-4462-0
    ISBN-10: 0-7546-4462-6
    1. Social change--Great Britain. 2. Social change--India. 3. Associations,
institutions, etc.--Great Britain. 4. Associations, institutions, etc.--India.
I. Title. II. Title: Stories, visions, and values in voluntary organizations.

  HN385.5.S38 2006
  303.40941--dc22

2006018457

ISBN: 978-0-7546-4462-0 (hbk)
ISBN: 978-1-03-283771-0 (pbk)
ISBN: 978-1-315-61085-6 (ebk)

DOI: 10.4324/9781315610856

Contents

Acknowledgements

This book has been in gestation for many years and there are many people who have contributed enormously to its creation. First and foremost are the people who I interviewed, from voluntary organisations in the UK and in India; chief executives, trustees, workers, volunteers, beneficiaries. Their stories were inspiring and also humbling. I hope that I have done some justice to the extraordinary passion, sacrifice and commitment that these people bring to their work.

I owe an enormous debt of gratitude to Mike Locke, from the Centre for Institutional Studies at the University of East London. Mike is a gifted supervisor and has read and commented (usually trenchantly) on many drafts and redrafts.

I also want to thank Rajesh Tandon and the staff at PRIA for support, advice and their excellent library in New Delhi. Anil Singh and the staff at VANI were also enormously helpful in providing contacts and information about the voluntary sector in India.

S. K. Chakroborty, from the Institute of Human Values at the Indian Institute of Management in Kolkata and Gouranga Chattopadhyay, formerly of the IIM also gave important advice.

I also want to thank staff and members of the Elfrida Society in London and KeyRing Living Support Networks. Richard Gutch and Dorothy Dalton from ACEVO also provided important support at an early stage.

Richard Kay's work on the use of metaphors by chief executives of voluntary organisations was an early inspiration, as were our discussions over lunch. Colin Quine, from the Grubb Institute, also gave me many helpful comments and advice.

My trips to India would have been much less pleasant without the extraordinary hospitality of my very good friend Urmilla Lanba and her family.

Finally, a project such as this takes its toll on those who least deserve it. Many thanks and love to Doug – and of course also to Abelard and Heloise who covered many a draft with cat hairs.

Earlier drafts of some of these chapters have been published in the following:

'Founders utopias and dystopias: the paradox of complicity' in the *Proceedings of the Sixth Conference of the International Society for Third Sector Research: Contesting Citizenship and Civil Society in a Divided World,* 11-14 July, Toronto available on <http://www.istr.org/conferences/toronto/working papers/index.htttml>

'Leaders' founding stories as creation myths' in Boje, D., Brewis, J., Linstead, S and O'Shea, A. (eds.) (2006) *The Passion of Organizing* (Malmo: Liber/ Copenhagen Business School Press).

'Stories, mythmaking and the consolation of success' in Satterthwaite, J., Martin, W. and Roberts, J. (eds.) (2006) *Discourse, Resistance and Identity Formation* (London: Trentham).

Chapter 1

A Genuine Voluntary Organisation ... Setting the Scene

This is the federation of primary fish marketing societies of fishermen, in this district. The primary societies were organised throughout the 70s and early 80s by another voluntary organisation, a genuine voluntary organisation of a group of social workers who were working with fishermen. So they had organised these fish marketing societies to help fishermen get out of the clutches of middlemen and money lenders, to control their own marketing and credit.[1]

Introduction

This is a story about the founding of a voluntary organisation in Southern India. It encompasses, in three fairly brief sentences, the key themes of this book: the contribution of voluntary organisations to social change, the use of stories told by participants to explore their different visions of the good society, and the ways people create organisations to achieve these visions.

This book is about voluntary organisations and social change, and in particular the work they do to empower people marginalised by the structures and institutions of society. The book uses stories, the stories that are told by people who create organisations, work in them and use their services to shed light not only on what they think about organisations but how they think about them. The stories come from people working and living in two countries, the UK and India, that each have a long tradition of voluntary organisational activity but also very interesting differences in the ways in which this contribution is understood. The stories reveal the ways in which people imagine a more just society, how those images inspire people working within voluntary organisations and the values they bring to management and leadership.

For the purposes of this book I am using the term 'voluntary organisation' to refer to organisations that are formally constituted, independent of government,

---

1   From an interview between the author and the chief executive officer of a voluntary organisation in Southern India. All quotes from my interviews are italicised throughout the book. I have generally kept the names of the organisations and the people being interviewed confidential except in instances where I am discussing the significance of the name of the organisation and in all such cases I have received permission from the interviewee.

governed by a voluntary board, not profit making – with any surpluses re-invested in the organisation rather than distributed to shareholders – and established for the fulfilment of some social or community good.[2]

I have organised this book into two sections. The first section explores social change in the wider society that voluntary organisations seek to influence. It explores the ways in which their visions of a better society are manifested and concentrates on the themes of why and how organisations are founded, their role in empowering people on the margins of society and how their work affects the social landscape. The second section looks at how organisations develop value based management practices that pose alternatives to the hegemonic discourse about good management, particularly in the areas of creativity and innovation, participatory leadership and governance and organisational change. The chapters in the two sections complement each other, in the manner of a dialogue, and can be seen as a conversation between the outer and inner experiences of organising and between the organisation and its environment. My proposition is that leading and managing vision(s) requires attending to the values that are inherent in their chosen ways of working.

In this chapter I introduce these key themes and their importance to managers, researchers, policy makers, users and members – in short, to anyone who aspires to creatie a more just society.

Firstly, I want to provide some personal background in order to explain how I have chosen to position the book in terms of its theoretical orientation towards a social constructionist perspective. My reasons for pursuing the research that led to this book were initially self interested. I have worked in voluntary organisations for over 30 years, occupying a number of roles including volunteer, paid volunteer organiser, development worker, manager, chief executive and currently, researcher and trustee.

When I began to venture into the academic world, initially as a postgraduate student, I was looking for ways of making sense of the some of the experiences I had had in those roles and particularly those that hadn't been addressed by the various management training courses I had attended. These courses did very little to explain,

---

2   I have borrowed these criteria from the report of the Commission on the Future of the Voluntary Sector, *Meeting the Challenge of Change: Voluntary Action in the 21st Century*, published by the National Council of Voluntary Organisations (NCVO) in 1996 which contains a good introduction to the issues involved in creating a set of generally agreed criteria for voluntary organisations. The collectivity of voluntary organisations is usually called the voluntary sector – here again language is contested. Other common terms include third sector (the corporate sector being the first and the public sector the second), civil society organisations, the non-profit sector, social enterprise, voluntary and community sector, or VCS. Debates rage as to whether these terms are synonymous or whether they demarcate specific families, or subsets of organisations. For simplicity I will be referring the all of these organisations as voluntary organisations because a defining feature is the voluntary impulse of concerned individuals that leads to their inception. However, in discussions about organisations working at an international level I will also use the term NGO (non governmental organisation) as this is more common usage.

to me anyway, how things really happen in organisations. They didn't provide ways of understanding some things that are commonly encountered in voluntary organisations such as the potential for people to reinvent themselves through volunteering, the passionate belief in social justice that motivates so many people working in the sector, the conflicting expectations of managers, the importance of organisational culture. Neither did all of they relate to my own perceptions of organisational life as messy, complicated and confusing, but also full of passion and excitement.

I began pursuing a literature about organisations from a very different paradigm from either the functional orientation that underpins most traditional courses for managers, or the primarily political focus of all lot of writing about voluntary organisations. The books and articles that interested me were (and still are) a fairly eclectic mix but all were written from a different perspective than that of the rational, functional and scientific paradigm. These alternative approaches were variously described by such names as hermeneutics, social constructionism, symbolic interactionism, critical theory or postmodernism.

The debates about whether these approaches are overlapping or distinct are interesting but beyond my current remit.[3] For the readers of this book I am only going to sketch some of the shared underlying assumptions and explain why I think they are particularly relevant to voluntary organisations.

Firstly, these approaches all share a belief that reality, or anything that we can know as reality, is constructed rather than given and that our understanding of it is created not discovered. Therefore, methods appropriated from scientific research are inadequate for the world of human affairs. The search for different methods has drawn organisation theorists into alternative theoretical worlds such as hermeneutics (originally a methodology of religious exegesis; the study of the interpretation of sacred texts) and anthropology (as applied to the study of organisational culture) to name but a few.

Interest in the interpretive, or hermeneutic tradition in particular owes much to the growth of Romanticism (expressed by philosophers such as Hegel, Schleiermacher, Dilthey and Husserl) as a reaction against the rationalism of the Enlightenment with its emphasis on the material world (Burrell and Morgan 1979). The French philosopher Paul Ricoeur has suggested that hermeneutics can be seen as a metaphor for the social sciences (Ricoeur 1992b). The application of postmodern theory to organisation studies can similarly be understood as a response to the limitations of the scientific and 'modernist' approach to management (Linstead 2004, Usher 1996).

All share a belief in the centrality of language. Gadamer, another hermeneutic philosopher states that 'the role of language assumes ontological status...language is more than a system of symbols for labelling the external world, it becomes an expression of the human mode of "being in the world" '(Gadamer cited by Burrell and Morgan, 1979). Social constructionists are particularly interested in the social,

---

3   For more on these debates see Crowther and Green 2004, Usher 1996.

or relational aspect of reality creation; critical theorists are more interested in the role of power and ask questions about whose interpretations matter and whose voices are heard.

The task of interpretation involves looking at the means by which reality is created through such mediatory devices as story, metaphor and symbol and to:

> ...reconstruct the ways in which human beings go about this interpreting...a task which involves *direct intuition* as the source and final test of all knowledge and *insight* into essential structures derived from such intuition. (Speigelberg cited in Morris 1977, 10 italics in the original)

Throughout this book I draw heavily on these and similar theorists. I have been particularly influenced by the work of Paul Ricoeur, the French hermeneutic philosopher. In each chapter there is a brief discussion of particular writers that I have found helpful to the topic under discussion; for examples the debate between Scott and Stone-Mediatore (2003) on the reliability of the stories that people tell about their own experiences, the ideas of Ricoeur and Nandy on utopian thinking and the visions of a better society that inspire founders of voluntary organisations and Burrell and Morgan's paradigms of social change. These emphases on imagination and creativity and the rejection of the certainties of the scientific approach to management were what attracted me. They offered a way of understanding those aspects of organisational experience that are not so amenable to functional or rational explanations. These theoretical approaches also seemed to me to be particularly relevant to understanding *voluntary* organisations.

Firstly, the suggestion that reality is created rather than discovered implies that there are many realities rather than one. This belief resonates with the plurality of beliefs and perspectives that are inherent in the voluntary sector,[4] the collectivity of voluntary organisations, comprising as it does, organisations founded by people from all walks of life and possessing all manner of competing and contradictory beliefs. The 'rejection of the grand narrative' (of an absolute and universal knowledge (Usher 1996)), that underpins these various schools of thought, is therefore particularly apposite.

Secondly, the search for non-rational explanations of organisational phenomena makes particular sense in organisations that are populated by people motivated by a passion for social justice (however they may define it).

Thirdly, the emphasis of the critical school on issues of power and emancipation is enormously relevant to organisations that work amongst the most marginalised people in society. Similarly relevant are writers from feminist and postcolonial perspectives because their interest is in the uses and abuses of power as experienced

---

4   The phrase 'voluntary sector' is also somewhat problematic as there are a number of complicated debates about its usage. These primarily comprise debates about which organisations are included or excluded and debates about whether there are subdivisions (such as community organisations or peoples' organisations). These issues are developed in more detail in Chapter 5.

by people who are historically located in disadvantaged positions.

Yet despite the obvious relevance of these schools to voluntary organisations I have found very little research that utilises their overlapping theoretical approaches.[5] The majority of theorising of voluntary organisations seems to be primarily developed from a modernist perspective and to be mainly concerned with their role in the political environment.

Meanwhile, although there is a substantial literature that applies constructionist perspectives to organisations generally very little has focussed on *voluntary* organisations. This is also surprising given the significance of voluntary organisations to our notions of the good society and the emancipatory interests of the critical school (Perriton and Reynolds 2004).

Voluntary organisations make concrete our changing views about moral and ethical behaviour. They have been a significant part of our social landscape for a very long time. They are amongst the oldest existing institutions, predating the establishment of the public sector.[6] As fashions and ideas change so new forms of organisations come into existence whether they be philanthropic, charitable, mutual aid or self help organisations, user or member controlled – these all represent different ways of coming to terms with the questions of suffering and inequality and with different ideas about the most ethical answers. These organisations can be seen as occupying a social space in which societies and cultures construct questions about the good society and test out new and evolving responses. This space is contested and fought over and its boundaries are endlessly debated. Issues about which organisations, or families of organisations are included in the sector (sports clubs? trade unions? hospitals? pressure groups?) have always been a feature of voluntary organisation research and are inherently incapable of resolution.

Interest in voluntary organisations is growing, and arguably, so are their importance.[7] Voluntary organisations occupy an increasingly prominent role in policy discourse in the US and the UK and a significant place in international economic and

---

5   A notable exception is Harris's (1998) study of the management of faith based organisations.

6   The report of the Commission on the Future of the Voluntary Sector, *Meeting the Challenge of Change: Voluntary Action in the 21st Century,* published in the UK by the National Council of Voluntary Organisations (NCVO) comments that organised voluntary activity 'predates the appearance of the state...equally they are wholly different from market exchanges, in not being embarked upon for financial profit' (15). The earliest legislation in the UK regarding the regulation of charities dates from 1601.

7   For example, Paul Boateng, the then UK Minister for the Home Office: 'The Government is passionately committed to the work of the voluntary sector. We believe that voluntary and community sector organisations have a crucial role to play in the reform of public services and reinvigoration of civic life.' Introduction to The Role of the Voluntary and Community Sector in Service Delivery: A Cross Cutting Review, published by the Treasury and the Home Office in September, 2002.

trade policy.[8] They are being courted and their expertise enlisted in the service of the private sector (in pursuit of its corporate social responsibility agenda), the public sector (in search of organisations to take up the role of service provider) and policy makers (in search of solutions to such perceived social ills as urban decay, decline of civic responsibility and neighbourliness).

The expectations of voluntary organisations are, therefore, tremendously high. The phenomenon of people coming together voluntarily to create institutional arrangements to alleviate some social ill is immensely potent. This phenomenon is variously seen as the guarantor of democratic society, the means to include the excluded by increasing participation from marginalised groups, the way to restore or preserve our sense of communality with others, the best hope for the regeneration of deprived and despairing neighbourhoods and the enemy of corrupt and self serving government.[9]

For all these reasons voluntary organisations should be of great interest to people working within the social constructionist paradigm. Similarly, managers and researchers of voluntary organisations may find that exploring the role of organisations in the ongoing processes of reality creation may offer important insights into some of the critical issues they are currently facing.

One such critical issue is that with the increasing attention come increased risks and challenges including the risk of co-option by the state. People working in voluntary organisations are not immune to flattery. Many believe that change can be more effectively, if less dramatically achieved by working alongside policy makers, and through persuasion rather than opposition. Furthermore, the sense of involvement that comes from trying to change from 'within' rather than from 'without' is immensely seductive. Many organisations are engaged in a walking a tightrope between collusion and challenge. Where to position itself along this continuum is a decision for each organisation – and many find it very difficult to get that balance right. In a recent survey of UK organisations 'the proportion that wish to achieve an even balance between the roles (of campaigning and service providing)

---

8   At the Fifth World Trade Organisation Ministerial Conference in Cancun in September, 2003, where talks collapsed because of the 'failure of the WTO to reflect the concerns of the developing and least developed countries' (Arun Jaitely, Indian Trade Minister, *The Hindu* cited in <http://worldbank.org>) there were arrangements for approximately 3,000 accredited NGO representatives (www.ictsd.org).

9   These different roles and expectations underpin many UK government policy initiatives such as the National Strategy for Neighbourhood Renewal, the New Deal for Communities and the Treasury Cross Cutting Review into the Role of the Voluntary and Community Sector in Service Provision. The contribution of voluntary associations to civic renewal and 'social capital' finds many proponents, most notably Robert Putnam in *Making Democracy Work* (1993) and *Bowling Alone* (2000). Establishing how this relationship works and the mechanics by which greater participation in voluntary associations contributes to building social capital is a significant focus of much current and recent research, one recent example would be Leonard and Onyx (2003).

is twice the number that say they have already achieved this balance'.[10] However, as a prominent voluntary sector activist has commented, 'I never mistake access for influence'.[11]

For all of these reasons it is increasingly important that we are able to address the critical question of how voluntary organisations contribute to social change. We also need to ask whether their role is intrinsically distinct to that of public or private organisations. I refer back to the quote that opened this chapter:

> *The primary societies were organised... by another voluntary organisation, a genuine voluntary organisation....*

This reference to a 'genuine' voluntary organisation does imply some notion of distinctiveness but if there are defining features that distinguish voluntary organisations from other kinds of organisations what are they? And does it matter? All organisations contribute to social change in some way or another. Do we need the voluntary organisations to play a distinct role?

Many who do regard their role as distinctive also see that distinctiveness as under threat (Rosenman 2000). As voluntary organisations take on more of the roles and responsibilities of the state do they lose their distinctiveness? As social enterprises in the UK and micro-credit and self help initiatives in India create new forms of income generation are they in effect simply small businesses?

> *...they had organised these fish marketing societies to help fishermen get out of the clutches of middlemen and money lenders...*

Pursuing these questions about social change also requires us to engage with the issues of power and resistance. How are the relative states of power and powerlessness experienced by people in marginalised positions? How do people want to take up power and how do they resist its imposition by others?

> *... to control their own marketing and credit.*

Furthermore, when increasing global connections (in the corporate, the public *and* the voluntary sectors) seem to be fuelling a drive towards conformity to some hegemonic notion of one best way of managing does the plurality and diversity represented by the voluntary sector hold intrinsic worth?

---

10 Gribben, C., Robb C. and Wilding, K (2002) *The Third Sector: vision for the future* (London: NCVO). London. This is a report of a survey carried out by the National Council of Voluntary Organisations (UK) in collaboration with the Ashridge Centre for Business and Society. The survey included 250 UK based voluntary organisations and looked specifically at the balance between service delivery and campaigning. 'Nearly two-thirds described themselves as 'exclusively' or 'predominantly' service providers but only a quarter believed that this was the ideal balance.' (Gribben et al 2002, 3).

11 In a personal conversation with the author.

A further question that lies at the heart of any discussion about social change is that although voluntary organisations are set up to improve some situation or social condition, the increasing awareness that results from its work, perhaps even simply from its creation can lead to a sense that the original problem is actually getting worse rather than going away. If we live in societies where inequality is growing then what implications does that have for the judgements we make about the effectiveness of voluntary organisations?

The increasing centrality of voluntary organisations has brought increasing attention to this question of effectiveness. Funders want to know that their money is being well spent, that organisations can deliver what they promise. These demands seem wholly reasonable, after all why shouldn't organisations say what they do with the money they receive (much of which is donated by members of the public) and how they make a difference. But the tasks of measuring and accounting for empowerment and social change are not straightforward (Ebrahim 2005, Paton 2003).

Therefore we need to know more about how voluntary organisations contribute to social change and we also need new methods for pursuing these questions. The central proposition of this book is that exploring the ways in which reality and meaning are created within organisations offers new and important insights. The particular methodology I have pursued is the interpretation of organisational stories and storytelling

We make sense of our experience through telling stories, to ourselves and to others. Through stories we give our day-to-day events shape and form. We dramatise some, play down others. We give starring roles to certain characters and others only bit parts. We make choices about what to put in and what to leave out. We think in stories, we tell our lives to others as stories. As we tell our stories our experiences take shape and meaning.

It follows then that stories are a rich source of information about how people perceive and make sense of their lives in organisation and indeed there is a growing literature on storytelling in organisations. And, of course, there are dialogues, disagreements and profound differences of views about what actually constitutes a story in an organisational setting (Gabriel 2000), how such stories should be studied (Boje 2001) or even whether they should be (Hosking 2004). Some of the key questions raised by these debates are summarised later in this chapter.

Feminist and postcolonial scholarship are also areas where academics have engaged in the importance of such stories. Stories make audible the voices of the silent and bring multiple perspectives to bear. Through this focus on quiet, less audible voices (and by 'voices' I am referring to the whole range of ways in which people represent themselves and others) feminists, postcolonial theorists and critical management scholars share some common ground. Spivak comments that fiction, the 'singular and the unverifiable 'is a useful 'training ground' (Spivak 2003, 333) for understanding the experiences of society's 'subalterns'. Postcolonial theory, with its critical engagement with the problematics of identity, representation and plurality, provides a relevant and useful frame for evaluating the contributions of voluntary organisations many of which, whether successful or not, are engaged in the work of understanding and representing those experiences. Some of the key questions raised by these debates are raised in later chapters where they have particular relevance to the specific topics under discussion.

The stories in this book are those of people working in voluntary organisations from all levels: users of services, volunteers, workers, managers and founders. They come from people involved in large organisations and small, from the newly established to those with roots in 19th century philanthropy, from the UK and India. They are fragmentary and episodic. Some are carefully crafted tales, others capture some of the success, failures, ambivalences of day to day organisational life.

In this introductory section I have set out why I believe that a social constructionist approach has the potential to generate new insights into critical questions about the contributions of voluntary organisations to social change. In the following pages I set the scene further by providing some background to voluntary organisations, storytelling as a research methodology, and the particular relevance of storytelling to voluntary organisations. These brief summaries are not intended to provide a comprehensive overview but rather to provide a useful introduction to the themes of this book.

Voluntary organisations

Perhaps the first thing that is highlighted by applying a social constructionist perspective to voluntary organisations is that our understandings of what voluntary organisations are, are profoundly structured by the ways in which we position those organisations in relation to our other imaginative constructs of society, whether these are ideas or institutions. To demonstrate this point, in this section I describesome of the ways in which ideas about voluntary organisations are created through defining these boundaries.

The boundary between the religious and the secular

Research into voluntary organisations is a relatively young field. Although the phenomenon of people getting together to engage in activity to improve their current situation is hardly new, our efforts to develop theories that account for such activity are located within historical, social and political contexts. For example, in India and the UK there is discernible organisational activity expressing ideals of compassion and service stretching back centuries linked to religious establishments. However, historical accounts of the voluntary sector tend to give them only a passing reference. In each country the point at which serious analysis of the sector begins is linked to the de-coupling of religion and compassion. Kendall and Knapp cite the Elizabethan Statute of Charitable Uses of 1601 as the beginning of the 'formalisation and secularisation of philanthropy' (Kendall and Knapp 1993, 1). The Indian surveys (Sen, S. 1993, 1997, Tandon et al 1991) start at the beginning of the 19th century, when the ideals of liberty, equality and fraternity which influenced the European revolutionary movements of the late 18th and early 19th century, were given organisational form (although in India these early social reform movements such as the Brahmo Samaj were still primarily religious). Kendall and Knapp (1993) also link the growth of the voluntary sector with the effects of increasing industrialisation on a hitherto primarily agrarian society.

By denoting such a starting point the impression these surveys give is that the values of the sector are essentially secular and embody the ideals of the Enlightenment. However, a recent study of volunteering in faith based communities in the UK found that for many volunteers their volunteering was a direct expression of their religious commitment. The researchers wrote that they:

> ...encountered difficulties during our interviews because our questions about organisations, based on our experience in the mainstream voluntary and community sector, seemed to have little relevance to the experience of the interviewees... [who] usually participated in ways that were more organic and individual than formal, more based on habit and personal contact than on systems. (Lukka, Locke and Soteri-Proctor 2003, 1).

These observations demonstrate that the assumptions made by such surveys about the boundary between religious and secular expressions of compassion are not necessarily unproblematic or universally shared.

The boundary between political and non-political

There is a similar difficulty in identifying the boundary between political and non-political expressions of compassion and commonality. Many people writing and theorising about the voluntary sector locate it within the narrative of civil society (for example, Deakin 2001, Deakin and Scully 1999, Sassoon 1996) which Chakrabarty (2000b), an Indian historian, sees as inextricably linked to its modernist corollary, the nation state. In India the passing of legislation decentralising local government, the 'panchayati raj',[12] has led to a proliferation of programmes run by voluntary organisations offering training in democratic patterns of behaviour to newly elected members of the local panchayats.

Voluntary organisations also engage in campaigning work to influence the development of public policy. Therefore, the narrative of citizen and state structures their representations, even if only as an underlying backdrop. The institutions and the debates about civil society, regeneration, democratic engagement, etc, are structured by a hegemonic discourse of modernity.

---

12   The 73rd and 74th Constitutional Ammendments are commonly known as the 'Panchayati Raj' Acts, the word *panchayat* suggesting a small grouping of five villages or so to which local decision making powers have been devolved. Each panchayat must elect its own members, a proportion of whom must be women or people from 'scheduled' castes, many of whom are likely to have poor literacy skills and very little knowledge of democratic processes.

The linkage between the voluntary sector and political activity is not without its critics: Spivak (2003) is caustic in her comments about the proliferation of courses in 'election training' offered by international NGOs. However, much of what voluntary organisations do concerns itself with representations on behalf of those who have been left out of this narrative, or who have found themselves on the losing side. It is not clear what alternatives there are for the concerned citizen and perhaps this is an irresolvable paradox that lies at the heart of voluntary organisational activity. Even those programmes and initiatives designed to create spaces for quiet voices to be heard are themselves shaped and circumscribed by people in positions of relative power.

This raises a number of questions such as how that representation is done, who does the representing and with what kinds of legitimacy. What are the representations of the 'other' that are proposed and what constructions of the other are made possible (or impossible) by those representations?

Therefore the overlapping interests between compassion and concern with religious or political aspirations are at one and the same time taken for granted and problematic. No less foundational to our ideas about voluntary organisations (and no less problematic) are they ways in which we construct their relationship to their wider communities and their relationship to the state and market.

Voluntary organisations and civil society: centre or periphery?

Tandon and Mohanty define civil society as 'the sum of individual and collective initiatives directed towards the pursuit of common public good' (Tandon and Mohanty 2002, 6). Voluntary associational activity is increasingly regarded as the activity that lies at the heart of communality and such communality is regarded as a significant guarantor of democratic and civic engagement.

Attempts to 'measure' the contribution of commonality regard it as productive of 'social capital' (Jocum, 2003) such as social networks, shared norms and values of reciprocity and trust, quantifiable through surveying participation in groupings such as tenants associations, neighbourhood councils, community and conservation groups.[13] In this sense voluntary associational activity is seen as supportive of, and central to the creation and maintenance of the nation state.

However, voluntary organisations are also seen as working at the periphery, with people who are marginalised because of poverty, disability, social standing (or lack of it), attitudes, lifestyle, perspectives. Tandon and Mohanty suggest that it is the 'disenchantment with the ...political movements and the failure of political parties to articulate their interests' (Tandon and Mohanty 2002, 41) that have led to the creation of many of the newer associations and organisations emerging out of social movements. From this perspective voluntary organisations occupy the space at the

---

13   These dimensions come from the Office of National Statistics (UK) website: <http: www.statistics.gov.uk/about_ns/social_capital/default> cited in Jochum 2003.

margins, a space filled with conflicting voices where subtle challenges to hegemonic discourses are played out and resistance shaped.

There are inherent contradictions here between the growing centrality of voluntary organisations / NGOs in national and international policy making, the still potent image of the warm hearted but impractical volunteer with few professional skills, and the sector as the voice of the dispossessed. Robert Putnam's books on democracy in Italy (1993) and on the decline in community involvement that he perceives in the US (2000) have been very influential for both researchers of voluntary organisations and public policy makers in developing the metaphor of social capital and its proposed links with democratic engagement (although Jochum (2003) points out that demonstrating these causal links remains highly complex and uncertain).

The voluntary sector and the others

The different roles that we ascribe to voluntary organisations and their relative legitimacy are also determined by the ways in which we perceive the relationship between the three sectors; public, private and voluntary.

An analogy that illustrates this is Chakrabarty's (2000b) proposition that world history is always written against a 'norm' of Europe, a Europe of the imagination, in which the narrative of European civilisation, with its democratic nation state and the subject as citizen, defined by ideals of modernity, provides a hegemonic discourse against which other societies and cultures interpret their own narratives.[14] Voluntary organisations may be seen to support of this discourse through their maintenance of the construct of the citizen who participates in democratic engagement through increased involvement in local democratic structures and in those forms of organisational activity that encourage democratic norms of associational behaviour. These being, as described above, those which contribute to the Putnamite notion of social capital.[15] From this perspective other forms of organising, for instance those that are based on kinship or community relationships, appear inherently inferior.

Chakrabarty's description is of the way in which one country (in his case, India) understands its own history by reference to an idea of what constitutes a normalising

14   Chakrabarty cites as an example, a literary critic, who, writing about *Midnight's Children,* comments that Rushdie was influenced 'on the one hand, from Indian films and legends and literature and, on the other, from the West – *The Tin Drum, Tristram Shandy, One Hundred Years of Solitude,* and so on.' (from Hutcheon, L. 1989, *The Politics of Postmodernism,* cited by Chakrabarty 2000b, 264-265). Chakrabarty's point is very clear – the Indian references are not regarded by the critic as needing elaboration but the Western ones are given in much greater detail.

15   For example, many organisations and consultants are currently engaged in providing 'capacity building' support to smaller, and more informal organisations which are encouraged to develop formalised procedures for chairing meetings, electing leaders and officers, minute taking etc that mimic local and national democratic governance structures. Other modes of associational organising, such as collectives, seem rarely to be encouraged or seen as valid alternatives.

narrative, the trajectory of political, economic and social history through such (borrowed) categories as feudal, pre and post industrial, information age and globalization. Voluntary organisations too interpret their history in relation to such normalising narratives of their relationship to the state and the market.

One narrative is that of voluntary organisations in a relationship of constant reaction to the state, whether against state action or inaction, hegemony, corruption or indifference, or of 'filling the gaps' where the state retreats (or never went). In this narrative voluntary organisations do the things that government doesn't, whether it is running hospitals or schools or experimenting with innovative models of service delivery and civic engagement. They also develop their campaigning strategies in terms of what they want the state to do, or not to do. The state represents the norm against which the sector defines itself and evaluates its activities.

The competing narrative is that of voluntary organisations in relation to the corporate sector. It is increasing in popularity as the public sector is represented as failing; inefficient, bureaucratic and inflexible, and the corporate sector as providing the gold standard of effective, stakeholder, consumer focussed (and therefore anti-elitist) management.[16] These competing narratives are signified by debates about names; voluntary organisations are 'non-government organisations' or 'not-for-profits'. These are the narratives of difference.

The third narrative is about the distinctiveness of voluntary organisations and of the voluntary sector, seen as a collectivity; what the sector *is*, as opposed to what it is *not*. The struggle between difference and distinctiveness underpins many of the debates about identity. The narratives of distinctiveness concern themselves with identifying intrinsic qualities of voluntary organisations and carving out a role, or space, that is inherently unique. (Note again the phrase ' a genuine voluntary organisation' in the opening quotation.) Rosenman (2004) asked taxi drivers what came to mind when they thought about voluntary organisations. The qualities that were consistently emphasised were sacrifice, the voluntary giving of time and money and the meeting of urgent need.

Recently a debate about how to define social enterprises occupied much e-space of a voluntary sector studies e-mail discussion group. Are social enterprises voluntary organisations by another name or warm-hearted businesses? Where, if anywhere, are the boundaries between social enterprises and other organisations that combine a social and economic interest? How can micro-credit schemes, credit unions, savings clubs, charity shops, public service contracts be understood? Again, there is a concomitant debate about names. Black likes 'more-than-profit'; 'to replace the "horrible" term non-profit or not-for-profit' he writes in *Social Enterprise Magazine* (Black 2003: 19 in Wallace 2004). Black's comments seem to belong to the discourse of difference rather than the discourse of distinctiveness.

---

16 See, for example, Leat's (1995) study of dress in the voluntary and corporate sectors, which showed that voluntary sector managers were increasingly adopting corporate sector norms of appropriate work clothing.

What these arguments demonstrate is the ways in which the conceptualisations of voluntary organisations and of the voluntary sector are constructed through explorations of their boundaries.   These ongoing attempts to create a definition of the sector that satisfactorily includes all that should be included and exclude all that should be excluded have not satisfied. The definition has proved elusive. This should not surprise us because it is no easier to define the other sectors. After all, the public sector includes such diverse organisations as housing providers and scientific research centres while the corporate sector includes self employed individuals, cottage industries and Nike. However, the argument is often put forward that the sector would be stronger and more effective if it could find a united voice, that it could better articulate its values and could withstand threats from without.

> By not having a more discrete naming system the strength gained in the diversity of non-statutory organisations is lost and that very diversity becomes the greatest weakness...
> There must be a clear definition of charity and what is charitable. If those of us working in non-statutory services and community groups are to make the most of diversity then we need to name our own and own our names. (Saunders 1998, 8)[17]

The 'fundamental reconsideration now taking place ...of the role of the state' (Report of the Commission on the Future of the Voluntary Sector 1996, 17) is leading to its withdrawal from the provision of services and its encouragement of the voluntary sector to fill the vacated space. While in the UK these are mainly social services, in India they are more likely to be development and aid programmes providing sanitation, health, water and literacy. In both countries this trend is regarded as both a threat and an opportunity - a threat to the independence of the sector and an opportunity for more influence and increased funding. Against this threat, an expression of uniqueness may be a potentially powerful weapon to fight being insidiously co-opted into the public or private sectors.

Perri 6 defines this as administering 'border patrol', and it is fraught.

> Ironically, every country in the western world has by now developed detailed and complex laws attempting to administer border patrol, between non-profit and for-profit activity, and, particularly for associations in western Europe, to ensure democratic accountability of decision-making in associations to their members rather than to the state. (Perri 6 1994, 2-3)

Ignoring, just for the moment, the emphasis on the west (border patrol is also a significant feature of the discourse concerning voluntary organisations in India) Perri 6 does draw attention to the space between non-profit (including the public sector) and for-profit activity. Within this space there is the possibility of finding other ways

---

17   Interestingly, this article reveals an assumption that non-statutory organisations, community groups and charities are synonymous, as they are not. In the UK there are voluntary organisations that are not formally constituted as charities under charity law and in India the closest equivalent of UK charity law is the Societies Registrations Act 1860 and registration does not necessarily carry the same connotations of 'charity'.

of conceptualising the relationship between the activities of organisations and the wishes, aspirations and needs of the people who are involved in them or who benefit from their activities. The stories that people tell about their engagement in voluntary organisations may suggest some such alternative interpretations.

Stories and storytelling in organisational analysis

Although researchers have increasingly looked to stories and storytelling to increase our understanding of organisations very little of this work focuses on voluntary organisations. In this section I aim to provide a brief overview of some of the critical debates within this field and explore the particular relevance a study of storytelling has for generating insights into the questions I have posed about voluntary organisations and their contribution to social change.

Why have scholars of organisations become interested in stories? The 'narrative turn' (Gabriel 2000) can be traced to two, distinct developments. One has been the growing awareness of the significance of culture in organisations which points researchers towards the methods of anthropology. For example, Smircich (1983b) and Schein (1986) suggest that stories, myths and legends can be regarded as artefacts in which the values and basic assumptions of the members of the organisation are manifested.

The second important development has been the appropriation of research methods derived from the discipline of literary criticism. This has grown in part from the work of philosophers such as Ricoeur (1992b) and Gadamer (1975) who extended of the notion of a 'text' beyond the narrow confines of literature to any purposive human activity which thereby makes available the panoply of approaches to literary analysis from hermeneutic interpretation through to poststructuralist methods of textual deconstruction. For example, one of Czarniawska's books on organisation theory terms it 'a literary genre' (Czarniawska 1999 subtitle). Within the general approach of conceptualising organisations as texts there have emerged a number of different debates each with concomitant methodologies.

Stories or storying?

Boje et al suggest that 'organisation is a material and discursive formation. Its materiality comes into being through discourse, established in a multiplicity of stories and transformed by more stories' (Boje et al 2001, 145). A text, in this sense, is not a fixed object but fluid; constantly moving, transmutating. One of the most important debates concerns the distinction between studying the story-as-object or the story-in-context (Boje 1998).

The story-as-object approach focuses on content and is concerned with methodological issues of interpretation within an overall search for meaning and meaning construction. This search proceeds through interpretation and text deconstruction, uncovering latent or tacit assumptions. The story-in-context approach focuses more on the processes of organising (or storying) and how meaning emerges. Researchers focussing on storying (Hosking 2004, Boje, 1998) see it as an ongoing process of re-creating and co-creating reality emerging from the context and the relational activities that are going on within it. Storying is a shared activity, a continual praxis engaged in by multiple voices.

There are also questions about what even constitutes a story in an organisational setting, how it differs from narrative (Boje 2001) or folklore (Gabriel 2000), for example. Unsurprisingly, there are different views. Gabriel says that for an account of events to be a story it must possess 'poetic imagination and narrative complexity' (Gabriel 2000, 60). Boje argues that stories are more fluid than narratives and that narrative imposes a degree of structure and closure.

> Story is an account of incidents or events but narrative comes after and adds 'plot' and 'coherence' to the storyline. Story is an 'ante' state of affairs existing previously to narrative, it is 'advance of narrative'. (Boje 2001, 1)

However, it is hard to see how there can be any way of linking incidents or events without at least the suggestion of a coherent connection between them and it is in exploring these connections that much of the richness of the story is to be found.

All of these approaches have validity. To change metaphors for a moment, while there are differences between studying a play, directing it, performing it, writing a new play, creating a new play through a group workshop activity or participating in forum theatre all are nonetheless valid enterprises. They may, however, generate different insights.

These differing approaches also cast the researcher in different roles. Is the researcher an objective 'outsider' a reader of a text, analysing its meaning, divorced from the context in which it emerges, as Gersie suggests?

> Through the act of storytelling we allow someone else access to our experiences, to our inner world and the wisdom or folly we have gained. *Once the story has been set free the tale begins a life of its own, independent of the teller*. It becomes vulnerable to alteration and change. (Gersie 1992, 16 my emphasis)

Or is the researcher a co-creator in the on-going process of reality construction?

There are undoubtedly exciting things that can be learned by studying stories-in-context but also practical problems in gaining access to storying in process, and important questions about how the researcher handles their involvement, given that their presence must, inevitably, become part of the story. And the rich tradition of mythology and folklore tells us that some stories retain their capacity to impart meaning, inspiration, and consolation long after the first telling. Boje's work on story-in-context (1998) is an invaluable addition to the growing school of storytelling analysis but one which sits alongside other, no less valid approaches.

Austin and the three aspects of a speech act

One way of resolving these differing approaches to stories is suggested by Austin's (1975) work on performative speech. Stories belong to an oral tradition. Austin distinguished three separate aspects of a speech act; the locutionary, the illocutionary and the perlocutionary. The locutionary aspect of the speech act he defines as 'that which is said'. I take this to refer to the content of the story, the story-as-object. The illocutionary aspect, 'that which is done *in* saying', focuses on storying, storytelling as praxis, the story as it is told. The perlocutionary aspect, 'that which is done *by* saying' describes the consequences of the speech act, or the functions the story fulfils; how the world is changed as a result of the story having been told (Austin 1975, 109 my italics).

This offers a useful framework for locating different approaches to studying storytelling in organisations and also the opportunity to make use of all three perspectives while not losing sight of their differences.

Within the locutionary, story-as-object perspective one approach is to take stories, often well known, that have been created outside of the organisation and use them as interpretive heuristics. For example Gabriel et al (2004) use legends such as the stories of Orpheus, Prometheus and Demeter, Sievers (1997) uses a Melville short story, Smith and Simons (1983) use fairy tales such as Rumplestilskin and Chakraborty (1998) uses sacred texts, the Rg Veda and the Bhagavad Gita as 'a springboard for an analysis of contemporary social and organisational realities' (Gabriel 2004, ix).

Mead (2001) uses stories as a method of organisational consultancy and action research. Here the story used is constructed specifically for the organisation, or the subject being researched.[18] These stories are created externally and are likely to be well known to the participants. They are used as a reference point against which current experience can be understood.

Another approach is to generate stories about lived experience from organisational participants and analyse them for their use of language, metaphor, construction of plot, depiction of characters, what is included or excluded, how events are linked and their sequencing. This is probably the most dominant strand of storytelling research. Some examples include Fineman and Gabriel's survey of stories told by MBA students (Fineman and Gabriel 1996); Feldman's study of stories in the US Department of Energy (Feldman 1991); Martin et al's identification of similar themes in stories told in different organisations (Martin, Feldman, Hatch and Sitkin 1983); and Kay (1991) on the metaphors in stories about effectiveness told by chief executives of voluntary organisations.

There are fewer examples of the illocutionary aspect of storytelling, storying as praxis, perhaps because of the difficulties of access mentioned earlier (although Boje has written extensively on the theoretical implications). However one example might be the method of drama production known as forum theatre, devised by

---

18   See also Wallace 2004 for an application of this approach to social enterprise.

Augusto Boal (1998), that involves the audience in devising the ending of the play. An initial situation is set out by the actors and then the audience is asked to suggest various possible endings. Often some of the audience will join the actors on the stage and take on a role within the play. Forum theatre is often used as a way of working with oppressed and marginalised communities to expose the contradictions in their situations and the opportunities for action.

Some examples of the perlocutionary aspect of storytelling, the function*s* the stories fulfil in creating and sustaining culture (Morgan 1986 and Smircich 1983b) are; framing problems and generating solutions (Schon 1979, also Boland and Greenberg 1988), mediating between the ideal and the actual (Abravanel 1983), stimulating motivation and commitment (Wilkins 1983, also Martin and Powers 1983), and maintaining third order controls (Wilkins 1983, also Wilkins and Ouchi 1983)

I find Austin's ideas very helpful for clarifying both the differences between these aspects of a speech act while also recognising their importance. I have adopted his schema throughout this book. Each of the six main chapters has an introduction and a conclusion that frame three separate sections, each using stories to develop the chapter's theme from the perspectives of the content of the stories (the locutionary aspect), the processes of storying (and of storying as a metaphor for organising) and the functions that are fulfilled by the stories (and, again by metaphorical extension, by the organisations).

My intention is that through this approach it is possible to discern how stories construct our notions of reality in organisations, how the processes of storying, or narrating, experience contribute to maintaining and subverting those constructions and the functions that stories fulfil.

Storytelling voluntary organisations and social change

Earlier in the chapter I proposed that a focus on stories and storytelling is of particular relevance to voluntary organisations. In this section I will give some examples to demonstrate this.

Firstly, a voluntary organisation can be regarded as a manifestation of the founders' desires to create social change and the stories that are told about the founding represent their views about their society at that time. Voluntary organisations are established primarily by committed individuals who have given up time, money, sometimes status, health and even physical safety to make life better for themselves and others. They create organisations in order to create change. The sorts of changes desired and the nature of the problems they want to address, are culturally and historically contingent.

> *Well it was a group of people who were very incensed about the conditions of people with learning difficulties who had to live in mental handicap hospitals, especially during the 1960s when there were a whole series of enquiries into malpractice, abuse in some of the biggest hospitals.*

We all have different views about what matters most to us, what activities we would like to be involved in, what injustices move us – poverty, cruelty, the environment, beautiful buildings, the welfare of animals, better facilities in our community or the need for spaces where we can explore aspects of our identities and experiences, painful or joyful, with people who will understand. It is for this reason, if for no other, that the sector is inherently pluralistic. Athough policy makers and researchers (and managers) find it pragmatic to refer to the collectivity of voluntary organisations as the voluntary 'sector' any grouping of such disparate organisations is fraught with ambiguity. It is perhaps more helpful to think of the sector as a space of competing voices.

Storytelling and empowerment

As we have seen, stories are a useful vehicle for developing insights into organisations and organising. Another aspect of storytelling that is particularly relevant to voluntary organisations is that it is one way in which power is mediated and exercised.

Storytelling is one way in which people can take up power through making their experiences known, through validating individual and diverse forms of knowledge and through the process of critical conscience, or 'conscientisation' (Freire 1996). Freire built his model of education for liberation on the premise that people cannot take power until they become aware of the elements, or 'contradictions' in their current situation that dominate, or oppress them.

Bhabha describes Fanon's work on the experiences of Algerians under French rule as a 'meditation on the experience of dispossession and dislocation – *psychic and spiritual* – which speaks to the condition of the marginalised, the alienated, those who have to live under the surveillance of a sign of identity and fantasy that denies their difference' (Bhabha 1994, 63 my italics). Through telling their stories people can begin to reclaim that difference.

Storytelling also plays an essential role in developing critical conscience, as Freire terms it, the awareness that becomes the foundation for action. However, the reverse can also be true. Hall applied Gramsci's concept of hegemony to analysing the appeal of Thatcherism and the widespread consent that was given to the narrative that 'there is no alternative' (Hall, 1983). Power is exercised through winning our agreement to a hegemonic story. Many postcolonial writers have explored the importance of dominating narratives of power (for example, Nandy 1983). Postcolonial theory concerns itself not only with the experiences of people whose countries were colonised by others but also with *the colonisation of the mind and the imagination* (Nandy 1983 my italics) of people with relatively little political power by those with more. Stories can colonise as well as liberate.

All stories are fictions even if they are based on our lived experiences. When we tell a story we build the narrative through the linking of events over time. The decisions we make about the associations between these events are revelatory of the ways in which we structure our experiences and make sense of our world. Making a story requires 'substantial editing and hindsight' (Weick 1995, 128). Certain events are picked out and linked to others, while events that do not fit are discarded.

Ricoeur suggests that our sense of identity relies on the capacity to tell stories about ourselves which are 'intelligible, bearable and acceptable'.[19] The story is the creation of the storyteller and their choices about sequencing, role identification and time are personal choices. Nevertheless, these choices are continually influenced by the society in which we live and by our individual experiences, emotions and anxieties. Our choices may be simultaneously influenced by, and helping us to manage, the feelings of helplessness and anxiety (Sievers 1997 and Weick 1995) and of domination (Bhabha, 1994) caused by living and managing in conditions of ambiguity and complexity. So, the ways in which we tell stories to ourselves can empower us or numb our pain. They can help us to justify our consent and acquiescence to hegemonic meta-stories or they can awaken us to their flimsy foundations.

Stories and representation

Another reason why storytelling is of particular relevance to voluntary organisations is because the stories of the users, or beneficiaries of these organisations are frequently appropriated by managers. The increasing emphasis from funders and government on the demonstration of 'value for money', that public money is being spent effectively has created particular challenges for voluntary organisations because many, if not all of the things that they aim to achieve are hard to measure (Paton 2003) and perhaps can only be captured by the stories that people tell about the impact the organisation has had on their lives.

> CS: *Do you find yourself telling the story about how the organisation got set up?*

> *A lot, yeah. Certainly to funders. And to people who don't know us, and who think we're something we're not. Yeah, I do. Of course. I think it's a good way of starting a relationship.*[20]

These stories can be extremely powerful and there is a certain morality in appropriating them and letting peoples' own voices be heard rather than making assumptions on their behalf.

Stories can also be powerfully persuasive and provide a significant source of legitimacy to the organisation in making political representation. In this act of representation organisations make visible minority presences. But representation has become a somewhat unpopular activity. Spivak (1988) maintains that it is impossible to speak for others from our elite positions. Said argues that the '*act*

---

19   In an interview with Jonathon Ree for Channel Four, September, 1992

20   From an interview with the chief executive officer of a voluntary organisation working with homeless people in the UK.

of representing' does violence to the subject of that representation; 'the paradoxical contrast between the surface, which seems to be in control, and the process which produces it, [the representation] which inevitably involves some degree of violence, decontextualisation, miniaturization, etc'. (Said 2004, 40-41).

Postcolonial theory explores the dynamics of power as experienced from the perspectives of people in marginalised positions. It forces us to ask whose stories are heard, and whose interpretations count. It also requires us to look at complicity and collusion – where are subaltern stories reinforcing hegemonic discourses and where are they representations of resistance? How do we temper our interpretive role with a degree of humility and hesitance, given that there must always be a measure of distortion and manipulation? What alternatives are possible?

This use of the term 'subaltern' in this context needs some explanation. The term has been appropriated by the Subaltern Studies Collective, a group of historians, originally from India but latterly involving academics worldwide, which aimed to 'transform the writing of colonial Indian history by drawing on the fluid concepts of class and State articulated in the *Prison Notebooks* of Antonio Gramsci' (Guha cited in Chaturvedi 2000, viii). Their early work ambitiously attempted to construct an understanding of the consciousness of people engaged in acts of resistance against imperialism, even when the only record available was the absence of a record.[21]

In an early (1988), and very influential essay, *Can the Subaltern Speak?* Spivak was quite critical of this aspiration. She maintained that it is not possible for anyone in an elite position, who chooses (indeed cannot escape choosing) the very context in which the subaltern's word are framed, to enter into their consciousness. Das supports Spivak and their criticisms constitute a significant challenge to people appropriating users' and community members' stories even for the best of motives:

> Once we acknowledge that the traces of rebellion are embodied in the form of a record produced in the context of the exercise of bureaucratic and legal domination, we also have to accept that the speech of the subaltern, as it becomes available for study, has already been appropriated by the superior forms of authority. (Das 1989, 315)

This challenge focuses our attention on the problematic relationship between the colonised and the coloniser, the oppressed and the oppressor, the end user of services and those who are providing them. Similarly problematic is the relationship between voluntary organisations themselves and other key players. This is clearly relevant to campaigning and political advocacy.

Gabriel (2002) cautions us against replacing unquestioning trust of professionals and institutions with an even more unquestioned trust in the story of the user or survivor. Their stories may seen to be unquestionable. But if, as he also says, stories

---

21 Linstead (2005) described efforts to trace patterns of genocide by looking for absence, where people should be but aren't, such as in villages where the majority of the population are women, suggesting that something violent many have happened to the men. This is another intriguing use of the importance of the evidence of absence.

represent our own attempts to make what sense we can of our lives, including our most painful experiences, these stories may well require some critical analysis.

Seen within this context the relative paucity of research into storytelling in voluntary organisations seems worrying. Stories are powerful – it follows that their power is not always benign. The misuse of storytelling, conscious or not, bears an uncomfortably close relationship to propaganda. For example, in 1995 Greenpeace was forced to apologise to Shell when they dramatically overestimated the amount of oil on board the buoy Brent Spar.[22] Voluntary sector managers need to be aware of the risks and dangers of storytelling and they need the skills of reflecting critically on their own, and others stories. These skills are as essential to transparency and accountability, both highly vaunted virtues, as demonstrating clear audit trails.

Concluding thoughts

In this chapter I have attempted to set the scene by showing why I believe that the application of a social constructionist perspective and within it, a focus on stories and storytelling will shed new light on some of the most critical questions for people involved in voluntary organisations. Voluntary organisations are increasingly under the spotlight. Their activities are being scrutinised. Their effectiveness and even their probity is increasingly being questioned.

The stories that people tell about their experiences of working and participating in organisations can provide researchers with important insights into the nature of organisational activity. They are revelatory of the tellers' beliefs, fears, aspirations and concerns. They open up a space in which the non-rational as well as the rational aspects of organising are made available for reflection and for this reason alone they can provide insights into some of the dilemmas and paradoxes of voluntary associational activity.

Subaltern stories, the stories of the people for whose benefit the organisation was established are an important source of information about how people in marginalised positions perceive power and domination and what taking power means to them. Telling their stories to a listening audience is also, of itself an act of power sharing. These stories are fragmentary, conflicting and provisional. They do not knit together into a unified pattern. Postcolonial theory is a useful frame for interpreting these stories not only by providing a metaphor for the relationship between the dominated and the dominating but also because of its emphasis on plurality, on multiple voices.

Furthermore, managers and participants in voluntary organisations use stories, their own and others, in fulfilling the organisation's vision externally through campaigning and advocacy, internally in leadership and management. It follows that the skills of storytelling and also of critical interpretation are essential management skills.

---

22 A brief synopsis of this episode can be found at <www.emt.orst.edu/grad/course490590>.

A brief note on methodology

I carried out much of the research on which this book was based while I was working as the chief executive of a UK based voluntary organisation. Therefore I was seen by the people I interviewed as an insider rather than a researcher, a participant in the task of management and sympathetic to the joys, difficulties and complexities of that role. It was also, as I wrote earlier, through my work as a manager rather than through academic research, that I developed an interested in the 'non-rational' (Kurtz and Snowdon 2003) aspects of organisational life. This perspective undoubtedly influences the meanings that I encountered in the stories. As with all stories, there are many other meanings and interpretations that could be made. The interpretations offered in this book are only some amongst many.

Many of the interviews I carried out were with other chief executives but I have also interviewed participants, trustees and people using the organisations' services. The organisations represent a wide range of activities and were chosen to demonstrate this range rather than to facilitate tidy comparisons across the two countries. I wanted to capture some of the amazing diversity of the sector by aiming for as broad a cross section of organisations as possible. If the samples had been too similar the effect might have been to obscure the differences. Czarniawska (1997a) has said that what is lost in translation from one language to another is that for which there is no ready equivalent – it is the differences rather than the similarities that are lost, and yet it is from taking note of these differences that we are most likely to be surprised, to develop fresh perspectives; after confronting the unfamiliar we are likely to see the familiar differently.

Some examples: in my experience the proliferation of fisherpeople's organisations in India does not have a counterpart in the UK, while animal welfare organisations are much more common in the UK than in India.[23] Another example; SEWA (the Self Employed Women's Organisation) in Gujurat is an organisation that is formally registered as both a voluntary organisation and a trade union. This would be highly unusual in the UK.[24]

In each country there are is least one organisation that was established in the 19th century as well as some which are as little as ten years old. All of the Indian organisations were established and continue to be governed by Indians (as opposed to international organisations with offices in India such as OXFAM, Charities Aid Foundation India, the Aga Khan Foundation and the like).

---

23 This is an impressionistic statement because there are no overall systems for collecting data on the voluntary sector in India comparable to the National Council of Voluntary Organisations' Voluntary Sector Almanac for the UK. My impressions are gleaned from studies on the sector in India (Tandon et al 1991, Sen, S. 1997,1993) and the membership list of Voluntary Associations Network India (VANI Annual Reports 1995, 1996, 1997).

24 The report of the Commission on the Future of the Voluntary Sector in the UK (NCVO 1996) used the Johns Hopkins classificatory system of a 'broad' and a 'narrow' sector in which *unions*, recreation organisations and higher education were excluded from the narrow definition.

My other criteria were that the organisations had been in existence for at least six years and had a complex management structure (defined in terms of there being some structural distance between managers and other staff whether through hierarchical, regional or functional structures). These choices were based on Osborne's findings (1994) that organisations more than six years old, and with complex management structures were less likely to be innovative than newer organisations. Osborne had concluded that one of the reasons that organisations more than six years' old were less innovative was that they had grown beyond their founding impulse and begun to develop the accretions of complex organisations.[25]

The stories and experiences that I am drawing on come from two parts of the world that are often discussed in terms of binary polarities; north versus south, west versus east, developed versus developing. All of these terminologies bear in their wake contested ideologies, as does the very nature of a binary construction. I am not, however suggesting that the stories from each country are *representative* of a particular aspect of these positions which, for the reasons mentioned earlier, would be a fairly dangerous undertaking, inevitably bound to do violence to their complexities and ambiguities.

My intention is rather to explore whether, in the different ways in which people go about the work of imagining a better and more just society and in their attempts to make these visions real we can discover new possibilities. I regard these stories as being, in some way, in a dialogue with each other.

Applying hermeneutics

I have found hermeneutics to be a helpful framework for exploring ways in which we construct our understandings of other cultures. Hermeneutics, originally a methodology of religious exegesis, pursues the problem of the interpretation of sacred texts from different cultures and times. I have taken from my reading on hermeneutics a number of foundational assumptions that are worth spelling out. These are that:

1. we can only know in the 'other' (that which we seek to understand) that which we can know in ourselves; therefore all knowledge of other is self knowledge,
2. self knowledge and knowledge of other is iterative; the more we understand of ourselves the more we are able to see in the other; the more we understand of another the more we are able to understand in ourselves, and this process of

---

25 By 'complex' I am referring to a structure in which some staff are distanced from the chief executive, either through a middle management structure, a regional structure or a membership structure. This has the effect of diluting the direct influence of the chief executive. There was only one exception, a peoples' theatre company which has adopted an unusual organisational model in that they live together as a 'family' in a communal arrangement but, superimposed on this structure, still has a hierarchical, three tier operational structure.

coming to know is both circular and infinite,

3. we can only know ourselves and others indirectly – there is always a mediatory device, whether it be thought, language, emotion, between our experiences and our attempt to name them. These mediatory devices include stories, metaphors, symbols.
4. we construct the relationship between these symbols and experience through two, opposing kinds of logic – a philosophical, or rational, logic and an associative, or poetic logic. (Mei 1996, Ricoeur 1992b, 1991a and b, Bruns 1992, Gadamer 1975, Ihde 1971, Bolle, 1967)

Some relevant questions these principle raise are if understanding of another is dependent on self understanding in what sense is it possible to know and understand that which is different? To what extent is human identity and experience universal, and to what extent is it endlessly diverse? Do notions of difference and similarity also set up a binary polarity that fails to do either justice?

Much has been written about the question of validity in interpretive research (Rowan and Reason 1988, Kets de Vries and Miller 1987). If many meanings are possible how can one choose between them and how can we determine whether some are more legitimate than others? And by what criteria, themselves also value laden, would we make those choices?

One response is the awareness that both researcher and reader maintain of the provisional nature of interpretation. These stories are not offered as definitive statements of reality, they are provisional suggestions of ways of seeing that may, in turn, suggest new possibilities. They have no claim to universal truth.

For many of the reasons mentioned above, such as the need to tell a story that makes some meaning out of painful experiences, the authors of stories have themselves an interpretive relationship to their own stories – they are not the only authors of their meanings, nor the authors of all of its possible meanings. Critical friends similarly have their own tales to tell. However, the more interpretations that are made and the more multiple meanings are proposed and explored, the richer the interpretations can be. Research into interpretation and meaning is less about the discovery of truth and more about participating in a developing conversation.

Meanings are many and are contingent. Meanings may be shared by the members of small groups and communities but unclear to outsiders. The same words can mean different things to different people; different words can mean the same things. Meaning is elusive. Even within groups meanings may be contested.

Critical questions for researchers interested in issues of power and marginality are: whose stories count, whose stories are heard, what kinds of knowledge are given value and legitimacy. In the very processes of reality creating how is meaning determined? What alternative constructions are possible? What possibilities are excluded by the story?

Stories are always fragmentary forms of knowing. Despite Boje's suggestion that a story must have some kind of closure (2001) such closure can only be fairly arbitrary. Something always happened next. So knowledge mediated through stories must be provisional. There is always a next chapter or sequel.

PART I
Stories and Visions

> We need a third dimension of language, a critical and creative dimension which is directed towards the disclosure of possible worlds. This third dimension I call poetic.... Poetry and myth are not just nostalgia for some forgotten world. They constitute a disclosure of unprecedented worlds, an opening into other possible worlds. (Ricoeur 1992b, 54)

In this section I want to explore these 'other possible worlds' as they are imagined by those people who create and manage voluntary organisations and who benefit from their activities. I am basing this exploration on Ricoeur's (1986) proposition that imagination is constitutive of social reality. I am also making the assumption that people who create and work in voluntary organisations are motivated by a desire to change society in some way, whether that is at a local or global level. Therefore, the stories that people tell, regarded as vehicles of the imagination, offer exciting possibilities for revealing these visions of new and better worlds and how people work to realise them in an organisational context.

> ...the best function of utopia is the exploration of the possible. (Ricoeur 1986, 312)

I have organised this book in two sections. The first section looks at the impact that voluntary organisations have on their external environment while the second section focuses on their internal management. The founders of voluntary organisations take action because they want to alleviate suffering, protect vulnerable people or endangered species, create new approaches to social problems; to poverty, oppression and inequality. The first chapter of this section explores the impact that creating an organisation has on the social environment. From the very moment of their founding voluntary organisations are engaged in social change. The following chapter concentrates on the stories of individuals. In this chapter I look at how individuals take action to change the circumstances that constrain them, how they conceptualise the relative states of power and powerlessness and the roles that voluntary organisations play in their empowerment. The third chapter of this section looks at the ways in which voluntary organisations propose alternative ways of imagining society itself and the institutions within it.

Stories 'disclose' imagination at work. Regarding stories as 'speech acts' in the sense that Austin (1975)suggests I have organised each chapter around his schema in which he distinguishes between the locutionary aspect, or content, the illocutionary aspect, or process, and the perlocutionary aspect, or function.

Looking at the stories from the locutionary aspect, the content of the stories – or stories-as-objects in Boje's (1998) terms – in each ,chapter I present my interpretations of the underlying visions of society that are foundational to the storytellers' imagination. These include what they perceive as injustice and the visions of a better, or more utopian society that underpin their desires to create organisations. The stories of individuals tell us how they experience powerlessness and power, the ways in which they imagine their location within society and how even these are structured by underlying assumptions about the nature of society itself and of social change.

The illocutionary aspect of storytelling, or 'storying' (Boje, 1998) focuses on praxis, the moment in which the imagination is realised into action. In these chapters I look at the ways in which the visions that people have influence the ways in which they construct organisations, come to perceive new ways of imagining their locations within society and new possibilities for challenging the structures of thinking that constrain them. When people tell stories they create their own interpretations of reality. In this sense the very act of storytelling is an act of taking power and of social change. Stories can disrupt certainties. They can reveal the contradictions that constrain us in our current circumstances, as we imagine them to be, and allow us to see new possibilities. Similarly, as a voluntary organisation is formed from the conjunction of the founders' critique of the existing situation and their vision of a better world these visions determine the form the organisation will take and its choice of activities.

> All utopias, whether written or realised, attempt to exert power in a way other than what exists. (Ricoeur 1986, 310)

Looked at from the perlocutionary, or functional aspect of storytelling suggests that creating an organisation represents one such attempt to exert power to effect change. Voluntary organisations change the way we think about social circumstances by representing the perspectives and aspirations of marginalised groups. They provide opportunities for people to re-construct their own perceptions of their location within society. They construct alternative models of the institutions of state and market and even of our notions of community which allow us to perceive new possibilities, 'other than what exists'.

However, even well intentioned acts of power are not necessarily unproblematic. Each chapter explores some of the paradoxes of empowerment. Creating an organisation to address a social injustice can be empowering but the very process of naming a situation as unjust can increase our awareness of it and perhaps its very existence. Voluntary organisations may be founded to empower people in marginalised positions but in so doing the organisation may constrain them in those positions. Coming together to articulate shared concerns creates solidarity and commonality but also separation and difference. Voluntary organisations create new models and alternative approaches to social problems but over time these may become professionalised and institutionalised.

These paradoxes create specific challenges for the management and leadership of voluntary organisations. In the second section of the book I explore these challenges further. My proposition is that managing the paradoxes of empowerment requires managers to engage with the founding values of the organisation in a hermeneutic process of interpretation and reinterpretation.

Chapter 2

Something Has To Be Done ... Creating Organisations as a Response to Social Injustice

I suppose the first thing to say is that undoubtedly I'm in this work because of my son. I have a 24 year old son who was damaged through maternal rubella and he has partial vision and severe hearing impairment.... [my son] would be born in 1975 and... 1976 onwards [I] started taking interest in what was available to him... and then it was clear that really the sort of services I would want for him weren't up here.

Introduction

This is a brief excerpt from a story about why one woman started a voluntary organisation in Scotland that provides services for people who have sensory impairments.

This story contains many themes that are common to the founding of such organisations; the personal commitment of the founder and the almost accidental way in which she became involved, the lack of the services she wanted and, by implication, some emerging vision of what those services might be.

This chapter explores the founding of voluntary organisations and the impact this has on the social landscape. Very early on in my research I became fascinated by the stories people told about how and why their organisation was founded.[1] I have talked to people working in voluntary organisations in the UK and in India, asking them what they knew about the founding and I have rarely encountered a chief executive, even of organisations that were more than a hundred years old, who did not know at least the bare outlines of the story. Awareness is also often high amongst people working at different levels within the organisations including volunteers and trustees, although less consistently so. This has led me to propose that these stories may be of mythic significance to the organisation, that they are among its sacred texts.

---

1   In Chapter 5 there is a more detailed description about how I became interested in founding stories.

In some organisations these stories are constantly being reinterpreted and retold.[2] They are not written texts (although in some organisations written versions of the founding stories do exist), they belong to the organisation's oral tradition. They are both histories and fictions; they are the stories of those founding events that still hold meaning for the organisation in its present state. The storytellers make choices about what to include in their narratives and what to leave out. These stories are well crafted tales. Day to day experiences such as applying for funding, finding premises, organising meetings and minute taking rarely, if ever, feature important though such activities must have been.

The stories recount the founding events as they are remembered, if the founders are still alive, and as they are interpreted by organisational participants. Seen as historical documents they are of very limited use; as myths they are potent and they can help us to construct our understandings of voluntary organisations. They tell us what motivated the founders and what circumstances they wanted to change. They tell us how the founders constructed their notions of the social world.

For example, the founder in the story above was motivated by passion and commitment to her child. The story can also be located within a meta-narrative about the failure of the state and the entrepreneurial spirit of the concerned citizen. Dantwala, writing about voluntary action, says that:

> ...the motivations for action which is unrelated to one's self interest... are too varied and complex to permit their grouping in a well defined rubric. The only common factor prompting such action is dissatisfaction with the prevailing social order and an urge to improve it. (Dantwala 1998, 31)

Dantwala focuses our attention on dissatisfactions with things as they are and while these are often cited as the reasons why founders came together this focus takes our attention away from the varied, rich (and sometimes conflicting) visions of better alternatives that the stories propose. The stories about the founding of organisations are rich; they tell of passion, sacrifice, dedication and commitment, often in the face of apathy or active resistance. Some founders even risked their lives.

Firstly, they tell us what circumstances the founders wanted to change. This may indeed involve 'dissatisfaction with the prevailing social order' (Dantwala 1998, 31) or it may be the desire to preserve something valued such as a building or park or nature reserve. Even here, however, the stories imply that that which is valued is under threat.

Therefore the stories suggest that particular activities, attitudes, policies, behaviours, institutions are undesirable, inequitable, perhaps even unjust. In many

---

2   Several of the Indian organisations celebrate a 'founders day'. This is not a tradition I have come across in any of the UK organisations but many of the managers I interviewed talked about the importance they ascribed to the founding stories and the ways they used them to communicate a sense of the organisation's values. Some of these examples are described in chapter 7.

instances these activities may not have previously been regarded as problematic and the stories both construct new interpretations and problematise them.

Nandy writes that 'oppression, to be known as oppression must be felt to be so, if not by the oppressors and the oppressed, at least by some social analyst somewhere' (Nandy 1999, 23). Oppression is a strong word and many of the situations that the founders want to address would not necessarily be conceptualised by them in such extreme terms. However, their motivation arises out of a desire to change, or affect those circumstances in some way.

Secondly, since the stories about the founding of voluntary organisations tell how the founders took action to change a situation they regarded as problematic or undesirable, their proposal for the alleviation or remedying of these problematised situations contain the seeds of a utopian vision of a better world. These fragmentary visions, while not necessarily productive of easy generalisations, may contain tantalising glimpses of inspiring alternatives.

Therefore, these stories not only set out a theoretical position about the social circumstances the founders wanted to change, by extension they also propose a vision about what might constitute a more just society ('just' in the sense of there being within it the possibility of addressing the founders desires and concerns). These theoretical positions may not necessarily be consistent or well developed. However, they are revelatory of the underlying assumptions the founders have made about the nature of the social world. The founding stories, therefore, reveal the founders' theories-in-use[3] about the nature of injustice (again, in the broad sense that I have suggested above) and its remedy.

Thirdly, these remedies, their suggestions for the way in which this desirable state might be obtained constitute the beginnings of an ideology. Ricoeur (1986) uses ideology in this sense to describe the mechanism by which a utopia is built. For the founders the creating of organisations constitutes that mechanism – the organisation is the means by which the desired alternatives will be achieved. In this sense the organisations, at least in their early state, can be regarded as the ideologies that concretize the founders' visions.

From a social constructionist perspective therefore, these stories can tell us what situations people want to change, what alternatives they would like to see and how these alternatives might be achieved. This chapter explores some of these theories-in-use as revealed in the stories.

However, these processes are not unproblematic and the stories also reveal some inherent contradictions. When people come together to create an organisation they

---

3 Arygris (1992) distinguishes espoused theories (the 'rules' or principles, that people will describe as influencing or underpinning their actions) from theories-in-use (the rules that would appear to influence the way they actually behave). Arygris makes the point that theories-in-use are often profoundly different from espoused theories. Theories-in-use may be held at a level that is largely unconscious – Schein (1985) describes these as 'basic assumptions'.

are taking power to effect change[4] whether it is in terms of resistance to something they don't like or to a threat to something valued. The action taking is in itself, and of itself, an instance of *productive* power (in the Foucauldian sense).

> …power produces; it produces reality; it produces domains of objects and rituals of truth. The individual and the knowledge that may be gained of him [sic] belong to this production. (Foucault 1979, 194)

On one level what is produced through this taking of action is the organisation itself. Foucault's observation is relevant here because it implies that the organisation may be regarded as producing, and encoding, both the new reality it seeks and the domain of knowledge that surrounds that new reality. This is particularly observable in relation to organisations set up to campaign or advocate on behalf of a particular group or concern. They represent these concerns and increase our awareness of them and our knowledge about them.

This may be one way of understanding the paradox by which those who seek to remedy injustice may become, to some extent, complicit in the maintaining of that injustice through the structures of meaning they inhabit. For example, the Disability Action Network (DAN), a UK voluntary organisation, campaigns vociferously against other voluntary organisations, saying that they perpetuate patronising and devaluing attitudes about disabled people, the very attitudes they were founded to challenge. A press release on their website criticising Mencap, a large and well established UK organisation says:

> Mencap was set up to work with carers and people with learning disabilities. Mencap show they prefer to work with carers, listen to carers and act for carers first and people with learning disabilities second.

> Mencap don't think we can speak for ourselves. One of Mencap's chief executives thought we couldn't organise ourselves because animals couldn't organise themselves and because children couldn't organise themselves. I am 46 years old. You can see what Mencap thinks of me.[5]

And DAN is similarly vituperative about a number of other voluntary organisations. Foucault also asserts that power produces resistance. Here we can see that organisations established to alleviate a particular problem or situation can find themselves perpetuating the very problems they are trying to solve. Identifying some of the processes by which this can happen is a significant theme of this chapter.

One of these processes is through the telling of the story itself. In their telling the stories not only recount the way in which the social world is created but also contribute to the remaking and re-imagining of that world. And as the social world

---

4   Anderson (1996) helpfully notes the important distinction between power-over and power-to.

5   From <http:tripil.com/04003.html>//accessed on 14/10/05

is remade new understandings and structures of meaning emerge – which may themselves constrain and lead to resistance.

Here is an example of the way in which the story sustains a sense of the founding vision and prompts an answering response in the listener:

> *So it was started, a bit like Shelter[6] really, as a result of public outrage, something that's rare in this day and age.*

Even in this one sentence it is possible to see how the story can play a significant role in rallying the organisation's participants, many years after the founding event. It is, in part, the very distance of time that gives it its particular motivating force. However, in that rallying force is also a reinforcing of the particular conceptualisations of power and powerlessness that motivated the founders.

In this chapter I use these stories to look at how the creation of an organisation changes the social landscape. In the next section I use the content of the stories to reveal the founders theories-in-use about social injustice and also their utopian visions for a better world.

In the following section, I look at the praxis of founding, the developing of organisational responses, the structures of thinking that determine the actions required to achieve a desired state – the 'technology' of the ideal. Ricoeur (1986) suggests that ideologies and utopias are dialectically linked.

> ...the very conjunction of these two, opposite sides, or complementary functions [of ideology and utopia] typifies what could be called a social and cultural imagination. (Ricoeur 1986, 1)

It is in this conjunction that these 'ideologies' are encoded in the organisations themselves.

Thirdly, I suggest that one of the functions of founding organisations is to create new meanings of social inequity and injustice, and that this can lead to a paradox that is inherent in the founding of new organisations (as demonstrated by DAN).

Many organisations, as in the example that opens this chapter, are founded not by the oppressed, or by those who are (at least intentionally) the oppressors. The mother of the child disabled through rubella is not motivated by concern for herself, but for him. In such cases the founders are acting in the capacity of Nandy's social analysts; analysts and critics of the existing social order and also as entrepreneurs who are able to imagine and construct alternatives.

Subversive stories and utopian tales

> *In the city of course we are finding people who have been migrating from the villages and settling here, and they always look forward to going back to the villages where they came from after some years...they always dream of going back.*

---

6   Shelter is a UK based organisation that campaigns on issues of homelessness.

These villagers have come to the city in search of employment because there is no longer enough work in the villages to provide the income to sustain their families. This quote comes from the founding story of an organisation that works in rural areas to alleviate poverty and to campaign for sustainable wages to be paid by landowners so that people do not have to leave the villages for work. Here, the link between the identification of a social problem, the vision of a better world and the organisation's activities is clearly made.

Reedy writes that 'formulating answers to what the good life should be by painting narrative pictures is the practice of utopia…it possesses the capacity to de-naturalise the dominant reality by imaginatively transcending what are seen as current material limitations (Reedy 2001, 2). In this sense the founding stories, as the founders' answers to what the good life should be, are stories about utopias. Exploring the content of these stories gives us insights into how these different utopias are imagined.

However, utopian thinking contains elements of resistance, indeed Ricoeur (1986) in his writing on utopias suggests that all utopian thinking is inherently subversive. In this section I develop the proposal that the founding stories can be seen as both stories of subversion and utopian tales.

This development of new, alternative perspectives defines utopia's most basic function. May we not say then that imagination itself – through its utopian function – has a constitutive role in helping us to *rethink* the nature of our social life?….Does not the fantasy of an alternative society and its exteriorisation 'nowhere' work as one of the most formidable contestations of what is? (Ricoeur 1986, 16)

Here is one such example in which the vision is clearly articulated:

Because if you created a culture which really revered its children, and loved its children and had them top of the agenda, I think it would transform what happened to children. And it's easy to say that child abuse is intolerable but it's a big step to go from a theoretical statement like that for people in this country to say 'we're simply not going to tolerate it'.

The utopian vision is of a society in which children are truly loved. However, the 'contestation of what is' lies in the clear implication this is not the currently the case. This brief excerpt from the founding story also begins to set out the mechanism through which that utopian condition might be achieved.

In the following example the connection between the founding vision and its challenge to the status quo is even more explicitly stated:

… the organisation was founded with a very big vision of a just and sustainable economy, but also the idea that there were emerging strands of new thinking in relation to economics that could add up to a new economics to challenge economic orthodoxy.

Here it is clear that the founders did not believe that economic orthodoxy was going to lead to a just and sustainable economy.

Subversive stories

What do the contents of these stories tell us about the ways in which the founders critique, or contest the status quo and their underlying theories-in-use about the nature of injustice? Resistance to the oppression of the poor is a significant theme as in the following example:

> *... Most of them were landless people and most of them were oppressed by caste, you know, hierarchy.*

In this story it is possible to suggest that the founder is not only identifying oppression as a social ill but also proposing the suggestion, or theory-in-use that oppression is *caused* by caste, by a hierarchical structuring of society; similarly in the reference to the 'privileged group' in this excerpt:

> *... When we started work it was a totally backward area with illiteracy, poverty and various miserable problems dominating... this area was in a very bad condition. Illicit distilling and bonded labours, all the more exploitation by privileged group. This pathetic condition aroused feeling towards the hapless beings in me. As I am hailing from a family where all have the spirit of social work it was so natural.*

And in the quote that opened the first chapter (repeated below) oppression is theorised as residing in dependence of the fishermen on the very people who are exploiting them.

> *...so they had organised these fish marketing societies to help fishermen get out of the clutches of middlemen and money lenders...*

Cruelty towards vulnerable people and also society's indifference to suffering is another recurring theme.

> *And he was, basically, appalled by the way some children were treated and was particularly concerned that there wasn't any effective legislation protecting children from cruelty at the hands of their parents or carers.*

The use of such words as 'appalled' and 'exploitation' indicates the strength of feeling that the storytellers project onto the founders. The following quote demonstrates the continuing frustration felt by this activist at the slow progress in the implementation of UK government policy on the closure of long stay hospitals.

> *Well, you see there is a belief that that battle has been won, and it is true to say that many of the battles around that issue have been won, but the war itself is not won. And there are many other battles to be fought because there are still, in England alone, about 3,000 people with learning difficulties living in long stay hospitals, 4,000 in Scotland....*

Several organisations were created because the founders had become increasingly aware of the limitations of existing solutions and of the need for a new approach.

Here is one example from a story about the founding of the settlement movement in the UK in the early 20ᵗʰ century:

> *He* [the founder] *was fairly convinced that people were making things worse in the poorest parts of London by doing the Lady-Bountiful-doling-out act and wanted to do something much more radical than that, and challenge students...to come and live in the area rather than visit the area.*

This is a critique not just of a model of intervention but of the attitudes and assumptions that underpin it. The story clearly sets out the founder's theory-in-use that a class based, 'top-down' philanthropic approach perpetuates social injustice rather than alleviating it.

One Indian founder, a medical doctor who specialised in child nutrition, said that his motivation for setting up a new organisation came from his growing belief that in India malnutrition is a *social* problem rather than a medical problem. Its roots lie not only in poverty but also in the cultural attitudes to women that lead mothers to save the best food for the men and boys, therefore interventions based only on the provision of medical care were doomed to failure.

> *So as I studied more and more I realised that malnutrition was not a clinical disease but it was a social disease and it had social ramifications... And as I put my head round to look at more and more children, I could end up seeing two, three hundred children, and the same faces kept on coming back with the same problems. So I said, 'something has to be done!'*

I heard another example of the problematising of existing solutions at a meeting I attended in Delhi discussing international relief efforts following the 2001 Gujarat earthquake. I was told that although a lot of clothing had been donated many of the survivors were still wearing the clothes they had on when the earthquake struck, because they couldn't make sense of the donated supplies. These offered clothes were not in their colours or style and they couldn't understand them as clothes they could use.[7] Here the critique is of an approach to relief rather than of the circumstances that led to the earthquake.

Quite a different example concerns an organisation set up for young conscientious objectors, during the Second World War in the UK, who needed to be found something to do.

> *Most voluntary organisations start when someone identifies a need – this is an organisation that started because people needed something to do. Which is different.*

What they chose to do was to re-build the communities that had been bombed, in effect to re-create what the war had destroyed. They visited families who had lost all their possessions (and often some of their family members as well), offering

---

7   This was a comment made by a member of the audience at a presentation I gave in New Delhi, 6 March, 2001.

whatever help they could. From these initial beginnings the organisation developed a model of family case work with vulnerable families for which it has become renowned. The CEO who told me this story said that 'the whole definition and style of the notion of a problem family was part of [our] history'.[8]

The injustice being critiqued in this story is war and the destruction it causes. However this example is also particularly interesting because it clearly exposes how the creation of the concept of a problem (families unable to cope) is an innate part of the process of offering a solution to it (family case work). The creation of the problem becomes dependent on the prior creation of the solution. The problem follows the solution rather than preceding it.

These stories are powerful tales. The use of battle imagery, phrases about cruelty and oppression, the evocation of courage in the face of war, all these reveal the passion from which founders create, or dream, their utopian visions of a more just society.

Utopian visions

Ricoeur (1986) writes that utopian thinking inspires us to create imaginative variations of 'what is'. What then are these utopian variations? Many of these fragments are specific to the group of people about whom the organisation is concerned, as in the example previously given of a society in which children are loved and valued or a future state where fishermen are able to trade their own fish without being harassed.

Is it also possible to construct, from the fragments of these stories, some elements of a shared vision of the just society?

There are several common themes than run through many of the stories. One is of an underlying vision of an interconnected world. This holistic vision is often expressed through the desire to express solidarity and make links with others. These are two such examples in which founders are reaching out to make common cause with people in other parts of the world:

> *... a definite gap in terms of research and awareness... with regard to the causes of poverty and the links between north and south and how they interact... So the organisation started out more as a research, campaigning, lobbying type of organisation, very much driven by the then left wing of the '70s very much of the left wing concept of solidarity...*

The second is from a story about an organisation that was founded earlier to offer support to intellectuals fleeing from the Nazis during the Second World War:

> *...a bunch of worthy academics coming together, I think really as a sort of 'we must help out brother and sister academics in the rest of Europe'.*

---

8   In an interview with the author in February, 1998.

One Indian activist talked about the importance of locating AIDS work within a health 'package', rather than 'targeting the prostitute'.[9] Here this idea of interconnectedness is focussed on a problem rather than on a group of people, but the approach is the same, to locate it systemically within a context of interconnected issues.

This emphasis on a systemic analysis is in sharp contrast to the 'atomisation' of groups, issues and problems that Kwek (2003) has suggested is a rather western phenomenon. However, it is also worth noting here (and this is a point I will return to at the end of the chapter) that there is a paradox between the expression of a belief in an interconnected world and the establishing of an organisation that sets people apart from the wider society and identifies them in terms of a common interest, such as that of disability (DAN) or occupation (fishermen) to give but two examples.

Another common theme is the belief that in a utopian society all people are regarded as assets to their communities, the possessors of strengths rather than weaknesses. The circumstances in which they currently find themselves are not the result of feckless or immoral behaviour but of an unjust society that creates barriers rather than offering assistance. Many activists were profoundly critical of policies and practices that locate individuals in the role of the passive victim rather than that of a resourceful person with the strength and ability to act on their circumstances.

> This collective response to health [voluntary run community health initiatives] can be seen to be either an implicit or explicit criticism of the foundation of health service delivery; a foundation that asserts that people are ill because of something to do with them as individuals not because of how society is organised. (Watts in her introduction to Kenner 1986, 3)

Therefore, by extension, a utopian society would be organised in order to enhance peoples' strengths and create health.

These utopian visions are fragments and many are implied rather than explicit. Some are emergent; it is the recognition of the injustice or problem that motivates the founders that the desired response is being shaped and articulated.

Janeway says that 'the trouble with utopias is that they are full of brilliant ideas for desirable ends, but overlook the means for getting there' (Janeway 1980, 184). However all the founding stories tell of people acting on their social (and sometimes physical and imaginative) environment because they want to change it. While the stories all function as an implicit (and sometimes very explicit) critique of the status quo, they propose as a remedy not only individual and collective action but also the creation of institutions – the organisation which is the resolution of the tale. These founding stories move beyond utopian thinking to describe the creation of the organisational structures that are designed to achieve the desired vision.

---

9   In an interview with the author in May, 1999.

Creating alternative ideologies

> Ever since the Mayflower Compact was drafted and signed ... voluntary ssociations have been the specifically American remedy for the failure of institutions, the unreliability of men [sic] and the uncertain nature of the future. (Arendt 1973, 82)

Arendt is wrong, I think, in saying that this is 'specifically' American. Many of the stories about the founding of voluntary organisations are stories about people coming together to create their own remedy for the failure of the state either to provide what is wanted or needed, or to provide it in the way that people want or need it. Their remedy is the creating of alternative institutions, or ideologies in the sense that Ricoeur (1986) describes, alternative means of achieving their visions. While traditional utopian thinking, as Janeway (1980) comments, rarely moves beyond the depiction, in word pictures, of alternatives these founders don't merely dream about these alternatives, they set about developing institutional structures to realise, or 'concretise' their visions.

This section explores the 'praxis' of founding. My suggestion is that it is in this fusion between the founders' dissatisfaction with things as they are and their utopian visions for the future that the new organisational responses are shaped.

This is demonstrated in the following example in which the storyteller explicitly links the type of organisation he chose to create with his experiences of poverty. This organisation helps poor fishing communities to establish and run their own small businesses.

> *So, this was the background how it emerged, my own experience, my own vision... . Because [of] my family background also. I am from a very poor family, fisherman family. So I suffered a lot, as a member of a backward family, community, so all this helped me to come up with instituting this type of organisation....*

Following Arendt's observation that voluntary associations are a remedy for the 'failure of institutions' it is not surprising many organisations were founded as a response to this perceived failure. In may cases their response is to create an organisation to campaign for reform as, for example, in the case of one 19th century activist's efforts to ensure that legislation was created to protect the rights of the child.

Here, the need for a campaigning organisation is created by the belief that the government response to the provision of services for people with learning difficulties is inadequate.

> *And in 1971 the* [UK] *government published a paper called 'Better Services for the Mentally Handicapped'.... So this particular, small band of people, who had been sort of meeting together... felt so strongly that the government should go further, that they decided to actually do something about it. And they set up CMH, Campaign for Mental Handicap, and they produced a document called 'Even Better Services for the Mentally Handicapped'.*

Some founders respond to the perceived inadequacies of services not by campaigning but by developing alternatives.   Examples of these would be organisations that developed community based support for people with mental health problems or learning difficulties who were living in long stay hospitals (themselves, originally of course called asylums to suggest a place of safety and care) rather than campaigning for improved state provision. In the following story the parents of children with a then little understood condition didn't want their children to be taken away from them and put into residential care which was the only option available at that time.

> *It was parents coming together to make things happen because there were no resources for their kids, so they didn't think about 'how do you do that', they just did it one way or another, so they sold their houses and bought buildings and opened a school.*

Perhaps surprisingly, there were very few stories which actively promoted philanthropic responses although these are two such examples, the first from the UK and the second from India:

> *It was kind of, you know, active women and then it was an issue around philanthropy ....so it was just kind of women coming together and worried about, you know, poverty and things like that.*

And:

> *We have come from Bangladesh. At Partition....And our neighbours and villagers, they are all come to us. You know what is zamindar? We were zamindars there* [landlords under an essentially feudal system]. *So all the people came to us. That time I tried to do something for them.*

The first of these stories offers an interpretation of social responsibility that can be freely chosen while the second seems subtly different. In this the act of 'doing good' is presented as inescapable within a complex pattern of historical and cultural identity.

All of these stories could be interpreted as a response to the failure of institutions and the nature of that response is itself a response to the way in which that failure is framed and understood. However, there were other stories in which organisations were founded as catalysts to create the conditions for social change rather than to directly influence that change themselves. I have used the metaphor of the alchemical crucible to describe these catalytic organisations. In these stories there is no clear, direct causal relationship between action and consequence. They portray a more hermeneutic relationship between the prior and the desired state of affairs in which the organisation is established to play a catalytic role.

For example, there seem to be some organisations whose purpose is to be expressive, they exist in order to represent the needs and aspirations of a particular group or a particular perspective.

...my understanding is that it was just a talking shop of various organisations providing residential care, about what they thought they were about, what they were doing, why they thought they were doing it, what was the purpose of residential care, should you train your staff, was it a vocation or was it a profession, or was it just a way of earning a living....

While this could be construed as a solution to a problem, it is not entirely clear either what the problem is or what the solution might be. What is being described here is the creation of a space in which the meaning of residential care can be explored and named. Here, the locus of the transformation is neither in the organisation nor in its members, nor exclusively in the external environment, but rather in a fusion of all of these.

We will create a centre which creates social mobilisers ... a kind of change agent creating organisation, a social mobiliser organisation.

These stories are often short on content and long on process, but perhaps for these organisations the content is the process. They contain little detail about precisely what the desired changes might be. They do not offer an alternative vision but rather a way in which such a vision might be found. The organisation, in these stories is the crucible in which the conditions are set for the transformation of social inequity into social justice. In these stories the relationship between the solution and the problem is more symbiotic than linear; therefore the organisation has to play the role of mediator.

The objectives of the organisation were very, very broad indeed, but basically to act as help to the provider organisations, to act as a way of bringing together.

Many stories propose making connections either to achieve greater influence as in membership organisations, or to combat isolation, which is defined as a social ill in this example from the story that opened this chapter:

In the city, of course, we are finding people who have been migrating from the villages and settling here... And whenever they earned money they sent the money back to their homes. And they lived, you know, alone, as individuals, not as families.

The last sentence in that example is particularly interesting, that the people who had migrated from the villages to the cities now had to live alone, cut off from their roots and their families. The theme of building connections is also very strongly evoked in the following story about the building of a road. This story is worth quoting in length not only because of the way in which it links the identified problem, the isolation of the village both in geographical terms and in terms of the location of the villagers in the social structure, but also because it describes, dramatically, the risks that are taken by founders and activists.

We discussed matters regarding education, the condition of the village, the problem of illicit distilling, the problem of bonded labour and exploitation, the lack of transportation facility, road, electricity Then I asked them what we can do to change the situation. I suggested to start some action programme as the first step. So the next day... all of them brought some equipment and baskets and we started construction work. First was the construction of a road... We worked in groups [on] both sides and we connected the place to the main road by making five kilometres of road.

Problems also started with our work. The land where we started constructing the road belonged to some individuals who were the main exploiters in the area. They started troubling us saying that we have encroached on their land. Their ultimate aim was to kill us and especially me, because I was the leader. They gave a petition to the police to stop us from this work. They had enough money with them and they were successful in influencing the police and political leaders. But we were determined to continue the work...

The police accepted the petition and kept the place under close scrutiny. They gave protection to the area and kept two, three personnel there. But when they [were] not there we [would] work and the construction was completed very easily ...by the work of five months we connected the road to two places.

This fascinating (and also humbling) story is rich in metaphor and symbolism. The isolation of the villagers is geographical (because the village is cut off from the road), economic (because of their poverty) and social (because so many of them are bonded to local money lenders) and so the act of constructing the road together has meaning on all of these levels. Furthermore, the land on which the road was built 'belonged' to the local landowners, not to the villagers. Their action was therefore illegal and the police within their rights to reinforce the landlord's petition. The choice of activity, the building of the road, establishes an opposition between social justice and legal justice (reinforced, of course, by the telling of the story).

Whilst many organisations are founded to create solutions, or to provide the conditions for solutions to emerge, sometimes a new organisation is founded to create a change in awareness, so that a situation which had previously been regarded as unproblematic becomes problematised. The perception that a certain situation is acceptable changes; an example might be the changing attitudes towards domestic violence from private concern to criminal act (or, as in the above example, the suggestion that criminal acts can have legitimacy). These organisations are engaged in the work of reinterpreting the social environment.

What all of these examples demonstrate is that the ways in which the founders frame the situations they want to change and their visions of a better world influence the particular forms of organisational activity they create. However, the process of institution building is not unproblematic. While the actions of the individual founders may be radical, the organisations themselves may become conservative, the tendency of organisations to act to preserve the status quo rather than subvert it is well researched. This paradoxical relationship between the radical and conservative functions of organisations will be discussed in the next section.[10]

Changing the social landscape

This section looks at how the creation of an organisation functions to construct new meanings of social injustice and at some of the contradictions inherent in that process.

How effective voluntary organisations are at achieving the changes they strive for is a complex and difficult question. While each of the people I interviewed spoke convincingly about the successes of their individual organisations, in the larger context they did not always see improvement in the social problems they were aiming to ameliorate. They felt that many of the issues that voluntary organisations hold dear such as better access to justice, homes for homeless people, improved healthcare, improved literacy, more, and wider community participation were getting worse. This was best expressed by one person whose organisation is active in the field of child protection, who said, 'how do we live with the fact that we have been in existence for 113 years and yet there seems to be more child abuse occurring now that ever before?'.[11]

In many of the countries with active and diverse voluntary organisations social inequities such as the distance between rich and poor, demographics of health, poverty and inequality are widely perceived to be growing rather than diminishing.[12] In many countries both absolute and relative poverty is increasing. Euan Ferguson, writing in *The Observer* notes that '25% of households [in the UK] are benefit dependent ... the wage gap between the richest and the poorest is greater now than at any time since the industrial revolution'.[13]

How can we understand this? Is it merely that voluntary organisations are inherently just less powerful than the other great players on the social stage; governments, economic trends, multi-national corporations? Is it the methods they use that are at fault?[14] These are interesting and important questions. But is there also a sense in which in raising awareness of a social ill the organisation may actually be *producing* that which they are trying to eradicate?

---

10 See, for example Morgan 1993 and Clegg and Dunkerly 1984 on the ways in which the need for survival can distort all other organisational priorities.

11 In a conversation with the author in spring, 1997.

12 For a discussion on the relationship between increasing inequality and poor health in particular, see Wilkinson 1996.

13 30th September, 2001.

14 For example, there are continuing debates around organisations that provide emergency aid by working through corrupt local agencies and officials, such as the criticisms of many organisations involved in relief operations in Rwanda and challenges that charity increases dependency.

Ludema et al suggest that 'human systems grow and construct their realities in the direction of what they most persistently, actively and collectively ask questions about' (Ludema at al 2001, 191). This is reminiscent of the proposition made by Foucault that I referred to earlier; that power produces 'domains of objects and rituals of truth' (Foucault 1979, 194).

Cooperrider and Srivasta, writing from a social constructionist perspective (Ludema et al 2001, van den Haar and Hosking 2004) developed an approach they call 'appreciative enquiry' based on the belief that that on which we concentrate our awareness we bring into being. They therefore chose to focus their attention on the positive in order to create positive social change.

> Based upon the belief that organizations grow in the direction of what is studied (that inquiry is constructive) the choice of a *positive* topic for the inquiry is proposed – as a way to construct positive social realities (van den Haar and Hosking 2004, 1025).

Applying these ideas to voluntary organisations suggests one possible explanation for this paradox in which the very problems they try to solve sometimes seem to be increasing. There is a danger that voluntary organisations, which focus so much of their attention on what is wrong with the ways in which society is currently organised may be inadvertently creating a heuristic of deficiency for interpretation and losing sight of their crucial role in 'foster[ing] constructive change [which] relies on the capacity of a group to see and produce alternative realities' (Ludema et al 2001, 91).

The creation of a new organisation changes the social landscape. It intrudes into it. Before its creation it did not exist, afterwards it is there. It both emerges from its context and changes that context – and becomes part of the context it seeks to change. The complexities of this process can be illustrated by looking at the dynamics involved in the naming of the new organisation.

Many organisations become named by the social problem they have identified, such as the National Society for the Prevention of Cruelty to Children or the Child in Need Institute. Their very names create, in our social consciousness, a new concept with which to understand our world. Heidegger describes this phenomenon:

> Language, by naming beings for the first time brings beings to word and to appearance. Only this naming nominates beings *to* their being from *out* of their being. (Heidegger 1971, 73)

But the process of naming is complex. In Hacking's (1999) discussion of the social construction of child abuse he identifies how certain behaviours in certain contexts have come to be labelled abusive while others have not; specifically that child prostitution is rarely referred to in the media as 'abuse'. Similarly, the construction of 'child' varies from culture to culture. Hacking demonstrates clearly the culturally contingent nature of such problem construction.

'Child abuse' is a potent metaphor because it has the property of instantly oncealing its use as a metaphor. Once something is labelled child abuse you are not supposed to say wait a minute, that's stretching things. Which labels stick depends less on their intrinsic merits than on the network of nterested parties that wish to attach these labels. (Hacking 1999, 152-153)

One of those interested parties will be the voluntary organisation itself. The search for an institutional response to a problem requires that problem to be named and yet the naming itself is not value free but is an interpretive fiction. The name creates a new metaphorical understanding which allows for some new possibilities to be conceived while excluding others.

Hacking says:

What happens to the woman who now comes to see herself as having been sexually abused? I am referring to her entry to a new world, a world in which one was formed in ways one had not known. Consciousness is not raised but changed....She now has a new concept in terms of which to understand herself. (Hacking 1999, 142)

Hacking's observation can be extended more widely. When an organisation creates a new world in which a new concept exists our understanding of our society, our experiences and our place within it changes.

Here are two examples: for many founders their motivation comes from a growing belief that some social practice is unacceptable. Sometimes this represents a significant cultural shift in perceptions about what is or is not a social ill. The following example concerns an organisation that was founded in the 19th century to protect children from cruelty.

I understand that there was legislation protecting animals but not children. And... he [the founder] *recounts a story where he is going about his business and he comes across a young boy... who was literally dying in the gutter, and I think had been very severely beaten up, I think it was by his father, but by a parent, and, in desperation,* [he] *took the child to the local magistrate who said: 'Well, if it was a dog I could help you but it is only a child'.*

At this point in time cruelty to animals had been perceived as a public ill but not cruelty to children. (The CEO who told me this story went on to say, perhaps apocryphally, that a similar organisation in the US, at around the same time, took out a court case against a man who was abusing a child on the basis that the child was an animal and that therefore legislation to protect animals should apply to children.)

The following story refers to the identification of youth homelessness as a problem:

I think the organisation's put youth homelessness on the map as a social issue, and in fact it's probably done more than that, it's put youth deprivation on the map as a social issue... I don't think anyone else was doing it at the time, and I don't think anyone else has done it since. In the same way that Shelter invented homelessness, in a sense, or were about homelessness, I think we did that for young people, youth poverty and youth homelessness as a specific issue.

However, here again is the paradox I referred to earlier – that as voluntary organisations name and problematise situations they regard as undesirable they increase our awareness of the problem as much, or perhaps more, than the solution. In Hacking's words, we now have a new concept in which to understand ourselves and our society.

Maintaining this tension between the constructive and destructive potential inherent in raising awareness of society's injustices and deficiencies must be very difficult. Storytelling may help to reinforce a sense of meaning and purpose.

> If human action always achieved the results it intended, there would be no space for stories. Nor would there be space for stories if we lived in a perfectly ordered world, like Plato's *Republic.* But the world (both outer and inner) is irrational, puzzling, and threatening, our actions often lead to unanticipated results....So, we turn to narrative forms of explanation, interpretation and sensemaking. By attributing motive, agency or purpose to our human predicaments we may not always make them enjoyable or tolerable, but at least we make them sensical, capable of being understood. When motive, agency or purpose cannot be found we lapse into meaninglessness and despair. (Gabriel 2000, 239-240)

Morgan, in his description of the meta-metaphor of organisation-as-flux-and-transformation says,

> Any phenomena implies and generates its opposite... . Good defines evil and life defines death. Opposites are intertwined in a state of tension that also defines a state of harmony and wholeness. (Morgan 1986, 255)

Therefore we can begin to understand the complex nature of naming a phenomenon and the interaction between the power of naming to simultaneously make action possible and render it impotent. Bradshaw's review of Mike Leigh's film *Vera Drake*,[15] about a woman performing backstreet abortions in 1950s Britain, captures this tension:

> Vera's vocation as an abortionist exists entirely within the concentric circles of criminal concealment and euphemistic taboo. It is not merely that it is a secret from the authorities: it is a secret from Vera herself. She has no language to describe what she does or reflect on it in any way. The closest she comes to telling the miserable women what will happen to them after their appallingly dangerous treatment is to say that they will soon get a pain 'down below', at which point they should go to the lavatory and 'it will come away'. So when one of these women is taken to hospital almost dying in agony, and poor respectable Vera is confronted by the police, she is as hapless and hopeless as her victim-patients, with no way of defending or explaining herself. Her only response is mutely to absorb unimaginable quantities of shame. (Bradshaw, 2005)

---

15 Peter Bradshaw's Review of Vera Drake, directed by Mike Leigh published in *The Guardian*, 7th January, 2005, London.

This is a profoundly evocative description of the powerlessness that comes from the lack of language and of concepts with which to understand our world. Yet, until her arrest, the Vera Drake character is able to act on that world and arguably it is her very lack of language that makes such action possible.

Eliot (1943, 4) said that 'humankind cannot bear too much reality'. If the founding stories are stories of hope they also contain intimations of despair. Tandon (in a discussion in Delhi in March, 2001) suggested that the prevalence of discourse about values and vision in the sector may be a way of mediating our suspicions that we are not achieving the goals we set ourselves. So, too, may be the creating of yet another organisation – the intoxication of the new.

This highlights another paradox. The experience of coming together with likeminded individuals to create an organisation out of a shared concern or sense of purpose can be intoxicating. This action taking is empowering because it involves people defining for themselves what problems they face and what changes they want, and the very creation of the organisation can seem to lend legitimacy to those definitions. With it comes the recognition of solidarity and common cause with others who share those concerns and the establishment of a shared endeavour, the excitement of creating some thing new. But this solidarity itself creates a boundary and a separation, and the excitement can serve to mask other, less bearable emotions of anxiety and pain.

Taking power to define your own needs and solutions legitimises the perspectives of the creators and also their uniqueness, the specificity of their visions – and also their *exclusivity.* The creating of an organisation involves establishing a hierarchy of its own – once the boundary is drawn there must be a way of determining where that boundary is and a privileging of the insiders to the outsiders.

> …discourses of 'difference' often operate to conceal their role in the production and reproduction of such 'differences', presenting these differences as something pregiven and prediscursively 'real', that discourses of difference merely describe rather than help construct and perpetuate. (Narayan 2000, 82)

Here again is a description of the dynamics that can lead to the production of that which is being resisted. These boundaries between the organisation and its environment and the discourses of difference that sustain them separate an issue or a problem from the wider whole of which it is a part. Kwek (2003) suggests that this process of 'atomisation' is reductionist, that 'breaking a system into discrete and atomistic constituents means it can be studied in a way that is unique to Western civilisation' (Kwek 2003, 132). Badrinath also regards this preoccupation with definitions as a peculiarly *Western* preoccupation.

> Practically every branch of Western human knowledge is rooted in definitions. To define a thing is to set limits to it. One result of this process of definition is that whatever human material does not fit into those definitions is either denied, or somehow forced into those definitions. In Indian tradition the emphasis is not on definitions but on what is called

lakshana. Lakshana are attributes.... We need not the definition of truth but the lakshana, the attributes of truth. (Badrinath 1996, 158, 159)

The reduction and essentialising of difference, the *increase* of the distance between the group, or issue around which a boundary has been drawn, and its surrounding social environment also raises an important question about the extent to which the constructs which give legitimacy to minority perspectives can also become imprisoning. This suggests a way of making sense of some of the contradictory processes at work in identity politics in which people organise around a shared identity (for example in social movements such as the women's movement, the disability movement, anti-racist or communal protests) with which voluntary organisations are often closely involved.

Therefore, we can see that in the very creating of a voluntary organisation there may be dynamics at play that will subvert the best intentions of the founders. We bring into being that on which we concentrate our awareness. By focussing on social problems or the problematising of a situation hitherto regarded as unproblematic we increase our awareness of them. The very naming of an organisation contributes to a this increased awareness and also to a new construction of reality in which new ways of interpreting our experience have been created but these may be heuristics of deficiency rather than of strength. Furthermore, by creating an organisational response to the needs of marginalised groups to articulate their own needs and aspirations the boundaries that the organisation sets may serve to increase their sense separation and difference.

Concluding thoughts

The stories about the founding of voluntary organisations tell us how people took action to change the social landscape. They describe the founders' theories-in-use about the circumstances they wanted to change and what they dreamt about creating in their place.

The stories also tell us about the founders' preferred means for achieving their visionary aims through the creating of new institutional arrangements. However, paradoxically, the very naming of something as a social ill can increase our awareness of it and perhaps even its existence. Names and labels are potent and by emphasising the problem rather than its solution organisations can become complicit in maintaining the very structures of meaning they are trying to challenge.

The 'moral' of these stories is that the concerned individual should take action against injustice to achieve a more desired state. But the subject of the story is not always the subject of the action (as in the story of the mother of a disabled child that opened this chapter). These are the stories of the concerned citizen, the citizen who cares. They are stories about people expressing their concern for others but there is a risk that in so doing they capture the 'other' within their constructs.

Nandy (1987) captures these paradoxes well when he writes:

Theories of salvation are always soiled by the spatial and temporal roots of the theorists. Since the solutions are products of the same social experiences that produce the problems they cannot but be informed by the same consciousness. (Nandy 1987, 222)

However, engaging in social action is a way for people to give expression to the anger and frustration they feel in the face of cruelty and injustice. It offers a remedy for the uncertainly and anxiety that comes with a sense of relative powerlessness.

Lipman-Bluman writes persuasively about the 'dual myth of powerlessness and omnipotence'. This duality comes from the fact that 'even the most downtrodden and disenfranchised control some measure of resources' (Lipman-Bluman 1994, 113) including the means of creating organisational arrangements and mobilising voluntary labour. However, this illusion of control, that sustains the 'myth of omnipotence' (Lipman-Bluman 1994, 115) stems *from* the existential anxiety generated by a sense of powerlessness.

The founding stories replace the images of the oppressive and dominant holders of power with those of the founders.

As Janeway points out, even the weak are not without power: they have the power to disbelieve, the power to come together as a group to act towards common goals, they have the power to organise for action. (Janeway cited in Anderson 1996, 69)

The needs of marginalised communities to express commonality and solidarity with each other, to define their needs for themselves, to create a space where their culture and identity is reinforced and valued, and to take power against what at times may seem overwhelming forces of uncertainty against which they feel powerless, all these are wholly rational reasons for creating new organisations.

Kenner points out that 'self definition of need makes every initiative unique' (Kenner 1986, 1). There is little point in inventing an organisation to do exactly what another organisation down the road is also doing, so the new organisation has to give itself legitimacy through carving out some particular space for itself. It does some thing that isn't being done already, it does it differently, or better than other organisations, it does it for different people with different needs and perspectives.

There may be great similarities between organisations but no two will have the same founding story. The stories sustain the sense of being unique. And yet the corresponding need to be part of a community is also expressed through frequent references to shared values. This theme plays itself out in these stories in the dialectic between the uniqueness of each individual organisation and solidarity with the voluntary sector as a whole or a sub-sector of it.

Martin et al (1983) used the phrase 'uniqueness paradox' to describe this tension between the desire to be both unique and simultaneously a part of a greater whole. They demonstrated how organisational stories 'managed' this paradox by reinforcing the claims of uniqueness while revealing commonality. The majority of the founding stories contained some explicit statement about how the organisation was unique – the first, the best, the only one in this area, the only one to take this approach. At the same time, there was often a strong desire to be identified with shared values, not necessarily with the voluntary sector as a whole but with organisations that share certain beliefs (note the quotation that begins the previous chapter about the creating of a federation of fish marketing societies, which, with its reference to a *genuine* voluntary organisation, is a good example of this).

It is in the creating of new organisations that the voluntary sector seems particularly dynamic. For example, in 2001 40% of organisations listed on the Charity Commission Register in the central London boroughs were registered within the previous ten years.

Funders and policy makers often express frustration about the proliferation of organisations.[16] Why don't they merge? Why don't people who want to set up a new organisation just look around to see if there is already an similar organisation, and if so, then join it instead? On the face of it these are sensible questions (although I can't help but notice that this rhetoric seems to be much less often applied to small business where the increasing numbers of new businesses seems to be used more as an indicatory of a healthy economy). They are clearly very important for funders who want to ensure that their money is being well spent. Having (and funding) five organisations, all offering a similar service in close geographic proximity, can seem a poor use of limited resources.

However, these pleas seem to be unheard. There may already be an organisation providing services for Turkish Cypriot refugees in North London – this does not stop people wanting to set up new organisations for Greek Cypriot refugees or Kurdish refugees – although the services they want to provide may be very similar. The irrepressibility and fecundity of the sector points to the satisfaction of other needs than efficiency.

Abravanel (1983) says that one function of storytelling is to mediate between the ideal and the actual. The founding stories contain elements of both; the 'ideal' as represented by the utopian visions and the 'actual' as represented by the new organisations. It is in this mediation that there is the potential for a new way of seeing. The founding stories are examples of this constitutive use of the imagination; they are subversive in their challenge to the existing social order; they are integrative in that they legitimate the alternative power and authority structures they symbolise. But within this tension there is creative possibility. Considered not merely as the stories of individual organisations but as representing a plurality of visions, in the tension between world views, as in the tension between the ideal states they propose and the fallible organisations established to fulfil those ideals, there exists the possibility of the emergence of a technology of diversity, a means of interrogating and transcending the limitations of any single world view.

---

16 For example the recent strategy document published in June, 2004 by the Active Community Directorate of the Home Office contains as a 'high level objective' 'to avoid unnecessary duplication a protocol on the creation of new infrastructure bodies should be established…' (ChangeUp, Executive Summary, 11)

Chapter 3

A Road from Periphery to Centre:
Stories of Empowerment

My name is Patricia. I was born in 1940 in Lahore, India. When I was a tiny baby I came on a ship to England. My Mum said one of the sailors told her to throw me overboard because I had a disability.... When I was eight I was moved to a big hospital. I cried. I didn't like it there. They moved me to another ward and made me drink salt water. They did this a lot but I don't know what for. It made me sick... A female nurse pulled my hair and pushed me onto the floor and dragged me right across the ward. I cried and screamed... .I lived in the hospital for 40 years. There were some good things about it. I liked looking after the babies and I had some friends there. But there were some nurses who were cruel to us. They would force you to drink medicine that made you dopey. If you didn't want it they made you. That's enough about hospital.

When I was 48 I came to live with my Mum ... .One day at [the day centre] *Carl came to talk about KeyRing. I put my name down for a flat but I had to fight for it because my Mum didn't want me to go. I wanted to have my own place so I could do what I wanted at last.*

I've been in my flat for over a year and I've just had a letter from the Council saying that I'm in my flat for good. I have friends in KeyRing and I see them a lot. This is where I want to stay. I had to fight for my flat and I did it. I don't think I should have had to live in hospital for all that time but I had no choice.[1]

Introduction

KeyRing is a UK based voluntary organisation that works with people with learning disabilities who want to live in their own homes but need some support to be able to do so. Patricia told her story to KeyRing staff who were trying to create a campaign for restitution for the thousands of people who experienced the abusive regimes of long stay hospitals. Although the campaign was unsuccessful the many stories told by people like Patricia stand as an eloquent testimony to the organisation's work and to the achievements of people whose basic rights and potential had been ignored for so long.

---

1   Patricia Spry's story is published in one of KeyRing's publicity leaflets, *Go Back to Square One? Not On Your Life!* in use since 2001. KeyRing Living Support Networks is a registered charity with its headquarters in London. I am a member of the trustee board and have talked with Patricia on many occasions.

Power, for Patricia, is about not being abused, having choice and friends, and a place of her own. This chapter is concerned with the stories that people tell about how they have taken up power and how voluntary organisations have assisted then in their efforts. These are the stories of individuals; stories of collective struggles are the theme of the next chapter.

Dilemmas in interpreting stories of experience

When a researcher makes even tentative suggestions about the interpretation of someone else's story they need to be continually aware that that in itself is an imposition of power. Both the telling and the interpreting of stories are, in this sense, political acts.

Stories are amenable to multiple interpretations. Although my interpretations of Patricia's story are not hers they are not necessarily any less valid. My purpose in interpreting her story is not the same as hers in telling it but stories can serve multiple task mistresses. Before going on to explore these stories it is important to address some of the challenges inherent in interpretation.

One such challenge is posed from a feminist perspective by Joan Wallach Scott who argues that even when people tell their own stories these stories can only reproduce the very structures of meaning that constrain people. She argues:

> When experience is taken as the origin of knowledge the vision of the individual subject… becomes the bedrock of evidence on which explanation is built. Questions about the constructed nature of experience, about how subjects are constituted as different in the first place, about how one's vision is structured – about language (or discourse) and history – are left aside. The evidence of experience then becomes evidence for the fact of difference rather than a way of exploring how difference is established, how it operates and in what ways it constitutes subjects who see and act in the world. (Scott 1991, 777)

Therefore, when we claim the authority to speak on behalf of others we risk participating in 'discursive colonisation' (Stone-Mediatore 2000, 121) which may have the effect of validating these categories of difference rather than exposing the conflicts and struggles that lie behind them.

Scott (1991) highlights the danger of reproducing existing structures of power and avoiding this is the challenge for the interpreter. However, stories of 'others' that do not simply assign to them the roles of victim or dependent can contribute to challenging those roles and here the interpreter can also play a part in the process of empowerment by consciously exploring the possibility of alternative identities.

A limitation with Scott's position is that it doesn't explain how new discursive structures emerge and are formed and shaped. If there are no new frames through which to mediate our understanding of experience, how can new interpretations come to be and how can marginalised people contribute to their creation? Mohanty proposes that writing (and I would suggest, also telling) 'becomes the context through which new, political identities are formed' (Mohanty 1991b, 34).[2]

Mohanty sees the stories of third world women (the term is hers) as 'creative responses to tensions and contradictions of lived experience when this experience is conditioned by local, cultural practices along with globally organised political and economic relations' (Mohanty cited in Stone-Mediatore 2000, 111). In telling their stories people may be able to expose and challenge the circumstances that have constrained them in a marginalised position. This exposing of contradictions may be one aspect of what Austin (1975, 109) defines the 'illocutionary' power of the speech act, 'that which is done in saying' and Ricoeur (1991b) as the productive power of fiction to suggest the possibility of new possibilities.

Here is another story of a person with a learning disability, whom I will call Martin, who has moved out of residential care and into his own flat. Support has been provided by a volunteer and he has not only become more able himself he is also able to provide assistance to another tenant, Sally.

> *When I first moved in* [to my flat] *I needed a lot of support, but after a year I needed less support and when Sally moved in to her flat and needed help with her electricity and Mary* [a volunteer] *wasn't around she rang me and I was able to get the emergency services around for her.*

This story can be interpreted in many ways. It can be seen as a story about empowerment and a story about mutual aid. The voluntary organisation involved might see it as a story of success (evidence of Martin's increasing confidence and skills) while a funder, social worker or parent might read it as a story of failure (where was the volunteer?). And how would the volunteer herself read this story? How does Sally read it?

The context can influence the interpretation but in this case it isn't very helpful. Martin was participating in a discussion where people were being consulted about their views of the services they receive. When Simons (2000) carried out research into the lives of people with learning disabilities in the UK who were living independently or in supported accommodation he found very few who had any desire to go back into residential care. But Basil felt differently:

> Unlike many of the others, who are proud of their independence, Basil appeared to experience the lack of assistance not as a sign of his achievements but as neglect on the part of services that once governed every aspect of his life... .His views help remind us that not everyone would opt for 'independence' regardless of the costs. Not everyone sees institutionalised services as abusive. (Simons 2000, 22-23)

So Basil reminds us that we need to be quite careful with our interpretations. If Basil were the man who helped Sally with her broken electricity meter his story

---

2   I am indebted to Stone-Mediatore (2000) for her critique of Scott and her posing of Mohanty's work as a counter argument.

might indeed be a story about the neglect of services rather than of his pride in his growing confidence and independence.

How does Mohanty's suggestion help us in interpreting Martin's story? One possibility is that the story asks us to explore the significance of the volunteer's absence. It is her absence rather than her presence that allows Martin to discover how much he has learned. The tension between dependency and independence is not an unfamiliar one but it is one that both 'clients' and workers struggle with on a day-to-day basis. The story questions and problematises the very nature of the relationship between helper and helped because the implication is that if Mary, the volunteer, had been there then she would have taken on the role of helping Sally with her electricity meter, and so not only is it her absence that allows Martin to discover his own abilities, perhaps her presence would have made it more difficult for him to make that discovery.

A further point is that in telling his story Martin has become aware of how his knowledge and abilities have increased. In this sense the very telling of his story is itself an act of taking power. This process is clearly of great importance to the storyteller but how does the researcher / academic / social worker relate to such stories?

Mary's (the volunteer's) voice is important too if we are to develop our understanding of the dynamics of taking and giving power. The stories of people in marginalised positions are stories of experience but so too are the stories of the volunteers and workers that offer support to them. Both are valuable but neither is unproblematic and the stories of marginalised people can no more be taken at face value that the stories of concerned others.

When people tell their stories they assume responsibility for how their histories are represented. Each story is the product of an interpretive fiction. In each there are many interests being served by the creation of the story including, perhaps for both, the need to make sense of their lives and their work, the need to reassure themselves, the need for consolation. The events they recount, the moments of changed or increased consciousness are fragments and in imposing a shape and order on them there is the danger of distortion and 'discursive colonisation'.

Martin's story, and its possible interpretations, exemplifies many of themes that recur throughout this chapter including the centrality of relationships to the taking up of power and the difficulties of locating and naming the contribution played by the voluntary organisation involved.

In the following section I explore the stories told by people in marginalised positions[3] to look at what power and powerlessness mean to them. In the third section I then go onto look at whether these stories, and the act of storytelling itself create possibilities that allow them to renegotiate these positions, both with themselves and

---

3   Many of the stories I refer to in this chapter have been told to me directly. Several of these, such as Patricia Spry's story, have also been published in leaflets or reports. Those which come from secondary sources are clearly indicated.

others. The fourth section looks at the contributions of voluntary organisations to these processes.

The chapter concludes with a discussion of some of the contradictions and paradoxes that have been exposed. For example, the story that opened this chapter could be regarded as the story of Patricia's empowerment but the very term 'empowerment' itself is problematic. Patricia fought for her own flat. KeyRing didn't 'empower' her. KeyRing created a situation in which she was able to fight for herself. It is hard to write about the experiences of people like Patricia without falling into linguistic traps because there aren't ready phrases that easily express the nature of these joint struggles. Some of these linguistic traps, or paradoxes, are identified in the final section of this chapter.

Stories of power and powerlessness

> *They* [South Indian fishermen] *are* [now] *free of the large merchant control, and he* [the chair of the trustee board of this organisation, himself a fisherman] *says how years back they were more or less bonded to some of these middlemen who gave them money and they had no freedom to market their fish.*

This section explores the stories about power and powerlessness. Through interpreting the content of these stories it is possible to look at the ways in which power is imagined by those who perceive themselves as having very little of it. The above quote comes from an interview I had with three trustees of a fish marketing co-operative. I asked the trustees, all fishermen themselves, what difference the organisation had made to their lives. This reply (translated from Malayalum by a member of staff) incorporates two familiar themes that occur in many of the stories; the increased sense of individual agency (the freedom to market their fish) and their changed position in relation to others (the local merchants). Power (or the lack of power) in many of these stories is often described in terms of the ability, or agency to take up a new position in society.

In the previous section I explored Scott's (1991) argument that such stories can only reproduce the same structures of power that have oppressed people, and by extension, reproduce the same theoretical models of power. In the case above for instance, presumably Scott's suggestion would be that the fishermen's repositioned relationship with the merchants is simply a movement within an existing, and disempowering, structure and not the creation of a radical alternative. This is one valid interpretation of this story.

However, applying Mohanty's suggestion points us to what *isn't* said in this story, in particular, whether the fishermen are materially better off. They may or may not be, but that is not the emphasis of the story which is on the *freedom to market their fish,* in other words, in their increased sense of agency. In this story the fishermen are not seeking to reproduce the system that has controlled them, for example, by creating a new hierarchy in which some fishermen exercise control over others.

Furthermore, the possibility of failure, which must accompany the freedom to market their own fish, is also implied. Here the story could be said to have exposed a contradiction in that there is an increasing emphasis, in the regulation of voluntary organisations, on *removing* risk.[4] Therefore, this short story about the taking of power can be seen to suggest an element of subversion.

Stories about powerlessness

A sense of how people construct their own interpretations of power can often be discerned in stories such as this one that tell of its absence:

> T said that once a boy took his hearing aids and threw them in the bin. He was really upset. His brother and sister in law phoned the boy's family who were very concerned. (Grove 2004, 16)

We are not told whether the boy himself was repentant. The resolution of the story is ambiguous; power is mediated through T's brother and sister-in-law, as is its effect which is on the boy's family, and in this sense, supports Scott's criticism that the existing power structures are neither challenged nor dismantled. However, there is the possibility that in the telling itself the teller is able to realise some agency. Furthermore, the story's capacity to move us is perhaps especially potent because it is unresolved: no tidy ending here.

Similarly, in David's story:

> *When I was about 21 years old I had a toothache and was sent to the hospital dentist. He strapped me in the chair and used something that looked like a spanner to take out my tooth, and then he got a sharp knife and split my gums open and pulled out the rest of my teeth like a madman, my gums bled like hell. The nurse just stood there laughing at me because I had no teeth left.*

This story was told many years after the event. David goes on to say, 'since I've left [long-stay] hospital my life has changed altogether. I've got my own place and a job but what happened before should never have happened'.[5]

In each of these stories powerlessness is represented in terms of a lack of agency, but more poignantly, in their suggestion that pain and humiliation are funny – to someone else, of course. However both stories, David's in particular, also illustrate Mohanty's point that the telling itself can lead to the formation of 'new political identities' (Mohanty 1991b, 34). Through the telling people begin to challenge and disrupt:

---

4   For example, in the UK it is now an obligation of charity law that trustees carry out an assessment of the risks that the organisation might face and produce an action plan to minimise them.

5   'David's story' (undated) is another one of the stories collected by KeyRing in its campaign for restitution for people who lived in long stay hospitals.

... that deadly triad of definitions that the governed accept and use against themselves; lack of self confidence, a trivialisation of one's own values and goals and the isolation that invites a vision of oneself as a solitary individual, impotent in the face of the mighty. (Janeway 1980, 182)

Rosie, in the story told below does not accept the trivialisation of her own values but is nonetheless, impotent.

Rosie is a young women with learning difficulties who was recently discharged from long stay hospital. She wanted a dog for her birthday...not a special dog, just an ordinary mongrel... But Rosie lived in a staffed home... .The staff truly wanted to help but the hypothetical mongrel presented a myriad of organisational difficulties.

Could Rosie look after this animal? And if not, who was going to take responsibility for it and – this marvellous word – was it FAIR on those people?... Who would take financial responsibility for the vet's bills?

After two long staff meetings the problem was referred upwards... .The process took more than five months... her birthday came and went. The Dog File got thicker and thicker, the phone calls and meetings proliferated... . One evening Rosie came home tired from the Adult Training Centre and was presented proudly to the Home's new inmate. She passed it without a break in her step and, showing unerring zoological accuracy, said 'that's not a dog, it's a cat'. (Brandon 1999, 54)

Rosie's story was told to me by her advocate[6] who was extremely angry about it and in the telling the story became his as well as hers; reflecting his frustration and own impotence in the face of well meaning, but devaluing services where individuals own values and aspirations are, indeed, trivialised. What clearly angered him most was the attempt to pretend that the difference between a cat and a dog was negligible. Rosie is portrayed as disdainful, not complicit in her own devaluing but having no power available to her but her disdain.

These stories suggest that powerlessness, for T, David, Rosie and Brandon, Rosie's advocate, is conceptualised as a lack of agency whether in the face of theft (the hearing aids and the teeth), humiliation or even contempt (as in Rosie's case where it is her very ability to know what she really wants for herself that has been taken away for her). In each of these stories the storyteller is only able to realise agency through the telling of the story in which the possibility of a new political identity, as a campaigner in David's and Brandon's cases, or the refusal to accept the identity that has been thrust upon them, in T's and Rosie's is realised.

---

6 Pairing people with learning disabilities with volunteer 'advocates' who can support them in presenting their own views, particularly in meetings such as social work case conferences, is an established model of social work intervention in the UK.

Stories about power

People tell stories to position themselves... In the stories where power is conspicuously absent, the storyteller has a very clear idea of what constitutes powerlessness but sees themselves as having little ability to manifest agency or, in other words, to do anything much about it. Janeway writes that 'knowledge is power *if it can be implemented*' (Janeway 1980, 45 her emphasis). In T's story and David's story the power to act on their knowledge comes many years after the events described. However, when they *tell* their stories the image they present, of people of little agency, is subtly altered. At least they have the power to tell their own tale. Brandon, Rosie's advocate, may be consoled by the hope that his audience, professionals working in the field of services for people with learning disabilities, may be moved by his story and motivated to look at their own services more critically.

Janeway comments that 'the growth of self, the creation of a secure identity' is 'a process of learning to use power well, in a way that both serves the self and is acceptable to the human environment [including the wider society] in which the self is growing' (1980, 45). Janeway is referring to child development here but this is perhaps equally applicable to those who have been denied the opportunity to take on responsibilities at the same age as their peers. Gary Wrigle writes:

> I feel different in my own flat. I do my own thing. I love choosing and buying things to make it look nicer.... Recently I went on holiday to Edinburgh to see the tall ships. I chose it from brochures and went with a support worker. At home I only went away with my parents or with groups of people, and this was the first time away on my own. (Wrigle 2002, 16)

Many stories, such as Gary's and Martin's tell of people becoming more confident. This may be through the acquisition of new skills and the ability to use them in living independently and in managing one's own affairs, as the fishermen described. It may also be simply through an increased sense of having more possibilities.

> *I'm really busy now, I've made new friends and gone to new places. I've got a lot of confidence and am learning to speak up for myself more.*

The following story was told by a professional worker.

> *There was a young lad who we found living on the street... we worked with him, found him a job selling uddapams[7] to hotels, now he is earning Rs. 300 per day and he owns his own house.*

This story is an interesting contrast to the story of the fishermen who talked about the freedom to market their own fish before mentioning any financial benefits. Professionals and the people they work with sometimes have different priorities. I asked the chief executive of the fishermen's co-operative if he was surprised by their

---

7   A kind of South Indian bread.

answers to my question about the ways in which the organisation had affected their lives. He said:

A bit of a surprise is that they seem to put a higher, much higher value on non-economic gains than I might have expected.

All of these stories have described a change in the storytellers see themselves, from a person with little or no agency to someone who is able to take action in relation to their role within their wider society (in contrast to T, David and Rosie who are portrayed as very constrained with little room for manoeuvre). This changing perception of a self with little agency to a self who can take action is often expressed in terms of spatial metaphors. For example, David tells us that *now* he has his 'own place and a job'. Here are some other examples:

He [a poor farmer] *always thinks he has to work under a landlord...*

We can connect this place [an isolated village] *to the main road...*

...the organisation has given fishermen an opportunity to get linked to the outside world.

... they may be able to develop a project proposal and find resources from outside...

These examples of spatial metaphors, 'under', 'from the ground', 'from outside' are striking. They suggest that we 'build' an imaginative structure to help us position ourselves in relation to our different images of ourselves and others (the landlord, the main road, the outside world) and that taking agency involves a renegotiation (or a re-imagination) of the distances and the spaces between them.

The... story is about a boy...named Batilal whose parents migrated about ten years ago to Delhi as construction workers. Batilal worked on the construction sites alongside his parents and, as construction workers do, they moved from site to site, they never had a regular place to stay. When he was 12 Batilal went to a non-formal education programme where, for the first time, he learned alphabets. Over a five, six year period afterwards Batilal slowly began to master the urban slum environment. Today he has a small troupe of about 10 young boys from the slum who have founded a musical troupe. Batilal knew how to play a drum and over the years he improved on that and is now leading this troupe. They sing songs and they perform on religious and social occasions like marriage and childbirth, and earn a little income. Recently they were recruited to perform for a health education programme on polio. (Tandon 2003, 33)

In this story, told by a professional, Batilal's increased agency is a consequence of a change in his physical location as it becomes fixed (his parents no longer moving around from place to place), a change in his position within it ('he masters' his environment) and he also becomes metaphorically more embedded in 'the urban slum environment' through his new 'location' as a valued member of it.

Power, in these stories, is experienced in relation to something or someone, whether that 'someone' is oneself or another. Tandon says that the three necessary stages for overcoming the impoverishment of powerlessness, whatever the cause, are self renewal, the creating of opportunities and 'renegotiating with the context' (Tandon 2003, 33). It is in this renegotiation with the context that the potential for the creation of new political identities can be realised.

Batilal's story demonstrates all three of these in that it is through the acquisition of knowledge and skills that Batilal is able to create opportunities for himself to earn an income of sorts, but also, in his health education work, he is able to take an active role in changing not only his position in society and but even the very flavour of that society. In this example we can see clearly how the empowerment of one individual is itself a contribution to social change.

In the following story the spatial metaphors are particularly emphasised: the 'outside world', '*now* able to come to the city' – note that the context of this quote is of increased confidence, not of improvements in public transport.

> *He* [one of the South Indian fishermen] *puts a high premium on the benefit of fishermen now feeling the confidence of dealing with the outside world. He says we are now able to come to the Trivandrum city, meet people, explain our point of view, something we would not have even imagined or dated to do before all this took place.*

Ken Simons wrote a book titled *Living on the Edge* (2000) about people who fail to gain access to services in the UK because they are do not easily fit into the categories around which services are organised. The implicit image of society suggested by this title is one that has both a periphery and a centre. Some activists, such as Robert Chambers deliberately invert their metaphors, using phrases such as 'putting the last first' (Chambers 1997, subtitle) that relocate people from the margins to the centre. I noticed that many of the people I talked to in India used the phrase 'poorest of the poor' which has a somewhat similar effect in that it inverts an imaginary pyramid. These stories show that spatial metaphors play a significant role in the way we construct out image of society and our position within it. Whether we regard ourselves as being constrained or having some potential for manoeuvre is crucial to our sense of power or powerlessness. How we take up that potential is the subject of the following section.

Creating possibilities

> *...their stories* [of success] *were very few because they were poor, oppressed and they were living in a very bad situation ....So as a result, although they had good experiences of sharing their own stories of struggle, and so on, yet they were all stories of defeats, stories of failures. So we thought we should certainly help them to see life with a different perspective.*

This story illustrates two themes that reoccurred throughout; the use of the vision metaphor to create alternative images and the use of storytelling to create a new narrative in which new possibilities and identities emerge. The story demonstrates the storyteller's agreement with Mohanty's suggestion that it is in the exposing of contradictions (in this case between the good experiences of sharing stories and the bad experiences that were their subjects) that the founder of this organisation in rural India was able to look for ways in which new visions of a better future might be formed.

In this section I explore the praxis of empowerment, the processes of renegotiating a position in society and in particular, the use of storytelling itself, as in the above example, as a medium through which people are able to 'see life with a different perspective', one in which taking agency becomes possible.

In the following story a social worker tells how she began to realise that the very methods she had been using for years in her work with women and families were obscuring any alternatives. This story reflects the current international development policy debates about whether traditional approaches to the provision of aid end up creating dependency and how organisations can develop alternatives that support poor people in finding their own solutions.

> *...so I tried to look at ways by which I could put a twist on the traditional programmes in the centre.... because what I began to see was that women from poor homes face the crisis of dealing with day to day issues, and they develop very interesting survival strategies which nobody ever acknowledges, and that within those survival strategies are actually the seeds of a long term solution. But it requires an institutional arrangement which can stay with that and to lead it.*

This organisation is, in effect, problematising the traditional, welfare orientated approach to social inequity.[8] This debate is not restricted to the international arena, in the early 20th century a similar observation was made by one of the founders of the original settlement movement in the UK.[9]

She goes on...

> *...and what happened was that these women began to be treated as assets in their community because they now knew more about how to handle systems, how to go around difficult issues, so it's like the domestic help who comes to your house tells you how to go and handle the police - you can't look at her as a stupid woman any more who is very*

---

8   In the UK comments by Louise Casey, the then 'Homelessness Czar', that charities providing soup runs were perpetuating rather than 'solving' the problem of homelessness were very controversial. 'With soup runs and other kinds of charity help well meaning people are spending money servicing the problem on the streets and keeping it there.' (17/11/99 The Observer, available on <http://www.wsws.org/articles/1999.nov/1999/uk-n17.shtml> downloaded 14 /01/05)

9   The residential settlement movement was very influential in the US and the UK. In London, one of the earliest settlements was Toynbee Hall described by one of its founders as ' a clubhouse in Whitechapel occupied by men who do citizen's duty in the neighbourhood' (Dame Henrietta Barnet, cited in Knight 1993, 14). Most of the young men were university graduates and many of the settlements, for example Cambridge House and Oxford House, had direct links with universities. Although they could be seen as reflecting a rather 'top down' approach, their work is often credited with laying the foundations for community development.

poor and silly. So it transformed the way that thought of themselves, it transformed their position on their environment, and gave them the confidence to say, 'this isn't right,' and to do something about it.

Here, as in the story about Batilal in the previous section, the empowerment of individuals changes the society in which they are a part. In these stories the possibility of taking up agency follows a transformation in the way people 'see', or think about themselves. In the following example Mohanty's suggestion is overtly reinforced in the phrase 'see[ing] new avenues of freeing themselves':

A person who has been ploughing the land, as a landless labourer always believes that he has to work like a labourer and die like a labourer and he never thinks of other possibilities... so we talk about various situations in India ... helping them to understand and that politicisation would mean that if people come together and understand life from a political perspective they may be able to see new avenues of freeing themselves from the clutches of casteism, from the exploitation that goes on around it so that they can mentally and physically be free.

The vision metaphor, as in the sense of 'seeing differently' was commonly invoked in the interviews I carried out with phrases such as these:

...their vision is cleared...

...we drew ourselves a strategy

The vision metaphor was particularly strongly evoked in a discussion with an activist who was telling me about 'community exchanges', work they have done with people living in slum communities. In order that people might learn from each other this organisation obtained funding to take an entire planeload of people living in a slum in Mumbai to meet people living in Soweto and share ideas and experiences.

The other thing is the mirror image we use, especially with our exchanges when communities talk to other communities. We say it is like a mirror... because when you go, you can actually look at yourself, when other people are reacting and see how you look, so it's like a mirror when one community shares its experience with another community. And that in itself makes you grow because then you know what you look like, what you feel like.

The idea that it is through seeing yourself in a mirror (whether real or metaphorical) that there is the possibility of assuming new, and stronger identities, is also suggested in the following story about the paralyzing effects of trauma and grief on survivors of a terrifying cyclone.

In 1999 a 'super cyclone' struck the Indian state of Orissa with devastating consequences and an appalling loss of life. One of the organisations I had visited a year before, a theatre company, ran a series of 'creative camps' in jungle villages including one where they estimated that 60-70% of the population had died in the cyclone (Pattanaik 2000, no page numbers). They organised trauma counselling for adults and play activities for the children. They also filmed and presented a nightly news programme called *Lok Samachar* (peoples' news) showing footage of people engaged in reconstruction work that they had shot during the day in order to 'encourage people to be hopeful about life'. As there was no functioning electricity in these villages they carried video players, monitors and generators on their heads, and set them up, each evening, in the centre of the village. One villager said, at the end of the three week 'camp':

> In the deadly darkness [the theatre company] has given us light not only by the generator within the last 15 days, but for the next life to come. (participant, cited in Pattanaik, 2000)

(Note the use of the metaphor of light in this example.)

The main purpose of the news programme was to encourage people to overcome the paralyzing effects of trauma and to do this by showing them footage of other villagers, in similar circumstances, who were beginning to rebuild their lives. In his report Pattanaik says.

> *Sometimes the victims felt like being recognised as if they are important when they saw us using video and audio recorders to record them.*

With *Lok Samachar* the company was presenting the villagers with images of themselves that resemble the previous storyteller's metaphorical 'mirror' – they made it possible for the villages to see themselves in each other and those images hold transformatory possibilities.

> After a puppet show one person said 'we have laughed for the first time after the cyclone'. (Pattanaik 2000).

This company's regular work consists of creating plays that dramatise issues of current concern to villagers, telling the stories through local folk and art forms. Before creating a play they visit a group of villages where they will later be working. They stay with the villagers and talk directly with them about their problems. The company then undertakes what they term a 'cultural survey' to learn more about the specific dances, music and rituals that are used in those villages and they incorporate them into a play. They create stories about the issues the villagers themselves have raised, presenting them in dramatised form, using the villagers' own cultural language and musical instruments.

> *They record through tapes, through video, through photographs, through write- ups, through interview. Then this group comes back... then we get into a theatre making workshop...*

The director is saying is that for the villagers to be able to reflect afresh on the social problems that they are struggling with, to be able to 'see them' from different perspectives, they still need to be presented within their own cultural imaginary.

Similarly, in the UK the theatre group Cardboard Citizens, made up of people living on the streets, have adapted methods inspired by Boal's work (1998) on theatre for the oppressed. One such technique they call the 'rainbow of desires':

> This is a set of techniques akin to various elements of psycho-drama and drama-therapy. It is usually for a closed group. First of all, one or more participants will tell a story about an issue they are dealing with or have dealt with in their lives - unlike Forum Theatre, here the sense is that there are not outside oppressors, but still the protagonist is troubled, perhaps by internalised oppressors. The group will settle on one story; an improvisation based on a real encounter related to the issue will be played out. Then, depending on which technique is being used, the group will react to the story they have heard and seen by making images (Image Theatre); the story-teller will then interact in different ways with these images.[10]

The inference is that in the interaction the storyteller comes see their story anew, refracted in the perceptions of others, and from those images, new ways of responding. Many organisations working with people with learning disabilities also recognise the importance of visual media not only as an alternative form of communication for people who cannot read, but as a means whereby people can tell their own stories and strengthen their own self images. One such project works with people who have very little verbal communication.

> J shows a picture of himself in a fireman's uniform. He doesn't say much here but the others help out. 'He volunteered': 'It's a fireman', 'It was at the flower show'. (Grove 2004, 17)

J's story and T's story (cited earlier in this chapter) come from an article written by Nicola Grove (2004) about a storytelling project she developed with people who have great difficulty in communicating. She points out that the skill of storytelling is not only empowering in the rather abstract sense of identity creation that I have been discussing here – it is also essential if people are going to be able to communicate with doctors, social workers, shopkeepers, the police, the myriad of professionals who are the gatekeepers to services we all need. Their lives could depend on their ability to tell their story.

Storytelling and image making offer us new ways of seeing ourselves and our relationships with others; self images of increased agency and possibilities, and out of these can come the potential for transformation. One of the Indians who works for the people's theatre company, said about their work:

> *Whatever we are doing it is completely different from others. That is a kind of identity which we get from ourselves.*

---

10 Taken from their website <http://www/cardboardcitizens.org.uk/theatreoftheoppressed. php> downloaded 8/7/05

The spatial metaphors invoked in the stories about power emphasise the importance of the place in which we locate ourselves in relation to an imaginative construction of society. The visual metaphors used here suggest that our perceived ability to take up agency to renegotiate this location is enhanced when we become able to 'see' ourselves and our contexts in different ways. In taking up agency we not only change ourselves we change our contexts. In the next section I look at the roles that voluntary organisations play in contributing to this process of individual and social change.

A road from periphery to centre

Voluntary organisations are behind the scenes, in all of these stories. Sometimes their role is explicitly acknowledged (as in Patricia's story and also those of the South Indian fishermen). This section looks at the way their roles are constructed in the stories.

One voluntary sector chief executive described his role in metaphorical terms as being 'on the bridge of the Queen Mary' (Fletcher and Kay 1994, 14). This is an interesting metaphor of leadership but it also captures the sense of the voluntary organisation itself as in between destinations, located in the space between one place and another, or, in the examples cited previously, from one image of self to another.

One thing that an organisation can do to make it possible for people to move from the margins to the centre is to provide some help in making the journey. This help can be in both abstract and practical terms as described in the following quote from a refugee woman in the UK. She is commenting on a training scheme she had participated in, that was run by a voluntary organisation:

> I think also it's good because you are empowering women to get into the job. I was thinking that before I was not able to apply for any job apart from in my community but when I did get on that course... refugee women can make themselves confident and move on and so it's good for women to let them know that they are not under men, they can move on and be very important within the society and make a difference. (Erel and Tomlinson 2005, 47)

She seems to place equal importance on both the abstract (increased confidence, transformed self image, being 'not under men', an integral place in society) and the practical (a training course which makes it possible for her to apply for jobs).

Organisations can provide access to 'the centre' whether to jobs, education, services, information, even buildings ('access audits' were developed by organisations run by people with physical disabilities). This example is taken from an interview with another refugee woman for whom volunteering had provided a route into employment:

> ... I know them you know, I was working for the community organisations, other community organisations, I was attending meetings on a voluntary basis... so it was like it

was for me it helped me when I applied for the job you know because it's like oh, I have something already for the organisation so they took me in. (Tomlinson 2005, 10).

Tomlinson notes that working as a volunteer provided the woman with both confidence and connections and that 'the experience of being "different" (a refugee) is used not to account for failure but for success in finding employment' (Tomlinson 2005, 10). In this example, again, there is the notion that the ability to take up a new role is as dependent on a transformation in the notion of self as on more practical things such as the acquisition of new skills.

Another way in which an organisation can mediate is in providing access to information. A number of organisations working with people with learning disabilities in the UK have pioneered innovative ways of making information accessible pictures, large text and short sentences. Organisations can 'translate' policy documents, tenant agreements, minutes of important meetings such as case conferences, sometimes employing people with learning disabilities in making and approving the translations. This makes it possible for people to participate more fully.

In the following example Ted had difficulty imagining time and this caused him to have problems in looking after his much loved snake, Sid. This story is taken from a report of an action research project[11] that piloted community based approaches to teaching literacy skills.

> Ted loves animals and works on a city farm one day each week which is where he got the idea of keeping a snake. He was very keen to demonstrate that he could look after his snake in the face of some scepticism from family, neighbours and some of the city farm staff. Alex [Ted's support worker] discussed with Ted using a simple calendar to help him look after Sid, his snake, properly. The first non-snake use of the calendar occurred at the end of the project. Ted had a doctor's appointment the following week and marking it on the calendar served to illustrate the difference between this week and next week – it was also the first time such an appointment had not been in Alex's diary but on Ted's calendar, put there by Ted. (Cairns 2001, 6: emphasis in the original)

Here Ted has learned how to imagine time, time is the 'space' being mediated and the effect is to empower Ted not only in terms of his ability to look after Sid (and demonstrating that to the sceptics) but also in his ability to manage other important dates.

KeyRing has developed a 'travel buddies' scheme which makes travel accessible to people who have difficulty in understanding routes, buying tickets or reading bus timetables. Travel buddies are also people with learning disabilities who find such tasks fairly easy and they are paired with people who need to make a trip, to offer support and advice.

---

11   This was funded by Department of Education and Skills through an initiative of the National Institute of Adult and Continuing Education (NIACE) and run with the Elfrida Society (where I worked as chief executive for 13 years) and the Learning from Experience Trust.

A number of organisations in the UK have developed schemes to help people gain access to health services by advocating on their behalf, accompanying them to meetings and bringing groups of people together with medical professionals to talk about the difficulties they have in getting the services they need, perhaps exacerbated by language or cultural differences, an 'invisible' disability that is not recognised, as in the case of people with learning disabilities or mental health problems, or perhaps because they are homeless and therefore have no fixed address.

In all of these examples voluntary organisations provide a road to those things that are often perceived as being at the very heart of society; friends, employment, health, the opportunity, whether through formal volunteering or simply by caring for a pet, of having some impact on the fabric of that society. But the role of connecting the margin to the centre can also be more abstract; as well as building roads between people and services, the road can also connect ideas.

Our core business clearly means 'at risk' of homelessness but you arrive at homelessness through being at risk of, you know, no job, poor mental health, poor health facilities, leaving school without educational attainments, being thrown out – there 's a lot of risk factors. But we just say that the worst thing that can happen to a young person is to be on the street as a result of those risk factors... the range of services we offer can deal with resolving or reducing the influence of some of those factors on a young person's life. We can't really think about risk but we can think about unemployment. We can't do anything about disability but we can do something about employment training. And so it's about ensuring that we do build a structure which actually aids young people at risk of becoming homeless.

It is interesting to contrast this comment to the story of Ted and his snake because for many people with learning disabilities the process of breaking down difficult and intimidating tasks into small component parts is what makes it possible for them to master the task. However, that same compartmentalising can also be profoundly oppressive when it denies the connections that people know and experience. For the organisation working with young homeless people it is in that connecting that opportunities for agency arise.

The director of the Indian peoples' theatre project described his organisation as not only providing, but in some senses being the road:

The government is doing work and giving services to the people. But we have gone to such remote places through our bicycles that the government doesn't reach.

They take their shows through the jungle on bicycles, complete with costumes, musical instruments and props. During their cyclone reconstruction programme they brought the electricity as well.

Whether the organisation provides a road or is itself the road the implication of this metaphor is that the individual has to decide whether or not to make the journey or to stay on the road once they have embarked upon it. All of these activities can be either empowering or disempowering (or even both at the same time) depending on how they are carried out. What determines whether an initiative is liberating or constraining? Given the importance of relatedness and connections in these images of empowerment it is not surprising that the quality of the relationships that voluntary organisation construct emerges from the stories as highly significant.

The nature of the relationships

I suggested earlier that one possible interpretation of Martin's story, in which in the absence of the volunteer helper he discovered that he was able to help Sally with her electricity meter, was that it problematised the nature of 'helping' relationships as they are constructed in social care. In Brandon's story about Rosie and the ersatz dog Rosie is living in a hostel. We are not told whether the hostel is run by a voluntary organisation or by a local authority. However, there are enough stories about abuses, and also just uncaring and disrespectful practices in voluntary as well as publicly or privately run institutions for us not to be too confident about the answer. Not all voluntary organisations are empowering, and not always empowering to everyone.

How are empowering relationships constructed in the stories?

Walking alongside One aspect of empowering relationships is captured by the notion of organisations 'walking alongside' the people they are working with.

> *It's much more about walking alongside people in a process, ourselves as the so-called professionals as much in need of being a part of that process as those who are... more isolated or marginalised than perhaps we are because of our economic situation, our political awareness simply the contacts we've got, simply the fact that we're employed.*

Merrifield's story about working at the Highlander Center in Tennessee during the civil rights movement also echoes this theme:

> You may have heard of Rosa Parks who played a key role in the civil rights movement in the United States. She came to a workshop at the Highlander Center, about six months before she sat down on the bus in Montgomery, Alabama starting the Bus Boycott. She said afterwards that the key thing for her was actually washing dishes with white people. She'd never been in a situation where there was an expectation that black people and white people engaged equally in the work that was needed to keep the group going. That was one of the important learning experiences for her that led eventually to her role in the Montgomery Bus Boycott. (Merrifield 2003, 28)

Obviously this is Merrifield's story, a story of a story. Rosa Parks might have identified many more significant milestones. However people working together across traditional boundaries is a common theme. Brandon (1999) talks about this in terms of the difference between saying that you are 'taking people to' and 'going with'. These two phrases suggest fundamentally different positions with regard to respect and dignity.

Assets or deficits?   If we unpick the notion of 'walking alongside' what seems to underpin it is the notion of people as assets rather than deficient in some way that requires fixing.

> *Her team could see that what she was describing was what they had overcome...and she began to say 'well it's the strengths we ought to be thinking about' and we began to see that as an opportunity...*

This is a very simple point and suggests that public provision should be based on acknowledging and enhancing peoples strengths or building on passions (arguably Ted would have found it much more difficult to learn how to conceptualise time if he hadn't needed to feed Sid, his snake). But often social work case reviews are based on someone's needs, on the things they can't do (Poll 2003).

> *We also realised that women need to be strengthened. They have the ability but because they had not been given the scope to recognise this ability in them they were found to be lacking.*

Community development intervention as well, while ostensibly interested in the strengths that lie in communities, is nonetheless often framed in the language of deficiency. Beazley et al's critique of regeneration initiatives is just this, that 'community capacity has, historically, been conceptualised through a "deficit" model approach, a deficit to be "corrected" if communities are to play an active role in the status quo of local regeneration' (Beazley at el 2004, 1). The deficit model, they suggest, operates at three levels; at the individual as social pathology, at the group as social exclusion and at the community level as the so-called 'democratic deficit'. These are very familiar terms in the discourse of public policy. Yet how many of us feel more powerful as a result of focussing on what we can't do, or do badly as opposed to the things we love and are good at? Beazley et al argue for a new approach to community building, one that recognises the latent skills and abilities of all its members.[12]

Professional or non-professional?   The 'voluntary' ethos of voluntary organisations comes not only from their use and celebration of volunteering but also because volunteers (in theory, even governing trustees) bring an 'ordinary' perspective – their capacity for empathy has not been influenced by professional training. Voluntary organisations also emphasise the importance relationships that are based on friendship, neighbourliness and general good regard rather than on professionalism (not to be confused with being 'unprofessional' which carries more pejorative connotations).

---

12 Similarly, the Asset Based Community Development Institute based in the Institute of Policy Research at Northwestern University in Chicago builds on the work of John McKnight, who has written extensively about the importance of basing development on the 'assets' that people bring. Although McKnight's work in known more in the US than in the UK KeyRing has worked extensively with him and McKnight has run several workshops for people with learning difficulties through KeyRing's aegis.

They are therefore, less likely to objectify the people with whom they are working and more likely to relate to them as neighbours than clients.

For example, the organisation cited earlier, that took a plane of Indian slum dwellers to meet and share experiences with slum dwellers in South Africa believes strongly that people learn more from each other, and that what they learn is likely to be more useful than anything professionals can offer.

Brandon touches on this quality of non-professionalism in a critique of organisations that have developed advocacy or mentoring schemes where the workers are paid rather than voluntary:

> Now I have a difficulty with paid friendship because the whole point of friendship is that its unpaid. I do not expect the prostitute in Islington to be my friend. She gets cash instead. So when people start talking about paid friendship I don't understand what they're doing – it's like this awful word befriending. Just think what Shakespeare would have done with this language. 'Is this a befriend I see before me?'. Here again we are sistoring [sic] the language. How many befriends have you got? For ordinary people in the Red Lion in Upper Street [a pub] this is a meaningless conversation. (Brandon 1999, 58)

The professionalizing of friendship is a very powerful way of reinforcing the distance between the roles of giver and receiver of care. There is little reciprocity and such 'friendship' even when genuinely well meant, is, at least in part, motivated by financial reward. Brandon would say that such professionalised relationships have much less potential to be empowering. at least for the person on the receiving end, because however well intentioned, they reinforce roles that constrain people.

Voluntary organisations can provide a road for people to take which can connect them to people and institutions in the wider society. But people have to choose for themselves whether or not to take the journey. And whether the journey is liberating or whether it reinforces the distances between people is, at least in part, dependant on the quality of the relationships that the organisation builds with people along the way. If these relationships are not based on these underlying values of mutual respect and dignity the initiatives will not be empowering.

Concluding thoughts

In the previous chapter I suggested that people create voluntary organisations as a response to social injustice. The organisation provides a means by which that injustice can be challenged and the founders' visions of a more just society realised. Many of the stories suggested that the founders equated injustice with oppression and powerlessness. In this chapter I explored the stories that people tell about their experiences of powerlessness and power to look at how these relative states are conceptualised and how the roles that voluntary organisations play are constructed.

The stories suggest that people conceptualise power in terms of their location within an imaginary construct of society and the extent to which they see themselves as having the agency to change, or renegotiate that position. Spatial metaphors construct these images of society, dominated by the notion of a margin, or periphery out of which people desire to move to a 'centre'.

Voluntary organisations can assist in this process by providing a road on which to traverse the metaphorical space (sometimes a chasm) that the individual perceives between themselves as they are and their image of a more powerful self. Organisations do this in both abstract and pragmatic ways. They create opportunities for individuals to imagine alternative roles and conceptions of self that allow for new ways of thinking and new possibilities for action. Voluntary organisations also provide access to people, jobs, services, information and political institutions.

Given that people imagine power (and powerlessness) in relational terms it is not surprising that the quality of the relationships that voluntary organisations build between themselves and the people they work are significant. If these relationships are not based on mutual respect then the organisation's intervention will not be experienced as empowering (as with the provision of Rosie' ersatz dog). Yet although policy makers and funders do talk a great deal about empowerment the emphasis they place on measurable outcomes tends to draw attention away from examining the quality of the relationships that are being made and the values on which they are based.

Paradoxes in the rhetoric of empowerment

In the last chapter I discussed some of the paradoxes inherent in the founding of organisations and in particular, the possibility that an organisation that is founded to alleviate some social injustice can find itself perpetuating or even increasing that which it desires to challenge. In this final section I want to briefly address some of the paradoxes of the rhetoric of empowerment.

The very words that we have to describe the ways in which people are assisted in taking up agency are value laden and inadequate. 'Help' 'advocate', even 'empower' all imply a hegemony of the powerful against which the only space for manoeuvre is determined and controlled by the more powerful. The following are some of the most problematic discourses.

The hegemony of efficiency Anderson says that empowerment and efficiency are in opposition because 'it is always quicker, easier, more "efficient" to do [something] for others than to enable them to do it for themselves' (Anderson 1996, 78). In the debate between them efficiency always wins out. It should be possible to talk about the efficiency *of* empowerment and in the long term empowerment arguably *is* more efficient because it reduces peoples' dependency on expensive services.

However empowerment, as described in these stories, does not follow a linear process nor does it necessarily lead to a neat and tidy ending. The discourse of outcomes and impact, so loved by funders and policy makers, carries with it an interpretive apparatus that doesn't easily apply to these stories.

For example Martin only discovered, in the absence of the volunteer support worker, that he was able to sort out Sally's electricity meter for her. (Nor does Martin's story support Anderson's comments because it wouldn't have been either cheaper or more efficient to wait for the volunteer to return.) But it is in this ambiguity of Martin's story, in the importance of absence that problems arise. How, within the discourse of efficiency are we to talk about this absence? How can we talk about the 'mirrors' put up by organisations such as the theatre company in which people can begin to frame new images of themselves? How do we capture the importance of the opportunities provided for black people and white people to wash dishes together? And what sense can we make, in policy terms, of Merrifield's suggestion that washing dishes together 'led' to the Montgomery Bus Boycott?

The idea that learning and empowerment cannot be done for others, that every individual and every community has to go through the processes for themselves, that perhaps it is the processes themselves that are empowering is not a view that has much support. It goes against the tenets of efficiency.

The hegemony of independence   We also need new language to explore the contrasting and overlapping meanings associated with notions of independence, interdependence and dependence. The identification of independence with increased individual agency, and therefore also with empowerment is one that I have made throughout this chapter and it is one way in which empowerment is described in the stories. However, the importance of relatedness comes across very strongly. Humphries (1996) comments that the price we pay for the failure to create relationships that are empowering is dependency. But the relationship between these states is very complex.

Most of the people I interviewed working in Indian organisations tended to talk about empowering groups rather than individuals. For example, one woman said 'unless you are able to get group participation you are unable to create a change in thinking'. One could argue that a notion of independence that focuses on the individual is a western concept that is of very limited use in exploring empowerment as it is actually experienced.

Humphries (1996) accuses the rhetoric of dependency as 'marking the most disadvantaged as always needing more and more, as inherently deficient and unstable' (Humphries 1996, 6). Of course advertisers and marketing departments delight in portraying those of us with spending power as always needing more but for them 'need' is not equated with deficiency or instability and this is Humphries point – that the poor are deficient and unstable while the relatively better off are simply in need of the most up to date consumer goods.

The hegemony of choice   The connection between power and choice is also an interesting one. For Rosie the ersatz dog is a symbol of her lack of both power and choice, she cannot even chose what kind of pet she would like, although she can, of course, choose whether or not to be grateful. Policy makers delight in offering us choice; choice in schools, hospitals, political parties. Amartya Sen's (2003) work defining the ability to exercise choose as an important indicator of relative poverty is well known. But choice is always constrained. Some choices limit or deny other choices or other people's opportunities for choice. Where choice is invoked to imply responsibility the effect can be to individualise issues of power and control and to distract attention from systemic issues and here the rhetoric of choice can lead to the pathologising of people whose choices are very limited.

Finally, Humphries (1996) asks whether the discourse on empowerment also serves to *contain* resistance. Does the state really want lots of empowered people? She notes that the discourse of empowerment has emerged at a time when government in the UK is becoming steadily more controlling. A similar trend is observable in the funding of international NGOs. The withdrawal of the state from the provision of public services has given rise to the phenomenon of 'contracting out' services to voluntary and private organisations, but with very detailed specifications on operational guidelines, regulated through a plethora of institutions and quality frameworks. Amongst the many dangers these pose are the risks to organisations' capacity to develop the very kinds of relationships that are deemed to be so critical for empowerment; relationships that involve people working together, jointly looking for answers; relationships built upon respect and admiration of strengths and desire to help people to fulfil their aspirations and their passions rather than simply meeting their needs.

Chapter 4

From Private Trouble to Public Concern: Voluntary Organisations and Social Change

I'm strongly motivated by this business of making a difference, to leave the world a better place whether by a garden plot or a healthy child or improved social conditions.

Introduction

In this final chapter exploring the contributions of voluntary organisations to social change I look at their role in creating possibilities for alternative constructions of our very ideas, or images of society itself, its institutions and structures and of the boundaries between them.

Earlier I described how the founders' utopian visions of a better society and how it might be achieved influence the kinds of organisations they create. Many of these organisations are directly involved in the work of assisting people in marginalised positions. In the previous chapter I looked at the stories that people told about power and powerlessness. The stories suggested that people conceptualised power in terms of their relationship to others and where they saw themselves positioned within an imaginary construct of society. Whether people regarded themselves as powerful depended on the extent to which they saw themselves as having the agency, or means to renegotiate that position.

Therefore, imagining social change must be predicated on more foundational assumptions about the very nature of society, from which flow ideas not only about how social change occurs but also what organisations can do to bring it about.

For example, in the brief quote above gardens and healthy children make up some of the elements of a good society. But when the speaker refers to 'improved social conditions' we want to know more about what she thinks are the conditions that need improving and what would constitute improvement.

Arguably, before we can explore how people conceptualise, and act on their ideas about social change we need to have some idea about how they think about society itself. Stories can communicate these often unconscious assumptions through their use of narrative or symbolic devices. In this chapter I use the stories about the founding and managing of voluntary organisations to look more deeply into the nature of these imaginative constructions of society and social change and of the roles of voluntary organisations in bringing it about.

I hope that the tables are turning for the people feeling that disabled people are just in the community and we have to tolerate them..., their social contribution to the colour of our society is huge.... It would be a sadder place without these wonderful people.

People with disabilities play an intrinsic role in creating this storyteller's image of the just society. However, she is aware that her vision is not necessarily shared (with people who just 'tolerate' disabled people). In the previous chapter I suggested that one aspect of the dynamics of empowerment on an individual level was the ability to perceive new possibilities for the imagination of self. How do voluntary organisations change the social landscape so that there are new possibilities for marginalised groups to imagine themselves and to be imagined by others? One means is through creating alternative images and even institutions that offer imaginative variations on the theme of society. These include the main institutions of society, state and market, and their relationships to people in marginalised groups.

> The idea of society is a powerful image. It is potent in its own right to control or to stir man [sic] to action. This image has form. It has external boundaries, margins, internal structures. Its outlines contain power to reward conformity and repulse attack. There is energy in its margins and unstructured areas. For symbols of society any human experience of structure, margins or boundaries is ready to hand. (Douglas 1976, 114)

Therefore, the power to create alternative images is the power to liberate. Voluntary organisations work primarily with people whose lives are likely to be lived in those margins and 'unstructured areas'. They provide roads for people to move from the periphery, or margins to the centre of their images of society, as described below:

> *This organisation has given fishermen the opportunity to get linked to the outside world. Learn many things. Develop leadership skills... Even in his own village if someone is from the society they get a certain respect...*

Membership of the fishermen's society changes the fishermen's images of themselves and the image that the other villagers have of them. They have become 'centred' within their village. The fishermen have changed but the image of the position of fishermen within the village itself has also altered.

The founding of an organisation is an event that has immense significance in terms of that organisation's collective imagination and the ways in which it perceives social change. Ebrahim (2005) refers to this as the *discourse* prevailing at the time of founding, the ways in which social problems and solutions were understood and the range of influences and power dynamics that affect those understandings.

> ...NGOs can be profoundly influenced by the conditions surrounding their founding. They are, at least in part, products of the discourses prevailing during their initial, formative stages.... .In short, the initial conditions surrounding an organisation's founding are persistent: they are not unalterable but they do inform future behaviour and change. (Ebrahim 2005, 50)

These 'initial conditions' include the cultures in which the organisations are located. The ways in which people interpret experience, define problems and shape solutions, are likely to be profoundly influenced by the cultures in which they live. Ricoeur suggests that stories can provide a means for penetrating the 'mytho-poetic' (Ricoeur 1991b) nucleus of a society in which the imaginative connections between individuals and the various institutions of society are imagined and constructed. As the stories I am using come from India and the UK they provide an opportunity for looking at different imaginative understandings of society and social change.

> It [the mytho-poetic nucleus] is indirectly recognisable not only by what is said (discourse) but also by what and how one lives (praxis) and... by the distribution between different functional levels of a society....And it is only by the analysis of the hierarchical structuring and evaluation of the different constituents of a society (i.e. the role of politics, nature, art, religion) that we may penetrate to its hidden mytho-poetic nucleus. (Ricoeur 1991b, 483)

If the hierarchical structuring of a society[1] is founded upon its myths and metaphors, which Schein (1986) terms as its 'artifacts', then the story of why an organisation came into being may be a vehicle for discovering how the social environment is conceived and ordered in that particular culture. However, making cross cultural comparisons throws up a number of difficulties.

Dilemmas in cross cultural comparisons

Hofstede (1980) conducted a very large cross cultural study of IBM executives in 40 countries which identified cultural differences in four major areas: 1) how power was perceived and handled within organisations, 2) tolerance of uncertainty, 3) an emphasis on individualism versus communalism, and 4) an orientation toward masculine or feminine values. Several more recent cross-cultural studies seem to confirm his findings (Hofstede 1994 and Jaeger 1990).[2] But while Hofstede's work has been very influential it is not without its critics who focus on issues such as methodology (McSweeney 2002), on Hofstede's essentialist perceptions of cultures (Kwek 2003) and his simplification of the complex dynamics between competing

---

1   I am using the phrase 'hierarchical' in this sense not to refer to class or caste but in the sense that I take Ricoeur to mean, of a prioritising of values and relationships, and as discovered by Hofstede (1980) when he suggests that some cultures place more emphasis on distant power relationships, and on feminine rather that masculine values.

2   Hofstede's important conclusion is that management techniques developed in one culture will not necessarily be effective in another. As the majority of management literature comes from the west (and the United States in particular) this argues for 1) caution in assuming that western management techniques are easily transferable, and 2) the importance of eastern and southern countries developing their own approaches to management. However neither of these are the focus of this study. I am citing Hofstede merely in order to lay the foundation for the assumption of differences across cultures.

cultures particularly those of organisational culture, occupational culture and intra–organisational subcultures (McSweeney 2002).

There are also studies that explore the connections between different philosophical traditions and approaches to management. Chatterjee, for examples, notes the influence of Confucianism, Taoism and Buddhism on Chinese organisations and management practices (Chatterjee 2001) and links specific management practices to these values. A similar study by Vittal explores '*dharma* and the principles for ethics in public administration as reflected in our tradition in the Vedanta, Upanishads, Manu and the Bhagawad Gita' (Vittal 2001, 5) although the main thrust of his argument is not that these values are inherent in the current system but rather that they provide a prescription to remedy its ills.

These cross cultural comparisons primarily look at the influence of different values and philosophical traditions on the ways in which we think about organisations. However, thinking itself may also be culturally contingent. Ramanujan asks whether there is an 'Indian way of thinking' (Ramanujan 1980, 41) distinguishing between cultures where thinking is 'context-free' (many Western cultures) or 'context sensitive' (India) specifically, whether morality and ethics are 'absolute' or contingent. Similarly, Kedia and Bhagat write;

> In associative cultures people utilise associations among events that may not have much logical basis, whereas in abstractive cultures, cause-effect relationships, or rational Judeo-Christian types of thinking are dominant. (Kedia and Bhagat 1988 cited in Kanungo and Jaeger 1992, 11)

Saying that associative thinking may not have 'much logic' sounds a little pejorative. Ramanujan (1980) notes that many writers (not exclusively Western) have regarded associative thinking as more childlike or primitive than abstractive, or universalist thinking.[3] Perhaps there are different kinds of logic. This contrast between associative and abstractive thinking sounds rather like the distinction that Bruns draws between poetic and philosophical logic. Bruns says that 'every hermeneutic situation has the structure of this quarrel [between poetry and philosophy] which is governed by a logic that is, by turns, exclusionary and allegorical' (Bruns 1992, 229), a 'quarrel' representing differing views about how understanding develops.[4] Philosophy is 'structured', 'rational', where one sentence follows another according to some principle of 'internal necessity' whereas poetry is 'anarchic', 'subversive'. One implication of these observations is that storytelling, and, in particular the construction of a narrative, may obey different notions of logic in associative and abstract cultures.

There are clearly dangers in making any such generalisations, not least of which is that they tend to obscure the differences and arguments that exist within cultural

---

3   Ramanujan cites Said in developing this point but also Naipaul and Kaker (Ramanajun 1980, 41-58)

4   See also, for example, the debate between narrative and associational thinking (Czarniawska (1997b).

traditions. Amartya Sen, for example, notes the existence of profoundly different schools of thought within the Hindu tradition, including the *Lokayata* school that was famous for its rigorous philosophical logic (Sen 2005, 23).

However, while recognising these dangers, if we don't even attempt to create a dialogue across cultures then the opportunities for rich learning will be lost. Hermeneutics offers some ways out of these dilemmas. A hermeneutic enquiry, write Mahajan, 'seeks to understand the other and...by making available the life of the other it opens up new worlds and possibilities to us' (Mahajan 1997, 64). Hermeneutics suggests that the ways in which we construct our understanding of an object (in this case a culture) are not static but are a continual process of interpretation and re-interpretation, a continual seeking to understand.

> The problem of intercultural understanding as a movement of living thought is not the problem of discovering a formula for the 'other' culture or of grasping it in a concept, but of a mutual sharing of horizons, however slightly. (Mehta, ed. Jackson 1992, 249)

With such cautionary notes this chapter explores differing constructions of the images of society, social change and the role of voluntary organisations in the UK and in India. In the following section I use the content of the stories to reveal these foundational assumptions. I then go on to look at how the stories, and the organisations themselves, create a space in which new possibilities can be conceptualised. Out of these possibilities organisations create imaginative variations on the theme of society, alternative models of the institutions of state and market and of the boundaries between them. The chapter concludes with consideration of the idea of social change itself and a comparison between the notions of change and transformation.

Visions of society and social change

Do the ways in which people look at institutional arrangements change their relationships with them, or is everything universal?

My attempts to uncover the 'mytho-poetic nucleus' (Ricoeur 1991b, 483) of the storytellers, and in particular, whether these described different ways of imagining the social world began with Burrell and Morgan's influential book in which they suggested that all theories, whether sophisticated or implicit, were predicated by 'meta-theoretical assumptions' or 'ways of seeing'.

Stories as revelatory of differing world views

> ...all social scientists approach their subject via explicit or implicit assumptions about the nature of the social world, assumptions which are ontological, concerning whether "reality" is of an "objective" nature or the product of individual cognition; and "epistemological" – how one might begin to understand the world and communicate this as knowledge to other human beings. (Burrell and Morgan 1979, 1)

Burrell and Morgan plotted these different assumptions on two axes. The first represents differing views about whether we believe reality (and in this case the reality of society) is subjectively constructed or whether it has an objective existence 'outside' of the perceiving individual. The second axis locates alternative ideas about social change and whether it occurs primarily as a result of radical change and upheaval or through a self-regulating process of maintaining equilibrium. From these two axes they constructed four paradigms; the functionalist, the interpretive, the radical humanist and the radical structuralist.

I read through the transcripts of the stories I had collected about the founding of voluntary organisations in the UK and India, and using some of the key referents that Burrell and Morgan defined I attempted to 'locate' them within these four paradigms. The results revealed startling differences between the Indian and the UK stories. The majority of the UK stories were located in the 'functionalist' paradigm (with a foundational assumption that society has an independent, objective reality) and the majority of Indian stories within the 'radical humanist' paradigm (based on the assumption that reality, as we perceive it, is socially constructed). These paradigms are located diagonally opposite to each other on Burrell and Morgan's schema, having no underlying assumptions in common.[5]

Differing assumptions about the nature of society

The majority of the Indian stories seemed to suggest that reality is subjectively constructed while the stories told by people working in the UK were quite different. This is demonstrated by contrasting the two examples below. In the first story, told by a UK manager, the impression given by the phrase by 'giving back to society' is that society is a fixed, objective entity. In the second, Indian, story the social world is imagined as being more fluid.

> *And she equally wanted to give back to society by providing volunteers in museums and galleries and historic houses…*

> *…So the social image has been created, in our society, about women as a sacrificing woman or a crooked woman. There is no woman who can fight for the rights of themselves…. and have a say in the decision making process. So that is why we started with a small project, a one year project, to identify interested women who want to write plays and who want to direct plays, who want to have their own poster exhibitions.*

Similarly, in the another Indian story, also about an organisation working with women, although in a different context, the idea of woman in society is being transformed.

---

5   The stories were not wholly consistent but over 2/3rds of each sample did suggest one dominant, underlying paradigm for each country.

...and what happened was that these women began to be treated as assets in their community because they now knew more about how to handle systems, how to go around difficult issues, so its like the domestic help who comes to your house tells you how to go and handle the police – you can't look at her as a stupid woman any more who is very poor and silly. So it transformed the way that thought of themselves, it transformed their position on their environment, and gave them the confidence to say, 'this isn't right,' and to do something about it.

However, another manager who founded an organisation in the UK for people with sensory impairments 'makes the case' for financial support by using numbers to identify need as if numbers and need were fixed and objective entities

...I approached the Scottish Office and found some people up there, eventually, that were willing to listen to us, and the advice I got from them was we had to evidence and really prove our case. So I conducted some research...

CS: And what was 'the case'? Was it that there just weren't the services up here that you wanted?

...It was the level of need as well as the kind of need, so it was both. Primarily it was really number research.

The correlation between India/subjectivity and UK/objectivity was not absolute but it was significant in the majority of the stories. Burrell and Morgan suggested that Western sociological and organisational theories that belong to the subjectivist orientation owe their origins to the German romantic movement which was significantly influenced by Indian philosophy,[6] so it is perhaps not surprising that many of the Indian interviews seemed to be so firmly located here. Western thinking is sometimes categorised in terms of the tradition of scientific thinking influenced by the Enlightenment based on an increasingly wide separation between the physical and metaphysical so it is perhaps also predictable that so many UK activists seemed to view the social world as having an objective reality.[7]

---

6   There are a number of interesting studies on the relationship between Indian philosophy and the Western romantic tradition (for example, King 1999). Therefore it is hardly surprising that these influences are detectable. J.L. Mehta comments that:

Just as Western literature, and through it a whole new, modern world of thought and sensibility entered, like a breath of fresh, welcome air into Indian consciousness...so India penetrated the European imagination also through the Romantic movement....The process of the East lodging itself in the very heart of Western culture has been going on since at least 1808 with the publication of Frederich Schlegel's *On the Language and Wisdom of the Indians*...which made a profound impression on the German Romantics and through them helped the blossoming of the Romantic spirit in Europe and England. (Mehta 1992, 152)

7   This is an interesting extract from a discussion between Einstein and Tagore:

Differing theories about social change

Below is a quote from an interview with an Indian activist who said that he had been profoundly influenced by the work of Paolo Freire, and the quote reflects the speaker's commitment to the Freirean concept of conscientisation.

> *We have a philosophy of social change. And the philosophy says sufferers will be united if they can think for themselves.*

Differing assumptions about the nature of society are likely to lead to very different views about how it changes. Burrell and Morgan's paradigms contrasted theories of social change that emphasised stability and focussed on society's 'underlying cohesiveness' from those (such as Freire's) that were concerned with radical change and 'man's (sic) emancipation from the structures which limit and stunt his potential for development' (Burrell and Morgan 1979, 17).

These contrasting perspectives were represented in the stories by a clear distinction between those organisations that focussed on achieving the inclusion of marginalised people into the existing structures of society versus organisations that questioned and challenged those very structures. These seem to indicate a difference in the underlying assumptions about the way in which society needed to change: on the one hand the view that what needed to change was for the structures of society to become more inclusive and more accessible to people currently on the margins, and on the other hand a view that structures and institutions that exclude are themselves inherently inequitable and in need of radical reform.

Again, there was a significant difference between the Indian and the UK managers with a tendency for the majority of the Indian activists to be engaged in a fundamental critique of the social order while the UK stories were more likely to

---

Einstein: There are two different conceptions about the nature of the universe – the world as a unity dependent on humanity and the world as reality independent of the human factor...

Tagore: The world is a human world...the scientific view of it is also that of the scientific man. Therefore the world apart from us does not exist, it is a relative world, depending for its reality upon our consciousness.

Later in the interview...

Einstein: Truth then, or beauty, is that not independent of man?

Tagore: No.

Einstein: If there were no human beings any more, the Apollo Belvedere no longer would be beautiful?

Tagore: No.

Einstein: I agree with regard to this conception of beauty, but not with regard to truth.

Tagore: Why? Truth is realised through men.

(cited in Dutta and Robinson 2000, 295-296, recorded at the time by Dimitri Marianoff who was present at the interview and probably acted as interpreter.)

focus on improvement. For example in this extract from a UK story the emphasis on inclusion is very strong.

> *3,000 people living in long stay hospitals, or whatever you call it, is too much. And it's our view that nobody, on account of their learning difficulty alone, needs to live in long stay hospital. They may need some form of temporary hospital care if they have a mental health problem which overlays their learning difficulties, or a very particular physical illness as well, but on account of learning difficulties on its own... those people can be supported in the community, and are being supported now in the community.*

However, in the Indian story that follows the emphasis was noticeably different. This manager did not talk about inclusion but in terms of a deeper critique of the structures that keep people in marginalised positions.

> [We] *brought together the most poor and vulnerable women in the city, in the area, and our collective explorations caused them to begin to look at all the issues and systems which threatened them, disempowered them....*

Here is another contrast between two interviews in which each person interviewed (the first from the UK and the second from India) uses the metaphor of the band-aid to describe solutions to the problems faced by poor families but in the first example poor parenting is analysed as an individual, or a family issue, in the second example the same issue is framed as a systemic problem.

> *Where do the causes of poor parenting lie? They lie in the parent as child, in their history. And what can you do about it to secure permanent change in that condition as opposed to what* [the founder] *still regards as an 'elastoplast solution'.... And so it* [the focus of their work] *moved... towards a model of securing permanent change in the cycle of destructive behaviour within families.*

And:

> ...the major difference between children from middle class households, lower income households and poor households and the impact that impoverishment had... I basically felt that I was located in a 'band-aid' environment; you sort-of put band-aids on people and move them on but it didn't create the conditions for people to question why they had to deal with this, and why so many children had to deal with this.

This distinction between helping individuals and groups to achieve inclusion into society, versus reforming society itself is very significant in terms of the decisions an organisation makes about where to direct its attention.

> ...orthodox sociologists have become much more interested in and concerned with the problems of the 'individual' as opposed to those of the structure of society in general. (Burrell and Morgan 1979. 11)

Many of the Indians I interviewed directly acknowledged the influence of Paolo Freire in the development of their work. Freire's (1996) notion of conscientisation, or 'critical consciousness', the process by which people reflect together on the attitudinal and institutional structures that maintain them in a marginalised position implies a radical theory of change.

> *We never in our organisation say that women are marginalised. We want to say that women have been kept marginalised because society has pushed them out of the mainstream.*

Conscientisation is perhaps also more compatible with the subjectivist view that society is not immutable but transformable through enhanced consciousness. itself more reflective of the Indian philosophical disposition towards relativism in which, for example, the morality of an action is determined by its context (King 1999, Lipner 1999, Ramanujan 1990,) as contrasted with the Judeo-Christian tradition in which morality is absolute and context free.[8] Freire is known in the West but I have rarely come across a voluntary sector activist, whether manager, volunteer or trustee, who regarded him as a critical influence and none that were interviewed for these studies made any mention of his work or his ideas.

This small analysis demonstrates that the decisions an organisation makes about its activities and the roles it occupies are a consequence of the underlying assumptions about the nature of society and of social change that influence its founders and managers. Locating the organisation within the context of these assumptions is essential to understanding its role in contributing to social change. Using a cross cultural perspective to explore some of the underlying assumptions that structure the images we create of our societies and the dynamics of social change does expose more clearly how influential differing understandings of society can be and, as Mahajan (1997) suggests, helps us to see our own context afresh.

Creating possibilities

In this section I want to suggest that voluntary organisations not only play a role in contributing to social change with the frames of reference in which they are located, but also create the opportunities for those frames to be challenged and overturned.

Chakrabarty holds that it is impossible to think about social change without taking into account the role of the state and how it is imagined.

> We live in societies structured by the State and the oppressed need knowledge forms that are tied to that reality. (Chakrabarty 2000b, 274)

To extend Chakrabarty's observation, we live in societies that are structured by *both* state and market. To what extent do voluntary organisations *also* structure our imagination? If you regard the social world as primarily socially constructed

---

8   Consider the Biblical Ten Commandments which are presented as universal and binding in all situations.

then you are likely to see individuals and groups as the main drivers of change and as having the greatest 'agency' over their destinies. If, however, you regard the institutions and structures of state and market as having a more 'objective' existence then you are more likely to focus on them.

> This emphasis on human ability to affect change is the force behind the term 'agency' – the capacity to act as agents of change... he oppositions between these two perspectives, with one favouring the influence of certain objective rules as determining human behaviour and the other placing importance on individual action and freedom is the structure – agency debate. (Ebrahim 2005, 14)

It is impossible to talk about the work of voluntary organisations in isolation from other sectors. Our imaginative constructions of the idea of society are structured by state, market and by the many relationships and affinities and associational arrangements, formal or informal, lasting or temporary that occupy the space between them. And our expectations about what voluntary associations can do depends on how we see these other sectors; whether we see them as all powerful (the despotic state, the rapacious market) or impotent (the failing state, the market that only delivers to the chosen few). These are some of the conflicting narratives that provide a backdrop against which a voluntary organisation's activities can be hermeneutically interpreted.

If we regard voluntary organisations as occupying an imaginary space between the state and market, or between the public and corporate sectors then within this space there are many possibilities for action.

The activities that voluntary organisations engage in can be regarded as broadly falling into two categories; on the one hand activities that are directed at state or market and that are located at the boundaries, such as access, advocacy and campaigning work, and on the other activities located within Douglas's 'unstructured areas' where the primary focus is on individuals and communities. The choices that organisations make about where, and how to concentrate their efforts are, at least to some extent, influenced by their meta-theoretical assumptions about whether the power to change 'our lives and society' (Ebrahim 2005, 14) is primarily located externally, in structures and institutions, or internally, in individuals and groups.

Many of the activities undertaken by organisations that direct their gaze on the state or market could be seen as belonging to the narrative of these institutions as despotic, or all powerful, where their power needs to be redirected, reformed, ameliorated. These organisations are likely to engage in activities aimed at structural change through lobbying, campaigning, influencing, persuading, advocating on behalf of each other or for the groups with which they work. They may work directly with these institutions through participating in working groups, consultative or advisory committees or they may play a mediating role by making it possible for people to gain direct access to people who are seen as having the power to affect change. The desired changes could be of global significance (as in the Make Poverty History campaign) or very local (increasing opening hours for libraries). These activities have in common that they acknowledge the power of the state and the market and that they aim to reform or channel that power to the needs and aspirations of people in relatively less powerful positions.

However, the narrative of the failing state underpins many other interpretations as in the debate about the role of voluntary organisations in the provision of public services. Commenting about a scheme that was set up by the local health authority to provide people with disabilities with specialist aids and equipment and then later given to the Red Cross to manage, the organisation's chief executive said 'equipment loan is traditionally *done very badly by the NHS and social services*' (my emphasis) while the Red Cross is able to 'offer a little extra that the state could not provide'.[9]

These contrasting narratives of the failures of the despotic or impotent state and market imply different understandings of power and dominance. Janeway uses almost messianic terms to describe the potential for people marginalised by the despotic state to be its salvation:

> ...what opposition to tyranny seems to require is unorthodox thinking: a sense of the value of non-traditional uses of power those that are 'often assigned in hierarchic and stratified societies to females, the poor, autochthons and outcasts'. If there is no-one to oppose despotic rulers except the ruled and the weak it is the natural – the autochthonous – powers of the weak to which society must turn. (Janeways 1980, 201 her emphasis)

Another example of voluntary organisations in the role of 'saviour', but this time of the impotent rather than the despotic state, comes from an article published in *The Observer* after several London underground stations were bombed in July, 2005. In the immediate aftermath of the bombings UK newspapers carried many articles about the importance of 'engaging' with the 'Muslim community' (all three contested terms). Following a meeting in which the prime minister announced the establishment of a task force, including in its membership many prominent Muslim leaders, one commentator, Abdul-Rehman Malik criticised this initiative, saying that it would have little effect:

> It is the *street level voluntary and community sector organisations* that represent British Islam's hidden civil society, working to meet the needs of neighbourhoods struggling with violence, drug abuse and teenage pregnancy. These are the front lines of the fight against militancy and desperation.[10] (my emphasis)

Clearly the expectations projected onto voluntary organisations by such messianic expectation can be enormous and there are serious risks here for the managers of these organisations in that failure, in some sense, is virtually guaranteed. This is a theme I will return to in the final chapter.

---

9   Sir Nicholas Young, chief executive of the Red Cross quoted in an article by Tash Shifrin in the Guardian Society 27/07/05. The 'NHS' is the National Health Service, the state run organisation set up to deliver free health care to all who need it, funded through taxation.

10   Abdul-Rehman Malik, writing in *The Observer* 24/07/05

Storytelling and challenging the frames

In each of the examples given above we can see voluntary organisations' activities are both constructed by their meta-theoretical assumptions about the state or market *and* as altering those assumptions. One way in which voluntary organisations can create the possibility of new ways of imagining society and new configurations in which marginalised people see themselves, and are seen by others in different ways, is through telling their stories. The stories of people marginalised, oppressed or simply excluded from the benefits of the state and market are an important weapon in the armoury of campaigning organisations. Sometimes, as in the example below, stories are 'borrowed' by a professional manager.

> *I mean you can talk about 'shouldn't we be valuing our children' but to come up with one or two stories, real stories about what children have experienced, makes it much more vivid than any statistics.*

Alternatively, organisations can play a mediating role so that members of the community can tell their stories directly to policy makers. For example, an alliance of organisations in the UK working with people with learning disabilities took several of their members to address the parliamentary All Party Group on Disability to tell them about the effects of certain government policies on their lives. The example below demonstrates both of these ways of using stories: here the founder is reliant on the impact of users' stories to gain support for the organisation – but it is precisely *because* those stories have such an impact on the audience that they are effective.

> *Everytime she* [the founder] *did another conference there'd be a wave of people wanting to open another centre because they'd heard the users speak, and that's our most powerful fundraising message.*

In these two examples the stories of the users or members of an organisation are a significant tool in winning influence. In fact, their power can be out of all proportion. The story of one individual can have more effect than any amount of statistical evidence to the contrary.[11]

What the organisation has done is to turn a private trouble into a public concern.

Martin and Powers (1983) constructed an experiment where sample groups were

---

11 One example is the story of 'Jennifer's Ear', the story of a little girl who, it was claimed, had had to wait for nearly a year for treatment for an ear condition. The story was used to promote the idea the health service had deteriorated sharply under successive Conservative governments. This story dominated the 1992 election coverage and was seen as archetypal. (source: <http://www.bbc/co/uk>) Similar stories have surfaced during each of the successive general election campaigns, usually focussing on one individual who has received poor service from a publicly funded organisation and promoted to create a political advantage for one party or another.

given different kinds of information about an imaginary organisation, including case studies (stories), policy documents and statistical data. They found that where the different forms of information supported each other, the stories were more effective at generating belief. This power of storytelling is clearly acknowledged by the manager in the following quote:

> *I certainly tell stories out there, when I have to give speeches, because I think a speech about social policy isn't as interesting as telling people about the effects of a social policy on a young person. People sit up and listen when you tell them a story about an individual rather than a policy.*

These stories have the potential to profoundly affect the ways in which people are perceived. The image of young people in society is being altered by the storyteller above. When the storytellers are the young people themselves this impact is greater still because the storytellers are engaging in a process of their own re-invention (in their own imagination as well as in others', as described in the previous chapter).

So, voluntary organisations create opportunities for groups of people located in marginalised positions to challenge the very imaginative constructions that maintain them in those positions and in so doing the relationships between these groups and the other structures of society are altered. This is an example of Mohanty's (1991) notion that storytelling is disruptive in the sense that it allows us the possibility of seeing our lives in new ways and questioning previously held certainties.

The power of the individual story is very strong indeed.[12] This power is not always used well – the ongoing debates about the images used to raise funds for emergency appeals is a case in point. Although pictures of starving children can move people all over the world to donate funds to famine relief the longer term effects of these images can be to reinforce the idea that people are helpless victims, perpetually dependent on the largesse of the better off.[13]

These stories can also contribute to the creation of overly simplistic interpretations of very complex situations. Weick (1995) suggests that stories reduce the pressure that is caused by ambiguity and complexity by implying that events are not haphazard, but 'tightly coupled'.

> When stories overstate the strength of causal ties they stimulate the effect of tight coupling in a complex world. (Weick 1995, 130)

This is an important point. Although stories can disrupt and challenge certainties they can also reassure. Perhaps both the voluntary organisations and the institutions

---

12 However, Martin and Powers also discovered that there were limitations to the capacity of stories to elicit belief. In their experiment when the participants were given either statistical evidence, or policy documents that didn't support the stories, the stories were not believed. They were dismissed as the exception that proves the rule (Martin and Powers 1983).

13 See also Davidson (2005) for a discussion about older people and their dislike of the media portrayal of them as passive victims of crime.

they seek to influence may want to ascribe more universal significance to a story of individual experience because it offers the possibility that a remedy can be found, and indeed, that the listener is powerful enough to deliver that remedy.

> *I've found out using members stories, is tremendous. But are you making a difference to changing the structure of society? What makes a difference? I mean, do statutory structures make a difference? Do ideas move society? What moves it?*

People can feel powerless in the face of ambiguity and complexity. This is as true for people working in voluntary organisations as it is for the politician or business executive. Each may want to believe in the omniscience of the other and to that extent each may be complicit in maintaining the belief that the state and the market are capable of producing solutions to the problems they have created. It may be more frightening to confront the possibility that complex situations are not so easily resolved. Perhaps politicians, business executives and voluntary activists alike share a need to believe that such solutions are possible.

Imaginative variations on the theme of society

Social imagination constitutes social reality (Ricoeur, 1992b) in the praxis of thought and action, which I have likened in these chapters to the illocutionary power of the speech act, 'that which is done in saying' (Austin 1975, 109). In the last section I discussed the ways in which voluntary organisations' activities are both a response to the frames of reference in which they are located and also a challenge to them. But voluntary organisations go further than creating the possibilities for new ways of seeing and framing our imaginative constructions of society. They also construct alternatives of their own.

In this section I want to explore the function of these new, imaginative possibilities, that are envisioned in the spaces between the state and market, in creating alternative models, structures and communities, even identities.

> ...we can differentiate between 'models of' and 'models for' (citing Geertz). 'Models of' look toward what is but 'models for' look toward what should be according to the model. The model may reflect what is but also pave the way for what is not. It is this duality of forces that may be constitutive of imagination itself. (Ricoeur 1986, 311) [14]

Voluntary organisations are often regarded as innovators, crucibles from which emerge new ideas, approaches and solutions to social problems. These are 'models for' in the sense of the quote above because they emerge from the organisation's vision for a better world.

Many of these models have become justly renowned, such as the Grameen Bank in Bangladesh, the Gujerat based Self Employed Women's Association (SEVA), a

---

14 Ricoeur is citing Clifford Geertz (1973) *The Interpretation of Cultures* (NY: Basic Books), p. 93

trade union for women working as rag pickers or bidi rollers, Amnesty International's letter writing campaigns, the 'buddying' model of care and support that emerged from organisations working with people with AIDS, Local Exchange Trading Schemes (LETS) in which people living within a particular geographic area 'buy' and 'sell' their skills and services to each other, using locally created alternative currencies (such as 'Bath' Olivers), – the list could go on and on. These are ideas that have significantly changed the social landscape. And the process, by which new ideas are formed and developed into new models, or institutions of their own, is not limited to such famous examples. Many of the stories told to me concerned this process by which an organisation had created a new way of doing things which had, over time, become an institution itself.

Alternatives to the state

Probably no single issue is as controversial as the increasingly prominent role that voluntary organisations are playing in both countries in the provision of services that have been 'contracted out' by the state. These debates can be regarded as emerging from the narrative of the impotent, failing state, or simply of the state abrogating its responsibility. The controversies primarily centre around notions of legitimacy and identity – whose role is it to provide the services society needs? These debates are culturally contingent; different societies have different notions of the legitimate sphere of operations of the state, market and of those organisations that occupy the space in between them.

One aspect of this debate that has received less attention is the notion of non-professionalism, already alluded to as a foundational value of voluntary organisations. (One very popular management guide produced for the UK sector is titled *Voluntary, Not Amateur*[15]). However, several of the founding stories described a process in which informal, innovative and experimental ideas rapidly became seen as professionalised activities and valued as such. This outcome was talked about with pride, as representing a significant achievement on the part of the organisation.

Here is one, clear example, in which the storyteller describes an informal activity becoming professionalized, and objectivised as health visiting, a profession that today is accredited and regulated.

> *So it was just kind of women coming together and worried, you know, about poverty and things like that. And from that it was used as a model for health visiting and the first health visiting project was set up in Kings Cross...*[16]

In the next example child protection work that was carried out by a voluntary organisation (the National Council for the Prevention of Cruelty to Children) was later taken over by the state.

---

15 Reason, J. and Hayes, R. (7th edition 2004) *Voluntary Not Amateur*, LVSC, London.
16 Kings Cross is in North London.

...So the NSPCC took parents to court. And so the role changed very significantly with the setting up of the Children's Departments after the Second World War, when a lot of that statutory responsibility was taken into local authorities and into Children's Departments. But before then, up to the Second World War, they had a big statutory role played by the NSPCC and no other charity played that role.

In an interview with the chief executive of an organisation set up to find opportunities to occupy conscience objectors during the Second World War, she commented on 'how influential [the organisation] was in the development of social work as a profession'. Their work with families in the East End of London provided the model for what is now regarded as family casework. Health visiting, child protection work, family case work are all regarded now as professional activities, regulated through professional bodies who establish agreed standards of good practice and maintain the right to accredit those practitioners who have reached the required level of expertise and training. But they originated as non-formal activities developed by voluntary organisations and often carried out by volunteers.

I think we've also achieved the development of new projects. I mean we invented foyers.[17]

Arguably this process of creating new professions is one of the voluntary sector's most significant contributions to social change. The following quote clearly captures this notion that voluntary organisations create new professions:

My understanding is that it [the organisation] *was just a talking shop of various organisations providing residential care, about what they thought they were about, what they were doing, why they thought they were doing it, what was the purpose of residential care, should you train your staff, was it a vocation or was it a profession, or was it just a way of earning a living,*

Here, it is the very meaning of residential care and how it is to be understood that emerges from the creation of the organisation.

Although all of the above examples come from UK interviews this theme was also reflected in the Indian interviews. However, the differences in the underlying assumptions about the radical or incremental nature of social change, that I described before, could also be discerned in the nature of these different activities. In the Indian stories the activity being 'professionalised' was participatory research, which some

---

17 The 'Foyer' concept actually originated in France at the end of the Second World War, to provide integrated housing and support for young homeless people and was not, in fact, developed by the organisation referred to above, as its chief executive later corrected. However, I have included this quote because at the time it was made the storyteller believed it, and it therefore illustrates the point I am making, that voluntary organisations celebrate the movement of unstructured, informal work into a more fixed notion of professionalised activity.

of the managers interviewed presented as being the defining activity of development and, by extension, of voluntary organisations.[18]

> [The organisation] *started as an organisation to do research about issues related to women. But we realised that just doing research isn't enough. And we therefore entered into action. Whatever we studied the problems that we discovered needed to be handled immediately. And therefore the* [organisation] *moved from just research to research and action.*

While the organisation in the above quote started with research and then moved into action, the organisation described below travelled the journey in reverse, starting with the need to improve the social and economic conditions of the people.

> *... involved in research not per se for generating knowledge, but application of the research for the benefit of the people. So this is how you see our displacement study. I mean we did the study and then some of the findings of this study we are implementing in organising communities to somehow struggle for ... restructuring the economy, which is lost ...*

Participatory research originated as a radicalising process, and in these stories it is still an emergent activity. But participatory research is also now a highly developed methodology which has spawned not only training manuals and courses but also its critics who claim that in its professionalisation it has lost its radical edge (see Cooke and Kothari 2001, for example).

Participatory research's more radical orientation may reflect Freire's influence (Chambers 1999). Most of the organisations that talked about participatory research and espoused its discourse were founded within the last 20 years but Shantiniketan, an adult education centre founded by Rabindraneth Tagore and reflecting many of the same underlying ideas and beliefs, is much older. [19]

The nature of these different activities in India and in the UK is reflective of the underlying meta-theoretical assumptions about the nature of social change (radical or incremental) that structure the imaginations of their founders and activists. They emerge out of the founders' desires to create alternatives that challenge existing models and they are shaped by their underlying ontological views about social

---

18   In its application participatory research overlaps with participatory rural appraisal (PRA) a methodology where people are encouraged to explore the resources available to them in the community, its priorities and aspirations for community action. Participatory research, as it was described in the interviews I carried out, maintained the emphasis on information being defined and collected by the people but often then used to produce highly sophisticated reports (judged by traditional academic and policy terms).

19   These underlying principles are the same as those espoused by most people I met who were working for what they termed 'people based development', many of whom regarded participatory research as the methodology of choice. They are also the principles that Tagore inculcated in Leonard Elmhurst when he established Dartington Hall in Devon, where Tagore visited in the early 20th Century.

reality. They emerge out of their context and seek to reshape and change it; however as they become professionalised they become paradoxically incorporated into it.

Alternatives to the market

The examples cited above all concern the development of models of working that could be regarded as falling within the overall purview of the state. These could be seen as approaches that emerge from the narrative of the failure, or impotence of the state. Similarly, the perceived failure of the market to create sustainable well being for everyone and eradicate poverty and social injustice has led to the creation of alternative economic models. Most notable is micro-credit, created by Mohammed Yunus, founder of the Grameen Bank, which has become so institutionalised that it is now promoted by major foreign donors and development agencies and even the World Bank.[20]

In the UK there is increasing interest in the idea of 'social enterprises', organisations which have an interest in social justice but also an intention to generate income. The UK government is especially interested. In 2002 Douglas Alexander, a junior minister in the Department of Trade and Industry addressed Social Enterprise London (SEL) with the following ringing endorsement:

> If we see our mission, as we do, of not only building a more dynamic economy but also a fairer society the Social Enterprises have a key contribution to make. In fact we see social enterprises as addressing a whole range of public policy goals – in areas as diverse as health and care, recreation and recycling and education and empowerment.
>
> Firstly, social enterprises are at heart, businesses, and offer economically sustainable business solutions to social problems. To be able to thrive and grow they have to be as innovative and entrepreneurial, and indeed more innovative and entrepreneurial than their mainstream competitors. They are more likely to be risk-taking in order to meet their social objectives and provide new models of new and socially responsible business. ... Indeed mainstream business can learn a lot from social enterprises; about being close to customers, and responsive to their needs; about employment diversity; about doing business better. (<http://www.dti.gov.uk>)

Social enterprises embrace a number of models from well established 'ethical' businesses, such as Traidcraft or the Co-operative Bank to tiny, local food co-operatives. Superficially, some of the smaller, more local models seem very similar to micro-credit initiatives, for example an organisation that a student of mine was working with, run by Somalian women refugees, that is exploring the option of raising part of its income through the provision of hair braiding services to its members. However, here again the differences in underlying assumptions between the UK and

---

20   'The related current challenge in small and medium scale enterprise (SME) development is to build on the success of microfinance, establishing good practices for SME financing and for the provision of non-financial services to SMEs.' (From the World Bank website: my emphasis. <http://wkin0018.worldbank.org/networks.fpsi/reference.nef≥>

India are noticeable in that the aims of micro-credit schemes are inherently more radical. Micro-credit schemes, (sometimes called self help groups) aim to empower their members, usually women, in all areas of their lives.[21]

Alexander describes social enterprises as 'businesses' but their status is not always so clear. The rhetoric surrounding these organisations is confused and contradictory sometimes implying that this is a new (and progressive) model of organisation on the basis of its income generating intentions and businesslike practices. Yet these characteristics apply to the vast majority of voluntary organisations that are reliant on any income at all. The tone of the some of these debates, as exemplified in Douglas's speech, sounds almost millennial in the expectations that are being projected onto social enterprises to provide a corrective to the excesses of the market.

Alternative communities

When people have lost their trust in the state or the market (or, arguably, never had that trust) they create their own alternatives, sometimes entirely new communities, often motivated by images of alternative utopias. Indian examples include the Gandhian communities and ashrams.

> *I do think we need a place in the community where people can try things out.*

In the UK the Steiner communities, sometimes as large as villages (and often given names such as Botton 'village'), where people with learning disabilities and their 'co-workers' live together continue to draw people even though such villages run counter to current, community based policy. In many of these communities there are no 'salaries', income is shared according to need rather than role or merit.

The following is a quote from an interview with one of the actors in the Indian theatre company that has established a theatre village where all the members live communally:

> *Here there is a kind of group life, group life in the sense that we are trying to imitate certain things from the family culture. So whatever decisions are made it is now democratically done, not as in conventional families but as a family where there is a say of everybody.*

For many who live and work in these communities the desire to create a new model for social living is very strong:

> *We are practicing a particular discipline, a way of life which is a kind of demonstration for others, which is a demonstration for society.*

These communities function as exemplars, or concretisations of the founders' ideals and representations of alternative possibilites. However, many of these

---

21 I spent several weeks in 2001 visiting an organisation in Uttar Pradesh that encourages women to establish self help groups to manage their own credit but also to resist landlords, money lenders and oppressive husbands.

utopian communities, such as the Owenite communities in Scotland and Indiana or the Kibbutz movement in Israel, don't substantially outlive the original founders. They are also not without critics. (I have met people with learning disabilities who have been profoundly glad to leave the Steiner communities.) These communities don't entirely follow the pattern I have described above, of 'professionalising' their activities, but the founding values can become institutionalised into practices that spawn new resistances.

Alternative identities

One of the most common reasons that people come together to create new organisations is in order to make a space in which some identity or role shared in common with others is given shape: identities determined by gender, race or ethnicity, perhaps by shared experience such as raising a disabled child or bonded labour. Taking on a shared identity with others offers new possibilities of affinity and a more visible presence in the social landscape. These organisations can have a profound affect on the social environment as noted by Okin:

> More than anything else, it seems, the grassroots-to-NGOs and NGOs-to-international fora contacts and discussions of the 1980s and 1990s, by which the previously silent voices of many women could be, and continue to be heard, have done much to change the way the world thinks about human rights. (Okin 2000, 42)

But the role of voluntary organisations in such 'identity politics' and the extent to which these represent a real shift is problematic. The question of when a shared identity becomes a ghetto and when it is a source of renewed strength is at the heart of many of the debates around identity politics. The influence of social movements and identity based voluntary organisations on human rights and anti-discrimination legislation is profound. However, events such as the destruction of the mosque at Ayodhya by Hindus, the Hindu – Muslim riots in Gujurat, the suicide bombings on the London Underground in 2005 and the riots in Birmingham, UK between blacks and Asians raise uncomfortable questions about the balance between empowerment through the expression of difference and empowerment through the expression of commonality. In the second chapter I touched on the argument that discourses of difference can have the effect of increasing difference (Kwek 2003, Narayan 2000, Spivak 1999). Janeway is more positive:

> Tokens can certainly become normal – but the way they do is by means of a *change in the situation* a real shift in the external world that forcers a shift inside the heads of the elite, *so that normality is redefined* by adjusting the premises of social thinking. (Janeway 1980, 239 her emphasis)

When voluntary organisations create alternative structures, models, ideas and identities they change the context in which they operate. They change society because they 'adjust the premises' of 'our social thinking' and the ways in which we imagine and construct our notions of society and the institutions within it. But they also risk becoming becoming a very part of the context they were founded to subvert.

Concluding thoughts

In this chapter I have attempted to apply Ricoeur's (1986) idea of the 'social imaginary' to explore the contributions that voluntary organisations make to social change. Ricoeur suggests that the social imagination is constitutive of social reality. I have therefore attempted to use the stories of founding and managing voluntary organisations as a vehicle for uncovering the underlying images of society and social change, and of the roles of the various institutions and structures within it, that contribute to the storytellers' visions for a better and more just society. I have also suggested that their choice of method and focus is dependant on these different imaginative constructions of society.

Drawing on material from two different cultures that tend to be located in different categories (west/non-west, north /globalised south, developed/developing, first world/third world) I was interested to find out whether there were noticeable differences in the ways in which the social world was conceptualised. My tentative proposition, based on a fairly small sample, is that the Indian storytellers tended to hold a more fluid and subjective notion of society while for the UK storytellers their image of society was of something more fixed, objectified and immutable. Similarly, their understandings of the process of social change differed with the British favouring incremental change aimed at the inclusion of marginalised people into society and the Indians favouring a more radical restructuring of society itself. These differences were manifested in the organisations' activities with the British organisations creating new models of work such as health visiting, family casework and child protection work that was aimed at the improvement of society while the Indians were engaged in participatory research with its fundamentally more radical approach.

These stories and traditions are created, perpetuated and reinterpreted within their own cultural contexts and it is therefore not surprising that some analogies can be drawn between the philosophical traditions of the two cultures and these different imaginative conceptions of society. However, I am aware of the risk of generalising from such observations (as is demonstrated by the tendency of many, enthusiastic students of 'cross cultural management' to use Hofstede's dimensions to diagnose and measure cultures).

Challenges to Burrell and Morgan's paradigms

> The discovery of the plurality of cultures is never a harmless experience. (Ricoeur 1965, 278)

Since its publication in 1979 there have been many criticisms of Burrell and Morgan's work, both of the approach and of paradigms themselves. Since I draw heavily on these paradigms it is important to touch on these criticisms, if only briefly. There are three linked themes that are particularly significant for this study: firstly, that they wrote from a Western perspective, secondly, that they reinforce binary, either/or polarities and thirdly, the proposed incommensurablity of the paradigms.

All the theories that Burrell and Morgan explored, in constructing their typology, were of Western origin, although in his book *Images of Organization* (1986) Morgan later develops the idea that the flux and transformation metaphor captures something of the sense of the yin and yang of the Tao. The polarity between subjectivity and objectivity, and between conflict and order may not exist in the same way in Eastern thinking which has sometimes been characterised as 'both-and' rather than 'either/or' (Miller 1990). In his study of neighbourhood relationships in India, Miller concluded,

> Order, at least relative order, starts to take shape during periods of crisis and social disruption. Then, things coalesce, link up, simplify and, more often than not, confront each other. Solidarities form at the expense of previously inter-textured, quasi associations. With conflict order comes to the fore. (Miller 1999, 155)

Thus, for him order is a consequence of change, not in opposition to it. Chaos is a feature of stability. Chakravarty also questions the conceptualisation of radical change. He suggests that any theories of change that focus on systems and institutions are less radical than deeper transformations that change the way people think. Symbols can change the way people think and if symbols and structures coincide, then perhaps real transformations can occur, but not through structures alone.

Chakravarty also offers a very different interpretation of Burrell and Morgan's proposed subjective / objective axis, distinguishing between the subjective as cause and the object as effect, in other words that the object is the concretisation of subjective thought and not positioned in opposition.[22]

We need to be careful of applying Western typologies to non-Western situations. There is a real danger of distorting the evidence that emerges and applying interpretations that simply don't work. Miller and Chakravarty both invert Burrell and Morgan's axes.

It is also important to point out that many of the people working in the Indian organisations I visited would be surprised to hear their work being described as having such a radical focus. All of the organisations are well established and enjoy at least a measure of good working relationships with state and national institutions. Similarly, many of the UK managers are very aware of the limitations of society's institutions to respond to the aspirations and reflect the experiences of people in marginalised positions. However, these comparisons do, as Mahajan (1997) suggests, help us to see our own world differently and that may be their greatest value.

---

22 This was in a conversation between myself and S. Chakravarty, the Director of the Institute for Human Values Research at the Indian Institute of Management in Kolkata, in March, 2000.

Change versus transformation

> ...the idea of revolution...has become associated with professionalism and managerialism, leaving no scope for spontaneity, ambiguities, intuitions, innovations or poetry. (Nandy 1987, 140)

Nandy's comment captures a sense of the paradox I have referred to throughout this chapter, that although organisations create alternatives based on the radical, or at least subversive visions of the founders and their desires to challenge the status quo, these can become captured by the seemingly inexorable processes of professionalisation. In this process they can lose their radical edge and become sites of regulation and control.

The Indian founder cited below regards organisations as having legitimacy only as long as these practices retain their capacity for 'transforming' peoples lives.

> *...And the larger tradition of romancing institutional arrangements, 'the institution lives longer than the individual' and all those things are probably realistic in the mainstream environment. But when you're operating in an environment where you're dealing with communities that are marginalised, are isolated, the arrangement is only as valid as it is capable of transforming those lives.*

This quote raises another question. So far, in this book, I have been writing about the role of voluntary organisations in promoting social change. But this Indian activist talks about *transformation*. What is the distinction between these two terms?

Armstrong writes that change is 'something experienced as brought about from without' while transformation is 'something released from within' (Armstrong 1991, 5). Using these definitions some of the stories seemed to be linked to a concept of change and others to transformation. In the stories of transformation this occurred not as a direct result of activity the organisation had undertaken, but because the organisation had sought to create the preconditions for transformation to occur. These stories seemed to imagine the organisation as a crucible where the power to effect transformation does not lie in the actions of the alchemist but in the crucible itself. Other stories promoted action, linked to a concept of change. This distinction between change and transformation may also reflect the distinction between the objectivist and subjectivist perspectives.

Lawrence (2000) makes a similar distinction between change and transformation which is particularly relevant here.

> ...the preoccupation of the politics of salvation is with change – that is, others holding power impose it from the outside on individuals or systems. The politics of revelation is preoccupied with the conditions and resources for the exercise of transformation that come from inside the person or system and are brought about by people revealing what may be the truth of their situation to themselves and taking authority to act on their interpretation. (Lawrence 2000, 173)

This may be particularly important in helping us to understand the dynamics at play in the paradoxes that I have alluded to throughout this section; that in creating organisations to challenge and subvert the status quo, the 'formidable contestations of what is' (Ricoeur 1986,16) that Ricoeur says is at the heart of utopian thinking, organisations can become caught within the very structures of thinking and imagination they were founded to subvert.

Voluntary organisations contribute to social change on many levels. The creation of an organisations changes its context, the empowerment of individuals changes the way they imagine themselves and the way they are perceived by others, the creating of alternative perspectives and models of social intervention provides new ways of conceptualising and imagining society. And these new imaginative constructions are constitutive of new social realities. Whether these changes amount to transformations may depend on the ways in which managers and leaders respond to the challenges inherent in the paradoxes that accompany these processes. This is the subject of the second section of the book.

PART II
Stories and Values

The more the voluntary sector is defined as just the 'third sector' and we become locked into the language of the business and corporate sector and that's fine, but I don't want to get locked into the philosophy of the corporates actually, if we embrace too strongly the philosophy as well as the language of the corporate sector then I think there is a tremendous loss.

In Section Two I want to explore the 'philosophy' and 'language', or values of voluntary organisations as it they are expressed through the ways in which managers construct, or coneeptualise their management role.

Stories are well understood as devices through which values are transmitted, in a narrative form. This section therefore, is primarily focussed on those aspects of management in which organisational values play a significant role in shaping the way those functions are carried out. Fletcher and Kay suggest that values are particularly important for the management of voluntary organisations because their overall purpose is the achievement of some social good.

> Voluntary organisations are better depicted as social value organisations because of the importance of social values to the sector. As an image of process the metaphor of 'journey' has particular qualitative significance for the sector in that the process emphasises the action and operationalisation of the values of the institution, the direction and the journey to achieve the valued purpose. (Fletcher and Kay 1994, 23)

This section looks at three aspects of internal management that are particularly relevant to those tasks of engaging in social change that I have discussed previously. In Section One I explored the external significance of creating new organisations and in the following chapter I look at the internal management of creativity. While in the last section I looked at stories of individual empowerment here I look at empowering, and in particular, participatory leadership. Finally, the last chapter in the previous section explored social change more widely and here I look at the management of organisational change.

Exploring stories of internal management from the locutionary, or content aspect reveals the underlying assumptions about the nature of organisations that structure managers' thinking. In these chapters I have made extensive use of Morgan's (1986) work on the foundational 'images', or metaphors, that influence the way we construct our understandings of our experiences in organisations and their functions. The following chapter looks at the metaphors of organisations that underpinned the stories that managers told about creativity within their organisations. The succeeding chapter looks at constructions, or images of leadership and the final chapter in this section explores the metaphors of organisational change.

> Many of our taken-for-granted ideas about organisations are metaphorical, even though we may not recognise them as such.... By using different metaphors to understand the complex and paradoxical character of organisational life we are able to manage and design organisations in ways that we may not have thought possible before. (Morgan 1986, 13)

'Using different metaphors' is one part of the illocutionary aspect of storytelling, in which new interpretations and plots are created out of the imaginations of the storytellers. These chapters explore how creative ideas emerge in organisations, how leading can be conceptualised *as* storytelling in which the leader creates, or narrates, new understandings of organisational experience, and finally, how organisations are re-created hermeneutically in an iterative process of interpretation and re-interpretation.

Aspects of the functions of storytelling in management include the use of the founding story as a creation myth, an icon of creativity within the organisation, as a means of managing meaning and negotiating consent and as a heuristic in sensemaking, a source of inspiration, guidance and consolation.

My proposition is that leading and managing the tasks of social change requires an engagement with the values of the organisation. Many of these stories demonstrate just such creative engagement. However, as in the stories used in the previous section, they also reveal dangers and paradoxes. While the creativity of voluntary organisations was highly valued by all the storytellers they also saw it as under threat. While storytelling can provide a way of creating and negotiating shared meaning between leaders and followers, and even of challenging those constructs, leaders can also use stories to reinforce their own positions. Stories, and an appeal to the organisation's history can facilitate change or inhibit it. The challenges of managing these paradoxes creatively are discussed in the final concluding chapter of the book.

Chapter 5

Playing Pinball with Ideas: Storytelling and the Management of Creativity

Innovation and creativity...is, I think, the lifeblood of the voluntary sector.

Introduction

This manager is expressing a view about the importance of creativity to voluntary organisations that, in my experience, is widely held. Voluntary organisations are often regarded as being inherently creative; they are seen as being less bureaucratic than organisations in the public sector and therefore more flexible, responsive to change and able to translate innovative ideas into action quickly. They are also perceived as being more aware of the views and aspirations of communities than the private sector. For example, Gordon Brown, the UK Chancellor of the Exchequer, recently said:

> ...we know that voluntary organisations have a long and proud history of identifying new needs, pioneering fresh solutions, often cajoling governments into action, often long before government has admitted that there is a problem... .new voluntary organisations are today also pioneering and leading the way in new directions: the hospice movement, the anti-AIDS campaigns, environmental organisations, the playgroup movement, the pioneering advocates for the disabled, the worldwide movement against debt.

> And we know that the innovation voluntary organisations show in meeting new needs is matched by innovation in the way they do so – voluntary organisations making the connections that others cannot – such as Comic Relief, Children's Promise, First Cheque, Streetsmart, and doing so independently and without fear or favour, free of government.[1]

Brown not only praises voluntary organisations for being creative in what they do but also for *how* they do it and this is specifically the concern of this chapter. In the first section I said that creating an organisation changes the social landscape, that the very act of creating is itself empowering and that this may help to explain the fecundity of the sector. Here, I want to explore the nature of creativity within

---

1   Gordon Brown, the UK Chancellor of the Exchequer, in a speech to the National Council of Voluntary Organisations (NCVO) in February, 2000: www.hm-treasury/gov/uk/newsroom_and_speeches/chancellorexchequer/speech_chex_90200.cfc

voluntary organisations; how managers define creativity and what processes they use to bring foster creative thinking.

I am basing my explorations on two research projects. The first was a small investigation into the ways in which five UK chief executives, regarded by their peers as having a particularly good track record in creativity, talked about and thought about creativity in an organisational context. The second project, which has also provided much of the data for the previous chapters, was a larger study of the founding stories of 30 voluntary organisations, in the UK and in India and followed from my observation that the story about the creation of an organisation may be of particular relevance to the way in which meaning is creating and sustained. The significance of founders is well understood (Schein, 1991). However the importance of the founding stories has been less well researched.

While creativity seems to be highly important to the way in which voluntary organisations understand themselves and are perceived by others (as evidenced in the quote from Gordon Brown) it is not necessarily well understood, either in terms of how it works or what is required to support it. Within the sector there are also important debates about the influence of government policy makers and funders. Funders in particular are accused of only being interested in giving money for new ideas on the one hand, and imposing conditions on organisations that serve to stifle creativity on the other (Ebrahim, 2005).

There are also tensions between the creation of new programmes and the preservation of the 'tried and tested'.   Symbolic of this tension is the debate about social enterprise (as I have mentioned briefly in chapter four) and whether it represents a significantly new form of organisation or a repackaging of the same sorts of activities that voluntary organisations have always done.

A very brief survey of theories on creativity in organisations

There is no consensus about the definition of creativity in an organisational context. Is creativity best understood as idea, process or outcome, or all of these? Can teams or organisations be creative or only individuals? And to what extent is it useful to define it at all or rather, in the interpretive sense, is it more fruitful to explore the meaning that creativity has for individuals working within organisations?

> Organisations need creative solutions to many problems because, in fact, no-one knows the best way to 'solve' these problems. In that sense creative solutions are unknowable in advance and thus, the exact way to manage the creative process cannot be specified... creativity is about the unknowable and... fostering creativity is about managing the unmanageable. (Amabile 1995, 78)

Three overlapping concepts are change, entrepreneurship and learning. These ideas have generated a great deal of literature examining their significance within organisational settings. In each of these creativity may or may not be involved. Change may occur as a result of the development of a creative idea but it occurs for other reasons as well. Entrepreneurship is sometimes used to define the creating of the organisation (Osborne 1994) but social entrepreneurship is increasingly defined primarily in terms of diversifying the funding base.[2] The literature on 'learning organisations' seems to describe a process that is very akin to the creative process. However, the emphasis there is on reflection on experience and again, this may or may not involve the creation of something new (Ebrahim 2005).

A more difficult issue is the distinction between creativity and innovation. Two contrasting comments demonstrate this complexity. Nystrom says that 'innovation is the result and implementation of creativity' (Nystrom 1995, 66) while Amabile says 'an idea or product is creative if it is a novel and appropriate solution to an open-ended problem' (Amabile 1995, 78). So Nystrom defines creativity as the idea or starting point while Amabile sees it as the end product itself.

Analysis of creativity in organisations tends to concentrate on three separate aspects; the personality traits of creative individuals, the characteristics of creative organisations and the process of creative management.

Characteristics or 'traits' tending to be associated with a high level of creativity include tolerance of uncertainty, self-confidence, unconventionality, originality, intrinsic motivation, above average intelligence and a determination to succeed (King and Anderson 1995). But the 'creative individual' approach has its limitations. One is that these studies have tended to concentrate only on very high achievers and have therefore shed little light on more 'mundane' creativity. Secondly, the relationship between individuals and organisations is very complex. But I have noticed much anecdotal evidence that within voluntary organisations there is a strong belief that 'charismatic founders', 'creative oddballs' and 'maverick personalities' play a significant role in fostering creativity and this is an area of investigation which warrants further research. However, the main limitation of this approach is that it places little emphasis on the organisational context.

> ...innovative organisations invariably operated in a complex and multi-agency environment and relied on collaboration with other agencies to help them achieve their organisational goals. (Osborne 1994, 2)

Stephen Osborne's (1994) study of innovation in the voluntary sector in the UK highlights the importance of the external environment, suggesting that organisations may feel under pressure to describe work as innovative because of funding requirements, government pressure, and the general high esteem in which innovation is held within the sector. He points out that there are many thoroughly valuable functions that voluntary organisations fulfil, other than being innovative. For Osborne innovation involves a change in the nature of the client group the organisation works with and/or the service it provides as distinct from the incremental development or 'gradual improvement' of an existing service. (But he side-steps

---

2   I attended a plenary session of a major voluntary sector research conference on 'social entrepreneurship in 1999 where every one of five presentations focused solely on income generating activities, many of which did not demonstrate new ideas or models.

the difficult question of the distinction between innovation and creativity ignoring creativity altogether).

> ... innovation must involve discontinuity between the 'before' and 'after' states that the innovation involves, produced by the introduction of a new element into the situation... [gradual improvement]... may well lead to evolutionary change over a period of time but it is a different one from innovation. (Osborne 1994, 35)

'Organic' organisations (Morgan 1986) are more likely to be able to respond innovatively to changing conditions. However, this distinction seems problematic. Where to place the boundary between gradual improvement and change is an interesting and complex question.[3]

King and Anderson (1995) and Mintzberg (1989) conclude that certain characteristics are much more likely to be found in organisations that have a good track record in creative work. Among these are democratic leadership which encourages participation,[4] roles that offer opportunities for employees to exercise discretion and autonomy, a relatively flat and non-hierarchical structure, a climate that is encouraging of creativity and tolerant of risk and failure, and a culture that is relatively free of rigid traditions and role demarcations. This may be relevant to the process of 'professionalising' informal activities that I discussed in the last chapter.

Kay's research demonstrated how chief executives of voluntary organisations used multiple metaphors in making sense of experience and he described this process as itself creative. This implies that management itself can be constructed as a creative activity (and here Mintzberg's (1987) analogy of a potter at a wheel which he used to describe the process of strategy making – or strategy *crafting* raises another question, of course, about the distinction between art and craft).

Reed (1995) hypothesized that creativity occurs in four, iterative stages. Creativity emerges out of periods of regression and fragmentation which, in turn, lead us to seek new symbols of self identification through which fragmented thoughts are brought together at the level of conscious (or more often unconscious) thoughts or dreams and expressed in myths, stories and metaphors (Reed 1995), a 'stage of culture formation where community members evolve rituals to create tribal identification' (Reed 1995, 12).

In this chapter I explore how creativity is understood and constructed in voluntary organisations from the perspective of the stories that managers told about work that they described as creative. In the following section I use the content of these stories to look at whether they suggest a particular understanding of creativity within voluntary

---

3   As I described in the previous chapter, this may be dependant on very differing assumptions about the nature of social change itself (Burrell and Morgan 1979).

4   Participatory leadership is discussed in the next chapter. However, it is important to note that Damanpour suggested that his research only showed a 'modest positive association between participation in decision making and innovation and no significant association between both the degree of normalisation and extent of hierarchy, and innovation' (Damanpour 1995, 128).

organisations. The next section looks at the process by which the understanding of creativity within an organisational setting is conceptualised through metaphors. I then go on to look specifically at the functions the founding stories, considered as creation myths, play in sustaining the culture of creativity within the organisation. The chapter concludes with a discussion about the place of creativity within the sector and whether that position is under threat.

Metaphors of creative organisations

Now many of them [voluntary organisations] *are locked into service provision, I wonder what's happened to the innovation and the creativity. The countervailing force to that may be that so many funders are looking to fund new work, project based and so on, so that may be a countervailing force...*

In Chapter 2 I suggested that the founders of voluntary organisations were motivated by their utopian visions of a better world and that the stories they told were revelatory of these visions. Here I want to apply this idea to an exploration of the underlying assumptions about the nature of organisations that structure, or frame managers' understanding of creativity. Early in my research I came across Kay's study (1991, Fletcher and Kay, 1994) of the ways in which voluntary sector chief executives used metaphors to conceptualise effectiveness within their organisations and also how these were influenced by the underlying metaphors *of* organisations that Morgan (1986) had developed in his then still excitingly new book *Images of Organization.* Kay's work was then, and to a large extent still is, one of the very few studies that employs a social constructionist approach to voluntary organisations. My study paralleled Kay's methodology but applied it to creativity rather than effectiveness.

Kay's methodology involved attributing words, phrases, sentences and paragraphs primarily to the eight key metaphors that Morgan developed (machine, organism, brain, culture, psychic prison, political system, flux and transformation and instrument of oppression). Morgan used 'metaphor' to describe the 'picture' behind the foundational assumption being made by the speaker about the nature of organisations. Kay classified words and phrases by looking for the images behind them and then locating them within one or another of these 'meta-metaphors'. The Kay study primarily used the same eight metaphors that Morgan wrote about but he also included additional organisational metaphors drawing on other writers such as theatre (Mangham 1987) and military (Pondy 1983).

Taking creativity, rather than effectiveness as my subject matter I analysed the stories to discover the underlying metaphor of organisation that was dominant. The organisational metaphors used most frequently were flux and transformation, organism, political system, psychic prison and culture. The organisation-as-instrument-of-domination metaphor barely figured at all. It was only used on three occasions and two of these were with reference to the government, not to the interviewee's own organisation. Organisation-as-machine was used primarily in reference to applying quality standards so as to ensure consistency across membership organisations.[5]

Comparisons between metaphors of efficiency and metaphors of creativity

Kay interviewed 26 chief executives and subjected his data to much more detailed analysis. For this reason alone it was not possible to make any detailed comparison however there were some interesting similarities and differences.

In Kay's analysis the five most frequently used metaphors-of-organisations were:

brain	21.4%	
machine	17.7	
organism	16.8	
political system	15.4	
business (market place)[6]	7.9	(Fletcher and Kay 1994)

These results were so unlike my findings that they suggest very strongly that chief executives conceptualise their organisations very differently when they are thinking about creativity rather than effectiveness. While the 'organism', and 'political system' metaphors appear in both lists, the metaphor that occurred most frequently in discussions about creativity, flux and transformation, did not even appear on Kay's list, while his most frequently used metaphor, brain, did not appear on mine.

Metaphors of movement

Kay also suggested that one metaphor might have particular significance for voluntary organisations was that of 'journey'. My later work on stories about empowerment supported this, especially the use of the metaphor of the road on which the journey takes place. Kay's conclusion arose from a separate analysis in which he looked not only at the frequency of usage but also at the context in which the metaphors occurred. He noted that the statements that evoked the journey metaphor were often quite emphatic, '"now look here" … "nitty-gritty" statements where the voice is firm and more controlled' (Fletcher and Kay 1994, 14).

Inns says that 'journey' can be interpreted in different ways, depending on whether the destination, the vehicle used to get there, the likely length of the trip and the route to take are known or unknown. I analysed the flux and transformation

---

5   Quality assurance systems were mentioned in other situations and were attributed variously according to the context. For example one chief executive referred to the production of a quality assurance system as a creative 'product'.

6   Kay's research was carried out during the late 1980s and it is arguable that the 'market' metaphor would be much more dominant now, especially in stories about effectiveness; perhaps less so in stories about creativity.

attributions in the stories told to me about creativity to see how many implied non-directed movement, how many journey (which I used to imply directed movement towards a destination which is at least partially known) and how many a balance between countervailing forces. While I found 46 metaphors that expressed some sense of a journey towards a known destination there were also 23 that described non-linear movement and 27 that invoked a sense of equilibrium.

Here are two examples of metaphors of non-linear movement:

Sitting in a senior management team meeting was quite amazing because someone would come up with an idea over here, it would pinball around the table, five minutes later it would be turned into fact and then it would be presented to the outside world as a fait accompli.

...take advantage of the ripple effect...

These are metaphors of movement but the destination is unclear. The 'ripple effect' metaphor even implies that, at least to some extent, it will never be entirely known, Some consequences will be beyond the organisation's reach. The 'equilibrium' metaphor conveys a slightly different impression, that of action and reaction.

Some examples of the 'balance' metaphor:

...so that may be a countervailing force.

But...having done that initial, pro-active move, they were almost overwhelmed with the import that brought with it...

Organisation as journey is not one of Morgan's metaphors although 'the journey metaphor is one of the central metaphors of Western culture, embodying notions of progress, direction and purpose' (Lakoff and Johnston cited in Inns 1996, 200).

Morgan's metaphor for change however is flux and transformation. Within this metaphor he locates ideas of change as cyclical, or rotational rather than linear such as the 'logic of mutual causality' of the *Tao*, (Morgan 1986, 225) which seem consistent with these storytellers.

The organisation as organism metaphor

It is not surprising that the organisation-as-organism metaphor featured strongly given the common poetic associations of plants with creativity. Minztberg (1989) in his work on 'adhocracies' the form of organisation he suggests is most creative, frequently uses a garden metaphor. Here are some examples of phrases I attributed to the organisation-as-organism metaphor:

... it was a matter of the climate being right at the time ...

...so I planted the seed in his mind...

...we come from those disciplines that ignore sometimes the social, economic and political environment of families, so you can be going to see child guidance and they can never know that you haven't enough money to buy a pint of milk on the way home.

The words 'climate' and 'seed' clearly belong to an organic frame of reference while in the third quote the emphasis is on thinking holistically.

The psychic prison metaphor

The role of the unconscious was a feature in many of my interviews. Morgan's psychic prison metaphor combines the idea that organisations are psychic phenomena with the idea that these phenomena can be imprisoning. He emphasises the restrictions and resistances that these processes can cause. However, in discussions about creativity and creative ideas, the role of the unconscious was not seen as imprisoning but as liberating and as a fruitful source for new perspectives and ideas. The role of the unconscious in generating creativity is also highlighted in Reed (1995) and in the many studies of creativity in organisational settings described by King and Anderson (1995).

Here is one such example which captures the liberating potential of the creative unconscious:

And what happened after that was a very creative coming together of a load of people who had been at each others' throats, really, it felt creative because their animosity was refocused into creativity and they had to come up with something that was in everyone's best interest to do.

In summary, the organisational metaphors of flux and transformation, organism and psychic prison were particularly relevant to the ways in which these UK based chief executives conceptualised their organisations in reflecting on creativity. They were not the dominant metaphors found by Kay (1991)[7] and the ways in which these metaphors are invoked, particularly the psychic prison metaphor are not entirely consistent with Morgan's conceptualisations. These findings suggest that the ways in which managers imagine their organisations are not stable but fluid and shifting.

Conceptualising creativity through metaphors

This section looks at the ways in which meanings of creativity are created metaphorically through the process of storytelling and explore the shared imagery in

---

7   The findings discussed in the previous chapter also suggest that they might not be the dominant metaphors that Indian chief executives would use when telling their stories of creativity, given that the Indian respondents were much less likely to see change as proceeding incrementally.

the stories that managers told about creativity and in particular, from the metaphors that were used by the storytellers. 'Creative' metaphors could be understood in three different ways; 1) metaphors that draw analogies with the arts, 2) metaphors that generate, or 'create' new understandings, and 3) metaphors which describe creative processes within organisations In the stories there were only a few metaphors used that drew specific analogies with the arts. Some that did used phrased such as 'drawing strategy' and getting a team meeting going by using dance. The clearest analogy drawn was in the following example:

> *So having freed up the organisation... without tight controls allowed something to emerge that has a sunshine about it, you know, a sort of Bonnard type image, which wouldn't have happened if* [we] *had been more dour about it.*[8]

However, the relative absence of such analogies suggests that managers do not automatically draw on learning from the creative arts when reflecting on creativity in an organisational context.

Many of the stories fell into the second category, particularly, as I have explored in the previous section, those that told about activities the organisations had undertaken which had created new images, or ways of 'seeing' the positions of people in marginalised groups. However, there were also a number of stories that looked specifically at how creative ideas emerged in an organisational setting and here there was an enormous amount of similarity in all of the interviews. The findings seemed to fall into two categories, identifying creative processes and managing those processes.

Identifying creative processes

From the metaphors of creative processes one process that emerged very strongly was synthesis. When asked where the creative ideas came from they were always described as resulting from a number of disparate things coming together, whether these 'things' were people, teams or circumstances. There was no evidence for the view that creativity in organisations is located in creative individuals. No chief executive said that the ideas came primarily from them. This was particularly striking because two of the five were the founders of their organisations.

> *We used to idea hop between each other, one of us would get an idea, we'd chat about it quickly with the others and the links would come.*

The passive construction of this phrase 'the links would come' seems to describe a state of mind that many artists would recognise, that of expectant waiting.[9]

---

8   Pierre Bonnard was a French, Impressionist painter.
9   The phrase 'negative capability' was used by the poet John Keats, in a letter to his brothers George and Thomas Keats, dated 21 December, 1817. He writes about negative capability as the state in which we are 'capable of being in uncertainties'.

However, it is not a concept that is commonly used in books about management, most of which are primarily written in the active tense, although Bate's (1994) work on emergent strategy is an exception.

In the following example the idea is described as having an agency of its own independent of the people in the room:

Someone would come up with an idea over here, it would pinball around the table.

These descriptions of the processes by which creative ideas 'emerge' seems to confirm Gioia's suggestion (1995) that creativity in organisations differs from creativity in the arts by being located in teams rather than within individuals.

In some stories the synthesis was not of people but of circumstances or events:

A number of things came together at a particular time... I think it was a matter of the climate being right, there being opportunities in the changes in the legislation [this is a campaigning organisation] *for new directions to be developed in the organisation, plus a history that needed sorting out and you could get something out of those two scenarios that might be mutually successful.*

...so we started pulling all the links together

...we put various bits together...

Many of the stories were about developing new ideas and new work out of bringing things together in new ways, such as new after school services being developed bringing together a traditional childcare organisation, urban regeneration policy and new funding regimes; using quality standards and peer appraisal to revitalise membership affiliation, bringing together new community care policies, volunteering and informal carers to create new parliamentary legislation.

In one interview the words 're-focusing', 're-imagining', 're-positioning' and 're-visiting' were all used within a few minutes of each other. It is striking that these images of movement are, as mentioned before, non-linear. They are not descriptions of a steady progress towards an identified goal. Mintzberg's (1987) analogy of the process of strategy making with that of a potter crafting clay on the wheel, seems very similar to the processes described in these interviews in which the pot is shaped and reshaped. But again, this is striking because it contradicts so much of the current management orthodoxy that emphases a linear pathway from actions to objectives to (known and desired) outcomes.

If goals and objectives do not figure prominently in the ways in which these managers describe creativity, having a clear sense of purpose and organisational identity emerge very strongly. For example, in each interview there was a reference to the organisation having recently gone through a process of reaffirming and rediscovering its identity following a period of confusion and lack of direction.

We started looking at repackaging... the organisation was at a particularly low point... [it] had to look at why it existed, was it needed, what other organisations were trying to *achieve... so it had its period of navel gazing in good time, got that out of the way and really started to develop. We knew what we had to do.*

We had a terrible early part of last year... I do think we are needing to see that our identity is not in direct offering of parents groups but in helping others to do that ...so we are in a creative phase in a sense because we are all thinking about how we, you know, is that where we want to be, and I think we got our identity blurred... we do now see our identity as a source of training, bringing some of the ideas in...

Although there was not always a clear sense of where the organisation was going each chief executive had an immensely clear understanding of the organisation's identity. There seemed to be an important distinction here between identity and purpose on the one hand and ways and means on the other. These findings reinforce the Reed hypothesis that creativity is located within an iterative oscillation process of regression (as described in these stories by the 'terrible time', the 'particularly low point'), identification ('we knew what we had to do') and realisation ('we are in a creative phase'). Reed locates creativity within the transition from identification to realisation (Reed 1995, 9) as do these storytellers. Perhaps it is this clarity about identity that is a necessary prerequisite for seeing the opportunities inherent in disparate circumstances.

If we're about to embark on a period of new ideas we try to review exactly where we're at before we start thinking about where we want to go.

There was also emphasis on changing thinking and new approaches Some metaphors for changing thinking were 'pushing out the frontier', 'pushing boundaries', 'rocking the boat'.

...changing thinking, changing the way you work with a range of audiences... I don't just mean 'work 'in terms of the services you deliver but in the ways in which you work with different audiences.

...new focuses on a traditional issue...

it's not that they need to be trained... but they do need to think about it differently.

What this organisation used as its basic principles on which to build an atmosphere that people could try and work differently...

Another defining criteria was the drive to be constantly doing new things suggested in phrases such as 'testing out new approaches', 'waving with the wind', 'testing the orthodoxy'.

These stories suggest that creative process in organisations are non-linear but a synthesis, or 'coming together', that they 'emerge' after periods of organisational introspection and a renewed sense of purpose (although not of outcome) and they resolve themselves in new ideas and approaches that 'test orthodoxy'.

Leading and managing creativity

How did the chief executives see their role in encouraging creativity? These leaders did not see it as their responsibility to provide the creative ideas but they did see themselves grasping opportunities and 'poaching' ideas. They also saw it as their role to initiate the process of re-thinking, re-imagining and re-positioning but again, this did not have to be carried out exclusively by them.

> *It was L really, who is a very energising young woman...the team could see that what people were describing was what they had overcome...and so she began to say 'well it's the strengths we ought to be thinking about' and so we began to see that as an opportunity.*

So what do managers do to encourage and lead creativity? Each stressed the importance of having high expectations of staff, of creating a culture that celebrates success and of participatory management.

In every interview there was some mention of the importance of believing in the potential of staff 'to do remarkable things' and giving them the responsibility to demonstrate that potential. Specific examples were of speaking at conferences, writing a book, developing the quality assurance system. So one way in which the chief executives nurtured creativity in the organisation was in giving responsibility to staff to take on pieces of work where they would have substantial control for shaping the finished product.

> *You come in here and here's your opportunity to make your career plan... you've got a good pad to launch yourself*

Creativity is reinforced by celebrating successes.

> *You need to win a few battles. You have to parcel up what you're trying to achieve into bite sized pieces.*

> *One cherry can put everyone's state of mind quite quickly in such a high place. It's quite extraordinary what you can get to when you've had a cheque in the post.*

There was a unanimous commitment to a participative management style.

> *It appeals to people because it is a system they owned.*

> *It's not the senior managers who've taken on the task, it's the grass roots workers.*

These findings reinforce King and Anderson's suggestions about the characteristics that are likely to be found in organisations with a good track record in creativity; participatory leadership, work roles offering opportunities for discretion and autonomy, relatively flat structures, groupings determined by task and purpose rather than role demarcation (King and Anderson 1995).

There was a constant emphasis on maintaining the belief that individuals at every level could have an impact on the organisation.

...a feeling that at whatever level you are you can change things, you don't have to go through hundreds of channels...

One of the key things is the ...stone in the pond, and how if you can actually make a bit of a difference the ripple effect of that is enormous.

These last examples may not just be metaphors of creativity in organisations per se but of *voluntary* organisations in particular. The emphasis on change and on 'making a difference' are significant. The process of change implied in the phrase 'ripple effect' is particularly interesting, suggesting as it does, that the organisation plays a catalytic role, also a significant element in the stories about empowerment described in chapter three. The connection between creativity and empowerment is my next theme.

Creativity and empowerment

I have said earlier that creating an organisation is empowering. The actual word 'empowerment' was very rarely used in these interviews. However, there was a myriad of imagery which seemed to contain this notion. Here is one example, which I used earlier in chapter three, in the context of the metaphor of the road:

We gave then a bus ticket home to re-affiliate.

The context for this an initiative to encourage lapsed or disengaged members to recommit themselves to recommit themselves to the organisation. This metaphor rather wonderfully captures the sense that the organisation itself can only do so much – the recipients have to make the actual journey themselves. Another example was of writing a draft bill for parliament 'on the back of an envelope'. Here are some other examples:

We dispensed with the trappings of the go-between, the professional, the desks and the names...everyone was a first name which...might not sound so particular now but at the time it was something.

It's been the grass roots workers who've wanted to get involved [with staff appraisal] *and that's felt really good because, of course, these are the people who are usually on the receiving end.*

These stories reinforce the importance of relationships based on mutual respect. These are examples of empowerment at many levels: parents, small membership groups, projects, staff, clients, even the empowerment of the chief executive herself drafting a piece of parliamentary legislation 'on the back of an envelope'. However, it is striking that volunteers as a group (as opposed to members, parents, trustees etc) were only specifically mentioned by one manager who works for a volunteering agency. She said 'the creativity is in the volunteers'. Reed also said 'the creativity in the voluntary sector is located in the volunteers'.[10] However, no other manager mentioned volunteering.

In this section I have explored creative processes in voluntary organisations and they can best be led and managed. I now want to look at the significance of the founding story in creating and sustaining the organisation's culture.

Creation myths and the culture of creativity

In this section I explore the some of the functions of one particular organisational story of creativity, the story of the founding of the organisation. I have used these stories extensively throughout this book. My interest in them was aroused while I was carrying out the research I have just been describing, asking chief executives to tell me stories about events in the organisation's history that they regarded as emblematic of creativity. In the second interview the example given was the story of how the organisation was established, the 'founding story'.

Briefly, this story was of parents of children with a particular kind of disability who had become so frustrated by the absence of appropriate services for their children, and so determined to resist their being sent away to generic psychiatric hospitals that they sold or mortgaged their own houses in order to buy a building and start a school. They did this with very little idea about how such a service should be run and before there was much knowledge about their children's condition. So, the school's practice and philosophy developed largely as a result of trial and error.

In analysing the interview as a whole I realised that elements of this story, such as the involvement of parents (who still largely make up the trustee body), their commitment to the children, opportunism and risk seemed to resonate throughout. As this story was told the organisational metaphors of organism and flux and transformation featured prominently, for example growth was always described in organic terms.

Analysing the metaphors used in the stories and comparing them with the metaphors used throughout the interview demonstrated that the dominant metaphors in each founding story were also the dominant metaphors throughout the interview. However, these dominant metaphors, while consistent throughout each individual interview were not the same across the different organisations. This suggested that the founding story may be of significance; firstly in terms of how the chief executive defines the 'meaning' of creativity within that particular organisation, and secondly, that it contributes to creating and sustaining its individual culture.

The following story comes from a very different organisation. The founders, both psychoanalysts, wanted to work creatively with people without their having to

---

10   Bruce Reed, in a conversation with me in February, 1996 (see also Reed, 1988, 1995).

assume the labels of 'patients', and of working with them in a way which built on their strengths rather than their illnesses.

> *We began to think about how you could...still be aware of Mr and Mrs Ordinary, who didn't necessarily have to be in that stage of pathology before you got a hold of them.*

Throughout this interview Morgan's metaphor of the organisation as psychic prison resonated strongly. This manager talked about emphasising successes, helping people to redefine their own experiences. An example she gave concerned a project with parents which started by looking at their problems but was refocused to identify and build on strengths.

In another interview the story concerned a merger between two organisations. The key elements were survival, clarity of focus and the need for a single voice to be an effective campaigning organisation. In this story, as in the interview overall, the organisational metaphor that resonated most strongly was the organisation-as-political-system. A story that reinforced the dominance of this metaphor was of writing a new piece of parliamentary legislation 'on the back of an envelope'.

Finally, I interviewed the chief executive of a volunteering organisation whose founder originally worked from home 'at the kitchen table'. From this table, so the story goes, he sent young people half way around the world to do voluntary work. Often the volunteers did not know where they were going, still less what they were to do until they were seen off at the docks with their boat ticket.

This story was told so often within the organisation that it was often just evoked by the words 'kitchen table'.[11] The story is potent with symbolism, suggesting adventure, excitement, the unknown, the value of service. The metaphor of the kitchen table evokes resonances of home and nurturance in a way that a study desk would not. The kitchen table suggests that however far away they went they would always be able to return home.

These findings suggested to me that the stories play an important role in establishing the culture and reinforcing the values of an organisation generally, but also that there may be a specific association between the ways in which the founding story is told and creativity is defined.

Founding stories as creation myths

Following this research project I carried out a larger study into these stories exploring the proposition that they might come to hold mythic significance for the organisation. As voluntary organisations are often founded because people feel passionately about a particular issue these stories may be seen as heroic tales and 'cultural artefacts' (Schein 1986).

To say that founding stories can be understood as myths requires some exploration of the concept of 'myth' and also whether stories about organisational events can

---

11 This observation is based on my own experience as I worked for this organisation for nine years.

ever achieve the status of myth. These stories originate in lived events rather than as fictions. However, Gabriel's (1991) study of stories told by workers in the catering industry showed that their 'truth' content became less important over time, when the stories were '...no longer simply true or not because the mythical core [might] be expressing a "truth" even if the telling of events [had] become distorted' (Gabriel 1991, 865).

This relationship between 'myth' and 'truth' would seem to be paradoxical. The saying that a metaphor is a lie which tells the truth is attributed to Picasso (cited by Miller 1988, 44). Pondy says that a myth can be regarded as an 'extended metaphor' if the story told 'stands in a metaphoric relationship to real events', and which offers some explanation of the present by reference to the past (Pondy 1983). A myth juxtaposes the past and the present in order to show both how the present resembles the past and also how it differs from it. Therefore, for an organisational story to claim legitimacy as a myth it must have some explanatory force in making sense of the present. The findings presented in the previous section, from my small study of creativity, did suggest that founding stories are useful heuristics for understanding how specific meanings of creativity are sustained within each organisation.

The functions of creation myths

In developing my argument that these stories come to hold mythic significance I have made extensive use of Joseph Campbell's (1988a) work on mythology. He identified four functions of mythology: the transcendental, the cosmological, the sociological and the psychological. Campbell's schema was a very helpful tool for structuring my observations about the founding stories. How do these functions, which Campbell draws from studies of sacred mythologies, relate to myth making in voluntary organisations?

The transcendental function of mythology   Campbell (1988a) suggests that all great mythological traditions have sought to make sense of suffering and evil and to offer some path for transcendence, or redemption. As voluntary organisations come into being because an individual, or a group of individuals have identified a social injustice, or 'evil' the founding stories respond by suggesting that voluntary action offers the possibility of individual or societal redemption. Within this overall theme, the various specific injunctions include heroism, risk, sacrifice, philanthropy, social responsibility and the transformation, and re-imagination of the existing social order.

The founders' response to a social concern is to take action. These stories play an iconic significance because they portray organisations that were not founded because of a profit motive or in order to achieve the aims of the state but through free will, consciously directed towards the betterment of society. They set out a mechanism through which individuals can act, together or alone, to challenge injustice.

Some of these stories about action taking are heroic tales, promoting the values of sacrifice and courage. Other examples propose the acquisition of knowledge as a way of overcoming suffering as in the following example. The founder's portrait hangs above the stairs:

The woman on the stairs is one Patricia Fay. She was a housewife. Had a bad back, so was flat on her back for quite a long time, I think, and wanted to extend her mind. And this was the mid-sixties, and she wanted to learn more about the decorative and fine arts...

The search for knowledge can help to overcome suffering but it also gives social issues visibility. It highlights the importance of bringing consciousness to bear on the problem of evil and injustice. The Gnostics believed that knowledge, gnosis, rather than faith, was the path to salvation (Holroyd 1997, King 1999). 'Gnosis' implies salvation through knowledge with its vehicle being the mind.

...they invited two of the member organisations who presented their work in the field of self management, Arthritis Care and Manic Depression Fellowship, and I was so impressed by it, it was a really interesting and innovative piece of work , and there were two, entirely different kinds of conditions approaching it in different ways, so I decided to go on learning about it and I went to a meeting of the Manic Depression Fellowship... and there were over 100 people there, and they'd all been asked to do a poster which showed how they self managed their manic depression, and so all around the walls were these, just little posters, just A4, pieces of paper, and people had drawn what helped them manage...

If a function of mythology is to make it possible to bear the fact of human suffering, these stories do so through offering a variety of ways in which we can act to alleviate that suffering.

The cosmological function of mythology Campbell (1988a) suggests that the second function of mythology is to show how all things are coherent and consistent with a single world view, and to reinforce and legitimate that world view by demonstrating this consistency.[12] The founding stories fulfil this criteria by illustrating how the actions of the organisation and its founding values have internal coherency, that the actions are understandable as 'vehicles' for these values. Echoing Abravanel (1983), the myth 'mediates' between the actual and desired state of affairs.[13]

Cosmologies start with cosmogonies, stories about how the world came into being. The founding stories all function, to some extent, as cosmogonies, in that they purport to tell the story of how the organisation was created. But, as Ricoeur points out (1991a), the question of how an event is defined as foundational, is itself

---

12 This idea has some similarity with Morgan's (1997) concept of the 'hologram' (which he includes in the organisation-as-brain meta-metaphor), where the whole is wholly present in each of the parts.

13 Although note that Abravanel is suggesting something more ambivalent – not that the myths show how these two states can be linked, but that they enable us to cope with our fears that the real and the desired are further apart than we would like.

an act of subjective interpretation. The boundary between the non-existence and the existence of the organisation is not always neatly drawn.

In creation mythology this process is usually described as the creating of form out of chaos. Sometimes this happens in a moment, in other stories there is a gradual separating of elements.[14] Similarly, many of the stories describe the organisation's creation as a long process, which can 'start' in the early personal history of the founder. Some stories suggest the organisation was a single entity created in relative isolation whereas in others, evoking the organic metaphor, the organisation grew or evolved out of others and was separated off, amoeba like.

The stories reflect a wide variety of views as to when an organisation actually becomes an organisation. For some the 'naming' is a significant rite of passage. For very few is the process of becoming formalised through a legal instrument such as registration or incorporation dealt with in any significance. The starting point for the founder chief executives was significantly further back in time than for those who had come into an already established organisation. In stories about the founding of secondary, or umbrella organisations it is not always clear whether the organisation has grown out of its member organisations or whether it has a clear identity and beginning of its own.

What is the significance for an organisation in the designation of one event, or series of events, as foundational? Ricoeur (1991a) suggests that 'calendar' time is an interpretive fiction and it is possible to suggest that the way in which the founding event is constructed serves to locate the organisation within specific symbolic meanings. In the story about the mother of a disabled child, which I used in the second chapter, this is clearly demonstrated:

> ...[my son] *would be born in 1975 and I suppose really, from 1976 onwards, I started taking interest in what was available to him... so it took a few years and then it was clear that really the sort of services I would want for him weren't up here.*

And,

> *I decided to go to Andhra Pradesh, where I grew as a very small boy. I knew the area very well. I knew the problems also...*

The parent / child bond is emphasised in the first example and loyalty to your 'native place' stressed in the second. Were other foundational events to be identified, as perhaps another storyteller would have done for each of these organisations, they would have communicated different symbolic meanings.

---

14   Werner writes on Hindu cosmology, 'The story of the origin of the universe... is envisioned not as a creation out of nothing but as a continuous process of periodic manifestations of the universe out of its divine source or the dimension of the manifest, and it has its duration of time which is followed by the dissolution of the manifested world back into the hidden source, only to re-emerge again and again in ever recurring cycles. This process has no conceivable beginning in time.' (Werner 1994, 52-53). Contrast this with Genesis...

Campbell (1988a) suggests that myths should show how everything serves the purpose, is the vehicle of the transcendent. Within the context of voluntary organisations this can be interpreted as being about the link between values and action. All of the stories contain explicit details about how the founders' beliefs and visions led them to a particular course of action, as I proposed in the fourth chapter. These can be seen as providing a heuristic for linking values and actions, a litmus test against which the organisation can evaluate its work.

These links serve a number of functions. They reinforce the sense of identity and uniqueness in that while the values and beliefs may be similar they will find expression in as many different ways as there are organisations. They provide a yardstick against which the actions of the organisation can be measured and a means for interpreting what is defined as success or failure. They may also, as previously suggested, serve to mediate, or manage the tension between what is desired and what is achieved (see Abravanel 1983).

Pondy (1983) showed how myths could facilitate change by acting as a bridge between the past and the future through the evocation of eternal beliefs. These stories offer a way in which the organisation can grow and change and yet be seen to be 'true to its roots'.

The sociological function of mythology   Campbell's (1988a) third function of mythology, the sociological, is to validate the existing social order. I have developed this theme in greater detail in the previous chapter and, in particular, the question about the extent to which organisations see themselves as part of a process of change that is incremental or radical. In this sense it could be argued that the founding stories do not function as myths, as Campbell suggests, because they are primarily about changing the existing order rather than reinforcing it. Campbell's concept of mythology here is a rather conservative one.

However, the question of whether myths seek to maintain or overthrow the social order offers too stark a choice. Most of the stories I heard implied that these organisations saw their task neither as maintaining nor overthrowing the existing social order but of re-interpreting it.

> *... and the essence was both to challenge the G8 Summit and the economic orthodoxy that that represented but also very much to portray positive alternatives, a strong emphasis on that, and I think for some of the founding fathers and mothers it was recognised that economics was a language of power, and it was there that much of the social and environmental issues that activists were concerned about would be fought out. The Foundation was then set up in 1986 to really carry on this work of The Other Economic Summit and to develop, essentially, a new economics.*

These stories describe a process of setting out alternatives, of stimulating Ricoeur's 'social imaginary' (Ricoeur 1986) to create new worlds. They promote an alternative social compact; between men and women, the state and its citizens, business and the community, and even solidarity between organisations with overlapping concerns and an alternative vision of a just society while working through existing structures.

The psychological function of mythology Campbell (1988a) suggests that mythology has traditionally offered ways of understanding and ritualising rites of passage along the journey from life to death, and provided a 'container' for the anxieties that are generated within us by the awareness of the imminence of our own death. The organisation-as-organism metaphor suggests that organisations have life cycles, and the founding stories, by telling the story of the 'birth' also implies that it will die.

For these stories to be fulfilling Campbell's criteria, we would expect them to offer some way of acknowledging and containing the anxiety that the individual worker will feel about working in an organisation that has a death as well as a life. Several of the stories seemed told how the organisation struggled with a 'near death experience' and how it was overcome, seemingly miraculously, by a gift of money from an anonymous donor. This is the first example. (Note the evocation of the life-cycle metaphor through the phrase 'seven year cycles'.)

> *...a near death experience, which was in 1989.* [The founder] *left, and he left because he thought he couldn't make the organisation work, he thought it wasn't going to work and that he would be better off pursuing other channels....And in 1991, the autumn of 1991, just after the second TOES[15] interesting rhythms to the organisation, since the first one, every seven years, 1991 then last year 1998 – each has kind of precipitated a different phase in the organisation's life – so after TOES in 1991 the trustees met to decide when to close down the organisation and at that moment one of the trustees came in with the news that he'd raised £40,000 a year for three years to bring in a director, so that changed the situation. That's where I entered.*

In this example as well, the gift of money coincides with the arrival of the chief executive who was telling the story.

> *And then it got to a make or break point where the number of people supporting the training scheme had been dropping off and people were saying 'this really isn't working' and so it got to the point where we hadn't got an executive secretary, the training scheme is falling apart, what are we going to do with the association? Which had pottered along.... And so there was a crisis, basically. And a trust came up with an offer of £10,000 a year for two years to see the association through and to re-establish the training course as a distance learning package. And so I resigned from* [another organisation] *and applied for the job. And was appointed. And it was sort of double or bust time basically.*

The final example of death and rebirth doesn't legitimise the position of the current chief executive as the other three examples does, but it carries the clearest evocation of a sense of the miraculous, that 'God is on our side'.

---

15   TOES refers to The Other Economic Summit.

... one story [tells] *about Benjamin Waugh* [the founder] *sitting down at a coffee table because he didn't know where the next penny was coming from and how to pay the inspectors, and some chap sitting next to him said, 'Well you look a bit miserable chum, what's wrong with you?' And Benjamin Waugh telling him, and this chap ended up as a benefactor who brought some money in.*

The similarity in these stories is striking. Sievers (1994, 1995) suggested that one source of tension in organisations may be the awareness that while we will die the organisation may not. However within the voluntary sector this may play itself out slightly differently because these organisations are supposed to have a death wish. If voluntary organisations are set up to ameliorate certain social ills, then, so the thinking goes, they are supposed to work towards putting themselves out of business.

Perhaps in the voluntary sector tensions arise not only because of the knowledge that the organisation will 'outlive' its workers but also because there may be a conflict in the minds of its members as to whether that is desirable.

These stories offer a way of 'managing anxieties' through the evocation of the archetype of the hero or rescuer, as demonstrated above, who shows that death can be overcome. These stories may also serve to offer consolation to staff, especially later on, when the organisation faces renewed crises.

Campbell (1988a) suggests that myths lose their power at the point when it becomes no longer possible to believe that the events actually occurred and this highlights one of the most paradoxical facets of mythology, namely that there comes a time when the listener or reader of a myth simultaneously believes it to be true and knows that it is not true. Myths have their greatest potency when the audience can consciously hold this tension between believing and not believing, between knowing and not knowing because it is only then that myths can be appreciated most fully as symbols, and that their symbolic potential to suggest new possibilities and stimulate the imagination, is at its apex.

The founding stories of organisations tell of events that are still close enough in lived time to be seen as recounting 'real' events while simultaneously communicating metaphorical truths about the organisation (and the process of organising) as perceived by the people who work within it. Perhaps they lose their potency as myths only if an organisation moves so far from its original purpose that the story fails in its function of helping to make sense of present experience. At this point the tension between believing and non-believing slackens.

Smircich (1983b) and Schein (1986) suggest that stories, myths and legends can be regarded as 'artefacts' in which the values and basic assumptions of the members of the organisation are manifested, and if we re-define the 'transcendent' as the 'universal' these values, as described above, are transcendent. These stories express a metaphorical relationship between lived events in the past and current experience expressed through symbolic representations of eternal, or transcendent values. My analysis suggests that the founding stories carry out the transcendental function of mythology by promoting voluntary action as a response to the problem of suffering.

They carry out the cosmological function by denoting a founding, or birth event, and by providing a heuristic by which the values and actions of the organisation can be seen as congruent. They carry out the sociological function by re-creating and reinterpreting our social environment and the psychological by offering a vehicle to contain our anxieties about the organisation's immortality and death. This is not to say that each story fulfils all of these functions equally and, of course, there will be many other stories that also carry mythic significance for the organisation.

Concluding thoughts

The stories about creativity, including the founding stories, suggest that within voluntary organisations creativity is still strongly defined as being about the changing of thinking and attitudes, challenging orthodoxy, developing new approaches to social problems. And the means for achieving these things are through empowering those who are not traditionally seen as occupying powerful roles in society and through the bringing together of disparate ideas, circumstances, groups, activities in new configurations.

Within organisations one role for the leader to play is that of bringing together disparate elements, looking for opportunities is unusual places and leads in the constant interpreting and re-interpreting of experience. While the leader does not always have to carry out those roles s/he has to make it possible for that leadership to emerge and thrive.

The telling of the founding story is one way in which the leader defines the specific culture of creativity within each organisation. Other leadership functions identified by the storytellers include celebrating successes, having high expectations of staff and allowing them sufficient responsibility to be able to develop their creative potential.

Perhaps the two most essential leadership tasks are consciously valuing creativity and ensuring that the organisation maintains a strong sense of its own identity. Creativity within organisations requires a clear understanding of overall purpose but not of the means for achieving that purpose. Creativity is located in the seeing of new possibilities and new opportunities and of retaining the capacity to be surprised.

From this emphasis on the changing of attitudes and the challenging of orthodoxy it follows that the impact or 'product' of the creative process is nothing less than the social environment itself, its attitudes, rituals beliefs and practices. These are constantly changing, constantly being re-imagined and recreated.

Is creativity important to the sector?

Those managers I interviewed for the first study all said that creativity was extremely important, something they consciously valued and worked hard to achieve. Whether creativity was particularly important to the voluntary sector was more problematic and this relates to the question I posed in the first chapter about the distinctiveness of the sector. They felt that the way in which we perceive the sector was changing and some felt that these changes threatened the place of creativity within it. This raises an interesting question about whether it is important for society as a whole that we can 'locate' creativity in particular places or institutions. If donor agencies or local government contracting departments are becoming more creative in the ways in which they devise contract tenders through promoting new models or identifying unmet needs, does it matter if the voluntary sector is no longer perceived as being particularly creative?

This blurring of boundaries is also taking place in the arts themselves where there has been an enormous growth of work that combines art and therapy, art and community development, even art and urban regeneration.

> *The old fashioned idea was that... you give some dosh to the voluntary sector and they'll create things and then the general services would take them on and implement them... I think that's gone out the window.*

Bion (cited in Pines 1961) tentatively suggested that societies establish institutions such as the army, church and criminal justice system to 'manage' certain anxieties and projections on behalf of that society as a whole. He did not develop these ideas very far before his death. But these observations suggest that we should consider whether it matters if certain institutions are perceived as being more creative than others and what might be the wider effects on society more generally if those perceptions shifting.

Threats to creativity

Each chief executive interviewed in the first study mentioned the 'blurring' of the boundaries between state, market and voluntary sector. Each saw creativity as under threat. However when each was asked where they located these threats they were not only different across the interviews, they were also seen as only affecting other organisations than their own. Their own organisation had surmounted those threats.

For example one person said that while the great temptation for an organisation with limited funds was to 'tie yourself down, look for a base line that is secure' she also went on to say that having insufficient funding *for her organisation* was a significant motivator towards finding new and creative ways of doing things.

Another said:

> *There is a danger, particularly for service providers, of being lured down this 'we've got to make more money, prove ourselves by volume'... and that does threaten the creativity.*

However, about her own, service providing organisation, she said:

> *We've decided we'd like to do innovative services that would show new models of delivery...we'll reposition ourselves vis-à-vis this contracting culture.*

So she saw *her* organisation responding to the contract culture in a creative way.

'Once you become the creature of the demands of the local authority' (tied to contracts for providing services) 'perhaps the creativity is at risk' said another. But for her organisation service provision provided the legitimacy for developing innovative training programmes.

All of the chief executives therefore identified the threats to creativity in the sector in the circumstances that their organisation had successfully resisted, but they were not the same circumstances. Two saw the contract culture as a threat but had turned it to creative advantage. Another located the threat in financial instability but admitted that for her organisation it had been a significant motivator. A third saywthe culture of the business world as a threat but also saw great opportunities in its techniques and approaches.

These stories may be expressing the sense that every crisis contains an opportunity. But it is also possible that what is really important is to have creativity as a conscious aspiration. Within the business world there are many highly creative organisations that take competition, limited funding, contract negotiation for granted. Perhaps it is not these factors that represent the threat to creativity but the ways in which the organisations respond.

Levi Strauss suggested that 'mythical thought always progresses from the awareness of opposites toward their resolution' (Levi Strauss 1970b, 321). Sometimes the resolution occurs through the actions of the protagonists and sometimes through the creation of mediatory figures such as clowns, serpents and other mythical beasts. I have shown that voluntary organisations come into being because of the founders' desires to resolve a contradiction between an existing, unsatisfactory condition and their vision for a better one. The organisation is created in order to mediate, in this sense, between these two states. Given the tensions and paradoxes that have been touched in previous chapters perhaps the founding stories carry out this mediatory role through representing action as the remedy for pain. This is a different response to the psychological than was demonstrated in Gabriel's stories which dealt with pain by 'soothing, consoling and reconciling' while the founding stories are battle calls which 'excite and release the forces of change' (Gabriel 1991, 865). But are all the founding stories heroic sagas or do they also contain elements of consolation – and do heroic tales console?

Chapter 6

The Dancer and the Dance:
Storytelling and Leadership

...when you tell your own stories, with ups and downs, with failures and successes, it's very strong for people to learn from each other. It's not something that you read. It comes out from your own life experience, so you tell it with emotions. So it is very, very important.

Introduction

In the previous section I discussed the roles that voluntary organisations play in helping individuals take power, or agency, to change circumstances that constrained them in marginalised locations. I suggested that the different ways in which people imagine society also influence the way they imagine themselves and their position within it. Voluntary organisations can offer new perspectives, new ways of seeing.

The stories people told about empowerment also emphasised the centrality of relationships, in particular relationship based on mutual respect, recognition of strengths and a real desire to help people to achieve their aspirations and their passions rather than a focus on needs and deficiencies. These themes were also echoed in the last chapter where they were described as integral to creativity.

These observations have significant implications for the leadership of voluntary organisations, both in terms of their work with people from marginalised groups but also in terms of their internal management.

In some respects the key debates about leadership in voluntary organisations are those in organisations anywhere: what are the ingredients that make for good leaders and how important are leaders to leadership - is leadership located in individuals, usually the chief executives or in the chairs of the governing bodies? However, in voluntary organisations, because these are organisations that exist primarily to enable people in marginalised positions to take greater control over their lives and of the systems and structures that affect them, there are also critical questions about the leadership role of users and communities. Is leadership, therefore located in those for whom the organisation exists or in the relationship between leaders and followers and the nature of the consent that binds them?

Leadership and participation

Much of the discourse around participation and participatory leadership in voluntary organisations focuses on the involvement of beneficiaries, usually described as users or members. This discourse can encompass all sorts of things from the involvement (often token) of service users in consultation exercises or on the board of trustees, to social audits, and, at the far end of this imaginary continuum, a particular ontological stance on the nature of existence.

There is also an important distinction to draw between participation in the internal governance and leadership of the organisation and externally influencing of public policy and practice. Of course, to some extent, these processes are complementary. For example, in a report of a conference on governance, organised to mark the 20th anniversary of PRIA, a leading Indian NGO, one participant commented that 'as women, dalits and adivasis began to assert their rights to participate in, and manage the development projects and resources, it became clear that the larger structures of governance need to be reformed'.[1] Similar trends, perhaps especially amongst disabled people, have also led to increasing belief in the rights of people to be involved in making decisions that affect their lives.

However, while the quote implies that participation in internal management leads to greater involvement in public governance, in the UK this process has occurred in the reverse order. The widespread recognition of the importance of user involvement in public policy and service delivery has only recently led an interest in creating the systems for achieving this internally (Robson, Begum and Locke 2003).

Participatory leadership, user involvement, accountability to stakeholders; all these are terms that are readily bandied about, especially by funders and policy makers, but the reality on the ground rarely matches the rhetoric. Participation 'is more often invoked to convey a warm glow than to illumine debate or practice' (Eade 2005, 10). Robson et al note that 'the presence of users at an event or meeting or simply through their use of a service did not necessarily mean that they were engaged or influential' (Robson et al 2003, 2).

For people who are not involved in the day to day running of organisations to be able to have real influence in the way things are done requires us to be very skilled at making organisational processes easily understandable to people who may have little or no management experience. One of the findings of Robson et al's study of user involvement in UK organisations was that leaders have not only to be committed to making their organisations more user-centred they also had to 'have a broad vision of what a user-centred organisation *would look like*' (Robson et al 2003, 2 my emphasis). They have to be able to imagine it.

---

1   Dalits are people from lower castes and adivasis are people who live in tribes, usually in remote, rural areas. This report is titled *Governance Where People Matter,* and was published by PRIA in 2003. The quote comes from the introduction, whose author is not named.

Participation also requires real commitment from those holding power and knowledge and a willingness to allow others to influence us. This becomes harder, not easier, as the demands of funders for strict and increasingly uniform accountability regimes continue to grow. There is another paradox here in that many funders want to see user involvement and participation and require organisations to demonstrate a commitment to it as a condition of funding.

There are many, small entirely voluntary associations (readers' clubs come to mind) that are run exclusively for and by their members. However, once an organisation becomes accountable for staff, for running services, for visible campaigning work, the locus of control can shift to professionals; staff, funders or both. Alvin Gouldner commented in 1969 that one of the 'secrets of organisations' was that although the board is responsible for policy and strategy and the staff for its execution, the reverse is far more likely to happen. More than thirty years on it is not only that professionals are generally the ones that define both strategy and policy they are also the ones that carry it out, leaving many boards essentially impotent; with a role that may be very clear on paper, but is impossibly confusing in practice. This is another instance of the pressure toward professionalisation that I have noted in previous chapters.

A very brief overview of leadership theory

This chapter focuses particularly on the significance of storytelling to the leadership of voluntary organisations. Storytelling can be described as a function of leadership as well as being a metaphor *for* leadership (Bennis 1996, Gardner 1995, Hatch et al, 2005). Stories can be revelatory both of the ways in which we understand leadership and of the processes involved in constructing that understanding. Storytelling is also one way in which leaders and followers negotiate shared meanings, from which can emerge the consent to act.

The academic work on leadership seems to fall into similar categories to that of creativity in organisations; the traits of individual leaders, the functions and responsibilities of leaders and the environment in which leadership emerges or occurs. Although all of these approaches could be applied to leadership in any context, within the voluntary sector specifically the extent to which leaders (wherever in the hierarchy they may be) are able to demonstrate their commitment to the values of the organisation and to negotiate the meanings of those values with followers are particularly important.

Smircich and Morgan (1995) and Sievers (1994) conceptualise leadership as the 'management of meaning' (see also Bennis, 1996 and Gahmberg, 1992). Leaders 'define the reality of others' (Smircich and Morgan 1995, 398). This is an *obligation* of the leader to which followers give their provisional *consent*. This consent and obligation must exist if there is to be co-ordinated action, so that competing interpretations can be, at least temporarily, set aside. Therefore, the leader's interpretation must consist of a viable basis for action that can win the consent of others.

> Leadership lies, in a large part, in generating a point of reference against which a feeling of organisation and direction can emerge. (Smircich and Morgan 1995, 394)

Gahmberg comments that the management of meaning takes place through the symbolic expression of organisational values, and it is partly through the expression of these values that leaders 'generate a point of reference' 'define' the boundary between the organisation and its environment and also enact a sense of identity for the organisation.

> Leaders make ideas tangible and real to others so that they can support them. For no matter how marvellous the vision, the effective leader must use a metaphor or word or model to make that vision clear to others. (Gahmberg 1992, 154)

Robson et al (2003) noted that leaders who were able to encourage user involvement were those who could 'give a strong sense of direction... and enabled others to translate them into action' (Robson et al 2003.1)

One way this can be done is through storytelling and many managers openly regard storytelling as an essential part of their role. Here are three examples which illustrate different aspects of storytelling. The first example shows how the storyteller defines leadership.

> *...my role is, being the founder and being a dreamer - I am a dreamer... I am only trying to, you know set up systems and processes in the organisation so that the dream does not become a vague dream and dreams become a reality through a kind of accountable, operational system.*

While here is a different example in which storytelling can be seen as one way in which the relationship between members of the organisation is sustained:

> *If you care to interview all of these fellows, even from peon,* [a title for a worker who does a range of fairly lowly tasks from cleaning to office junior] *you may be knowing what are the problems so far. Ask them about why we started* [the organisation] *and how we emerged in the state. They know...The organisation, the organiser, the visionary has his own vision. That has to be shared. And from that vision the mission emerges. Every member of the organisation should know what is the mission, that is the guiding principle of their work.*

The third example illustrates a more functional approach, to transmit knowledge and values.

> *I do tell stories about how the organisation started but most of the stories I tell would be to try and illustrate what's happened to children so I can get support for why we need to do something...*

This chapter explores all three aspects of storytelling and leadership. The next section looks at how leadership is portrayed in the content of these stories. The following section explores the notion that leading *is* storytelling, that leaders are engaged in a constant process of making meaning. In the section following that I invert the metaphor by looking at storytelling as a function of leadership, and in particular, how stories mediate the relationship between leaders and followers through their symbolic expression of the organisation's values, whether or not the leaders are formal or informal, individuals or groups.

Much of the material I am drawing on in this chapter, as in the others in this section, come from the interviews I did with chief executives. At the time I carried out the initial research I was working as a chief executive and was fascinated, frustrated (and probably at times infuriated) by the job, and in particular, by the fact that so little I read about management and leadership in much of the readily available management lore seemed to acknowledge the symbolic and interpretive role of managers as opposed to their much more obvious functional roles. Exploring leadership through the frame of storytelling offered me new insights into the job I was doing and new way of making sense of my own experience.

Stories and the construction of leadership

This section looks at stories as artefacts (Schein 1986, Smircich and Morgan 1983) in which the values and meaning of leadership in voluntary organisations is constructed and maintained. I have chosen to concentrate specifically on the significance of the founding story and the role of the founder as the first archetype of leadership within the organisation. I also look at the values of leadership as they are suggested by the stories and the differences in the construction of leadership between the Indian and UK stories.

Creation myths and the social construction of leadership

What is the particular significance of the founding story, or the creation myth to our understanding of leadership? The influence of the founder is well documented (Schwabenland 1996, 2006, Schein 1991, Wilkins 1983) and may be of particular importance in voluntary organisations.

> Stories about the founding of an organisation, about charismatic leaders or about any other significant events in the organisation may serve...a function of presenting an image of the organisation which many participants seem to value and which would therefore serve to unify them. (Clark 1972 cited in Wilkins 1983, 83)

These stories not only present an image of the organisation, as Clark notes above, but also of the individuals and groups that came together to create it and in this sense they may portray one archetype of leadership as embodied in the values and characteristics of those founders. These values, representing as they do the passion and commitment of the founders, may well serve to unify participants around a common sense of purpose.

The stories then may be one way in which the leaders can construct and maintain the values of that particular organisation. Are there also any common themes emerging from the stories that suggest particular understandings of leadership within voluntary organisations?

Similarities and differences in the construction of leadership

Within the stories there were many similarities in the way in which leadership was understood. In particular there was a shared agreement that leaders were required to create a fusion between vision and practice, that leadership involved demonstrating how vision and practice could be congruent. This is an example which comes form a n interview with a UK based founder of an organisation that advocates for people who care for ill or disabled relatives:

> *I always tell* [new staff] *the founding story and I always say to them 'its not because I expect you to remember it but I think this will give you a little idea of what the culture of the organisation is and what its about, moving it on for carers, committed for carers, can you do it for carers...*

Personal commitment to the organisation and its vision was a constant theme in all the stories but there were some significant differences too. One was the way in which individual managers defined the boundaries between the personal and the professional. In the Indian interviews two themes emerged much more strongly than in the UK interviews. Firstly, in the Indian interviews, the theme of individual sacrifice was much stronger, as in this example:

> *...because this is a voluntary organisation, we live with that, a lot of sacrifice will be there. I could have worked for any, any government job... But we are for the sector and we are sacrificing... See even my family members are complaining. I have two children. One is in sixth standard, he is sick, and yesterday in the evening I came, I saw my son, he was crying, 'papa, are you here for the next few days?' I said, 'No, tomorrow I am going. I will come* [back] *after three days'. So all family life is suffering.*

Secondly, several of the Indians said that the way in which members of the organisation lived their lives must embody the values of the organisation. Frugality and abstinence was often stressed. I stayed for three weeks in one such organisation where no alcohol or smoking was allowed, all the staff wore simple, locally made clothing and ate only vegetarian food. In the following quote the rationale behind this emphasis on abstinence is made explicit:

> *So when we did a play on savings we opened our own savings account first. When we did plays on drugs we started stopping cigarettes, tea – we don't offer tea, neither take tea, we stopped taking paan and all that. So whatever we will say to others, if it is applicable, we must try that...* [otherwise] *why should we advise others? We must experience that.*

In Chakraborty's (1998) work on Eastern values and their effect on perceptions of management he notes the influence of Rabindranath Tagore. Tagore wrote a letter to Leonard Elmhurst (the founder of Dartington Hall) saying that the fundamental values of rural reconstruction were 'the spirit of co-operation... and *a delight of sacrifice*'. He says that Gandhi shared this view, saying that we must 'impart *a sacrificial character* to our lives' (Chakraborty 1998, 134 emphasis in the original). This theme of sacrifice seems deeply embedded in the voluntary sector in India.[2]

I must be a kind of role model for others what should be a kind of artistic life, artistic choices, by own demonstration of life. So choice to cloth, choice to food, choice to the lifestyle is more important, I think as a leader.

Here we have the idea that the way in which you live your life must reflect the organisation's values. However, the way in which this theme occurred in the UK stories was subtly different. Several of the UK chief executives described themselves as in some way 'embodying' or 'symbolising' the organisation itself which suggests a different understanding of leadership. The emphasis here is not on behaviour, on 'doing', on right action, but on an more objectivised symbolisation as is demonstrated in these two examples:

I wear a suit, cause it actually helps me to make relationships with people who generally don't talk to you unless you wear a suit. But the fact is, I'm a six foot black guy, and not many organisations would have appointed me to run their organisation, but an organisation like [this one], *I'm the best thing that's ever happened to them. Because I fit the bill, really...*

Another example:

... So the director needs to be, well in many ways the director is [the organisation], I have to say... And if you look at what [the organisation] *has done under each of its past directors, it's always been different. It reflects the particular skills and interests and expertise of each director. And that's inevitable when you have a small organisation, as small as we are, dealing with a topic that we are in the way that we do, I mean we are about values, and so on. But having said that, although* [the organisation]*'s done different things under different directors, each of those directors would be able to lead any of the work done by the other directors... because there's always the same beliefs and the same principles and the same values that are always running through.*

Miller comments:

---

2   Of course this is not unique to India. For example if I had included an interview with the chief executive of one of the Camphill Communities, for example, which are run by people who are inspired by the Austrian philosopher Rudolph Steiner in my sample I suspect the same theme of living your life in a way which reflects the values or philosophy of the organisation would have been equally stressed. But it did not figure in my UK sample whereas it was a significant theme in the Indian interviews.

We, in the West, have learned something about ourselves through the influence of India. It may even encourage us in the near future to reassess the decision made during our Enlightenment era, in particular to reconsider the costs and benefits of our specific separation of the 'public' from the 'private'. (Miller 1990, 180)

And yet, these examples would suggest that this distinction is less about where the boundary between the personal and the professional is drawn, but how it is drawn with the Indian emphasis on doing, and the UK emphasis on a more objectified being. When the UK leaders talk about embodying the organisation's values they are not simply subscribing to a neat divide between the personal and the professional but they are interpreting it differently.

Embodying the values of the organisation rarely features in the person specifications produced by the specialist charity recruitment agencies, but it may be an important requirement of leadership and if so this sheds an interesting light on an issue that recurs on a regular basis about whether the sector needs to grow its own leaders or whether senior posts can be filled just as well (if not better) by managers from the public or private sectors.

The influence of the Bhagavad Gita, the 'song of god' a sacred text that is located in the great epic tale of the Mahabharata may go some way towards explaining the Indian chief executives' greater ease with process. In the Gita the god Krishna adjures the mortal Arjuna not to be concerned with the 'fruits of his desiring' (see Lipner, et al 1999), meaning that we should be less concerned with the consequences of our actions than with the motivation for those actions. This idea was explicitly mentioned in one interview and implicitly in another. This is the explicit reference:

> You see, if you search for results, this is not your work. You must keep working but never look for results....So don't tell me I may get nothing, fine, I have planted the idea that's enough... Gandhi said the same thing. Gandhi said the means are more important than the end. He kept saying that.., 'I am not interested in ends.' That's how non-violence goes. This is a means.

And it is implied here:

> CS: Where do you think [the organisation] will be in a few years?

> We don't know and we really don't care.

This is a very different philosophy to that which underlines performance management in which a clear focus on outcomes is seen as inherently good. It is, however, more akin to the descriptions of the management and leadership of creativity that I discussed in the previous chapter. In each case what is being described is working with emergent strategy, the process that Mintzberg (1987) describes as 'crafting'. But here it is given a philosophical grounding.

Leadership training

There are clearly implications here for the ways in which leaders are prepared and supported in their role. While all of the Indian managers were highly educated they had little interest in management training of the sort that is being imported from the West into the highly prestigious Indian Institutes of Management (the IIMs), and which is primarily based on a functionalist paradigm.[3] The chief executives seemed rather lukewarm about this training. For example:

> *I have not read many of them* [books on management]. *I know the concept behind it. You have to put it into practice and see how far it goes. In the early stages we had the group dynamic process, the 'T'.. what do you call it, 'T-group'. That has been for some extent practised. We never set aside anything that is new....we try to see if it could be understood, it could be practised. If it is not so helpful then we just kick it away. But if there is anything that is valuable, we take it.*

This is not exactly a ringing endorsement and neither is the following:

> *...the management training is a useful kind of background thing. But the real skills you have to develop on the job.., some of the concepts... I have to de-learn. Maybe they are not really appropriate, so ...I have been very lucky, that with this educational background I came here and got involved with a group of social workers, who had a very different world view, you know of development, who had a great concept of peoples organisations, and also somewhat, very political, left of centre, so I think it's a kind of, all these influences that has helped me.*

In contrast, this UK manager who is much more positive:

> *...my view is that management development needs are related to size not sector. And that for Unit Managers I wish there was more synergy with small business. It's running a small business.*

Leadership is not a job that can be left at the end of the working day, it is an expression of the congruence between personal and organisational identity. This may be difficult to address in management education but without developing leaders' attentiveness to these issues they may be unprepared for taking leadership roles. Mintzberg is highly critical of traditional MBA pedagogy which, in his view, does not prepare managers for the real challenges of the job.

---

3 Perhaps this is overly harsh as there are many schools and universities that teach management from a more critical perspective. However, there are on-going debates about the usefulness of management training and the ubiquitous reliance on primarily Western management approaches. The most recent books by Mintzberg (2004) and Vaill (1997) are good examples of current critiques.

...they were hindered by a lack of experience in making value-based decisions, a lack of comprehension regarding the consequences of their actions on society... and an inability to articulate their own values in a leadership role. (Mintzberg 2004, 42)

There are some challenges here. The idea of leadership that emerges from these stories is one in which there are no strictly drawn boundaries between the personal and the professional because these leaders see leadership as the embodiment of the organisation's values. Gardner (1995) says that leaders must embody their stories. If there is no congruence between the story that the leader tells and their own identity, then the stories will not be believed.[4] In the next section I look at leading conceptualised *as* storytelling.

Leading as storytelling

The metaphor of leading as storytelling has been used by Bennis (1996), Gardiner (1995) and Bate (1994). Bate describes managers as 'fiction authors' who, like poets and troubadours are professionals in the use of language for dramatic purpose, 'to create an illusion of life' (Bate 1994, 32). And Gardner says that 'effective leaders' are those who 'tell or embody stories that speak to other people'. Bate also says that:

Cultural change...[is] the process of giving an idea form, the unfolding of the human spirit and its ultimate realisation in new, collective practices and a different quality of 'in-betweeness' between the members of an organisation community. In this context we may define 'leadership' as any activity that assists in guiding, influencing or directing the passage of the idea or spirit through the life course of the cultural production process. (Bate 1994, 237)

'Giving an idea form' and 'directing the passage of the idea' are descriptions of storytelling (although not exclusively of storytelling). Constructing a narrative involves making meaning out of non-meaning. Storytelling progresses through establishing a sequence of events, ascribing roles, creating relationships between roles and between ideas through plot and though poetic devices such as metaphor and symbolism that suggest associations between events and ideas.

The construction of the stories

How do chief executives go about storytelling? How do they construct narratives? In any story there are a range of narrative devices, ways of creating suspense, emotional

---

4   Gardner says that by *embodiment* he is not suggesting a critique of the way in which people conduct their personal lives, unlike the Indian chief executives I cited earlier. However, he says that a general who urges bravery but is him or herself a coward, will not be effective. There is a sense in which a leader lives the story they tell.

engagement, sympathy, interest. This section describes some of the devices that were used by these storytellers.

Plot and structure   What makes a list of events into a story is plot, the proposition, overt or implicit, that events are linked and that there is a causal connection between them. One thing that distinguishes these stories from purely imaginative works is that the storyteller has a relatively limited repertoire of events from which to construct their story. They do still however, have great imaginative leeway over deciding what to include or exclude and how to present the events so that certain connections appear more significant than others. For the story to succeed, it must appear that these implied links are plausible.

Here is a somewhat astonishing anecdote from a doctor who established an eye cataract surgery.

> And then one day we wanted to go somewhere... very remote.... And so first day we went into that area there were five people who just hopped onto our van. And they never asked 'where are you taking us? And 'who are you?'.... so those five people, I still remember them, we brought them to the hospital, we dropped lenses into their eyes, we operated then, and when we took them back and they had a good word to say for us, and gradually we found that as we subsequently went back there were ten people, there were fifteen...

For plausibility this story relies heavily on the doctor saying 'those five people, I still remember them'. Otherwise the idea that five blind people leapt onto the van of complete strangers who just happened to be doctors operating a free cataract operation service would seem somewhat improbable.

Looking at how events are linked sequentially can expose the implied causality that the teller wishes to suggest. Here is one example:

> We requested the authority to take over the road and do the necessary service for the proper maintenance and development of the land. As for our part we have done the initial work and it is for the government to complete the remaining part. The people were also willing to allow the government to take over the road and develop it. As a result the Public Works Department took over the road and they sanctioned fifty thousand rupees in the beginning for maintenance work. And later there was the slow progress but now the road has become very good as if a highway. The next step was effort to get bus services to this place. That attempt was also successful and now four stations are sending bus through this way.

The way in which these events are linked; we built the road: we requested the government to take it over: they did: now there is a bus service implies that the road building efforts led directly to the bus service being provided. (And of course this may be true but it is also possible that other factors were involved.) The impression that is created by this sequence of events is of a powerful narrative of success.

The following example from the story of the founding of the UK based National Society for the Prevention of Cruelty to Children powerfully shows how linking events can reinforce a theme:

> *Benjamin Waugh [the founder] was particularly concerned that there wasn't any effective legislation protecting children from cruelty at the hands of their parents or carers. I understand that there was legislation protecting animals but not children. ... he recounts a story where he is going about his business and he comes across a young boy... who was literally dying in the gutter, and I think had been very severely beaten up, I think it was by his father... and Benjamin Waugh, in desperation, took the child to the local magistrate who said to Benjamin Waugh, 'Well, if it was a dog I could help you but it is only a child'. And I suppose part of NSPCC's driving force is that attitude, 'it's only a child'. Anyway, that was just one incident in a number of things which were causing him concern, and to cut a long story short, he went about forming the London Society to Prevent Cruelty to Children....And one of the first things, right from the start, the NSPCC was a mixture of providing direct services to children, it started appointing inspectors, they were then called, but also campaigning, and Benjamin Waugh spent hours and hours and hours lobbying for legislation to give children some protection from cruelty. And against a lot of opposition. And indeed even Lord Shaftsbury wrote to Benjamin Waugh and said, 'you'll never get such a measure through Parliament', mainly because there was such a strong feeling that you don't interfere in people's family life. You don't bring the state into it. But in fact it proved not to be right, and not long after the society was formed, the first success was to get some legislation passed.* (my emphasis)

This is a very powerful story – the impact of the phrase 'but it is only a child' is immensely strong and clearly consciously invoked. But additionally, these five references to legislation and the implied causal links between them reinforce each other. The have the effect of legitimating the Society's emphasis on campaigning work and also establishing a paradigm for interpreting success.

The structure of many of the longer stories was built around a number of digressions. The sequencing of events was rarely just chronological. These digressions often functioned to allow the storyteller to develop a theme, such as the link between the teller's personal and professional life, which served to demonstrate their commitment to the organisation. This story tells of the founder's growing realisation of the links between the exploitation of women and their social status. The teller originally worked in a university where, as a woman, she regarded herself in a disadvantaged position, but her status as a member of the upper middle class, protected her from the far greater disadvantages experienced by poor women, even those with prestigious employment.

> *As a university teacher I had been participating in the Teachers Movement for uniform pay scale, for students rights, and therefore I had in a way been involved in social action, and therefore had been exposed to problems.... when I went on a campaign to find out the condition of women teachers of the university in the rural areas.... I realised the way these women teachers were treated.... And that made me realise, for the first time that I was not in the land of reality. Because I lived in an entirely different plane and this was, I think, one of the reasons why, when I went to Bangalore, and a lady in the Department of Women*

and Child Welfare asked me, 'If you're not doing anything, why don't you come and help?' and she took me to a slum, and I realised that the women in the slums were almost in the same state. So same condition of discrimination and exploitation.

Here, locating the story of the founding of the organisation in her own, personal history reinforces her commitment, but also her identification with the organisation itself. The implication is that the organisation's values are her values.

In creating linkages choices are made about what to include, but also about what to leave out. It is impossible to know what is left out but there are some obvious omissions. Very few of the stories put much, if any emphasis on the point at which the organisation becomes formalised. Receipt of the first grant and employment of the first member of staff are more often depicted as key events. But much of the history is only alluded to in passing.

...So this particular, small band of people, who had been sort of meeting together and talking about these issues, felt so strongly that the government should go further, that they decided to actually do something about it. And they set up CMH, Campaign for Mental Handicap.

There is clearly a huge amount of information not given here. How did people get together? What was the relationship between them? How often did they meet? These questions may seem trivial but the actual processes of associational activity and in particular, how associations are formed are the subject of current research interest and much still remains mysterious.[5] These stories are not illuminating. They do not provide a 'how to do it' manual on setting up organisations. These stories have a different role. They cannot function as blueprints.

Metaphor and symbolism   There is a wealth of poetic imagery in the stories, much of which has been already referred to. There are metaphors of journeys, organic metaphors, metaphors of movement and containment. There are also interesting examples of stories within stories and of stories that seem to be metaphorical in themselves. Can stories themselves be metaphors? Pondy (1983) said that a story can play a metaphorical role within a larger story of which it is a part or to some other entity (which in these instances this would be to the organisations themselves). However, Czarniawska disagrees, saying that narratives are not metaphors, that they do different tasks.

Metaphors condense stories and stories examine metaphors.... A narrative is a mode of association, of putting different things together...whereas metaphor is a model of substitution. (Czarniawska 1998, 7)

And yet, in the very process of making the substitution, of saying that *A* is *B* a whole narrative is implied. For example consider the following story, Admittedly, it concerns a theatre group involved in social activism, so there is an added layer of

---

5   See for example Deakin and Scully (1999).

complexity here in that the group uses narrative as an intervention more consciously than might be the case in other organisations. But this example is interesting not only for that reason but because it illustrates this use of story *as* metaphor.

> *...And we did a play of 10-12 minutes named 'Wildman'. It says about how the village has come up in this world. Going back to Darwin's theory, when the monkeys have become apemen and then the prehistoric men, wildmen who were moving in the forests, and the whole of their work was to search for food and sleep. That was the only work. But they somehow felt the need of being united. That is how they started living together in different caves, under trees and nearby rivers, and then the civilisation came up. The village become cities... But nowadays, when we are thinking that we are most civilised, we are thinking that we are most modernised, we do not know who is there in our neighbourhood... Bhubaneswar is now imitating the culture of Delhi. The district headquarters are imitating Bhubaneswar and the block headquarters are imitating district...now the tribals have left... their dances. They have started searching for video films, where they will not get electricity for next fifty years, they are now getting a generator, a video and [carrying] their television by their shoulders....*

The story of the play, *Wildman,* seems to stand in a metaphorical relationship to the organisation, Natya Chetana, which keeps ancient cultural traditions alive by re-introducing people to the heritage they are losing. The company live together as a community because they believe strongly in the values of 'unity' and 'family' which they see as being under threat. They sign their correspondence 'Natya Chetana *Family'*.

Wildman, and similarly perhaps both the stories of the kitchen table, described in the previous chapter and the story of the child who had less legal protection than a dog, seem to stand in a metaphorical relationship to the organisation itself. These stories encode and transmit the values of the organisation and arguably, they are more effective at doing so than the most well crafted mission statement.

One example of the use of symbolism is the naming of Centrepoint, an organisation for young homeless people after Centrepoint Tower, an office building that was deliberately kept empty for tax advantages. The use of this name (the organisation was never located in Centrepoint building) serves as a vehicle to ensure that the link between capitalism and homelessness is constantly reinforced.

Another example is the reference to individuals who serve as symbols of particular ideological positions. One founder referred to 'the tradition of E.F. Schumacher'. Here is another example:

> *At one meeting they all sat in the front room, I think it was of Nancy Astor's house – she'd founded Virginia House – and I think they were discussing something about the school leaving age... at the end of the meeting they said, 'Well who's going to see who?' And they simply carved up the Cabinet between them'.*[6]

---

6   Nancy Astor was a member of the UK parliament. The 'cabinet' is the term used for the ministers who head the various government departments.

In each of these examples the reference to a named individual, Bertrand Russell, E.F. Schumacher and Nancy Astor is almost cursory and yet it serves to locate the organisation within a particular political or ideological orientation. Of course, as with symbolism generally, it is only effective if these references are recognised and the coded meanings shared. The audience has to be both familiar with the names and also the ideology they represent. In this sense the use of such symbols also divides the audience in to those who do and don't recognise and understand the intended meanings and privileges those that do. They both bind and exclude – they reinforce followership and they define its boundaries.

Dramatic devices   How the storyteller tells the tale is also significant.

> *They had this staff conference where it appeared – I wasn't actually there which was a pity – but it appeared from those who went there that the group rose up as one and said 'Give us training'.... And whilst you're about it, give our managers training too!' And from that the ARC Training Scheme was born.*[7]

This excerpt has an almost Biblical quality to the phraseology. The dramatic delivery of the phrases 'rose up as one' and 'give us training' serve to create a powerful impression in the listener that a story is being told. This subtly reinforces the authority of the storyteller and adds significance and emphasis to what is being said. Did they really say 'Give us training?' Probably not, but it sounds a lot more impressive than 'We would quite like some training please'. The stories that the leaders tell and the ways in which they chose to craft their tales can invoke a sense of the leader as a source of sacred authority.

Invoking the transcendent

The telling of the founding story may particularly evoke the sense of the leader as god. Naydlor (1997) says that all creation myths contain an account of the separation of heaven and earth, and of a being who effects this separation.   Prior to that moment all is formless. The creation of form, of a boundary is a divine act. This suggests that in telling the story of the creation of an organisation, the teller is evoking a resonance of the divine.

> Homified leadership must manage the paradox of enterprise which is based on itsmembers' mortality and on the fiction of the immortality of the firm....In addition the homified leader has to incorporate the paradox that he [sic] is a mortal agent of immortality. To live with and act from this paradox takes heroism and wisdom... (Sievers 1994, 284)

---

7   'ARC' are the initials of the organisation's name – it is perhaps a little fanciful to suggest that their use at this point in the story evoke resonances of the Biblical ark but it is an interesting thought!

Gabriel (2000) wrote an article called 'Facing God' about stories that MBA students told of encounters with managing directors. The students were asked to relate one story, from their six month work placement, that had particular significance for them. The preponderance of stories about leaders was very high.[8] In several of these stories the students' meeting with the CEO is described with almost religious imagery, which 'echoes the archetypal scene of meeting God on the Day of Judgement' (Gabriel 2000, 191). Gabriel says that 'individuals may experience their first meeting with a great leader or charismatic individual as a "liminal" moment, presaging an important moment in their lives' (Gabriel 2000,192).

Of course, in several of the stories, the expectations of the students were severely dented; reality did not live up to expectation, leading them to feel a sense of anger and betrayal. Any sense in which leaders are seen as godlike can only be understood in a symbolic sense, if the leader is not going to constantly fail.

Symbols and myths are not meant to be taken literally. Raine (1985) says that once we try to separate historical fact from mythical truth, we lose both. While the teller of the founding story may be evoking a *resonance* of the divine, this is, of course, only to be understood symbolically, and this is extremely important in considering the problem of leadership in a democratic society, let alone in an organisation that is actively engaged in empowering people in marginalised positions within that society.

Managing this dichotomy creatively is a serious challenge. Gabriel says that leaders may not fail if they manage to:

> ...read the unconscious wishes, emotions and needs of their subordinates...make conscious what lies unconscious and use power not merely to meet targets or to gratify personal ambition, but to achieve...realisation of collective purpose in unleashing real and intended social change. (Gabriel 1997, 340)

Of course 'real and intended social change' is exactly what the leaders of voluntary organisations are aiming to achieve. However, Gabriel's emphasis on the ability to make conscious the needs and aspirations of subordinates has to be understood in this context as primarily relevant to the users and communities the organisation exists to serve. Successful leadership relies on shared stories whose meanings are jointly negotiated.

> A key dimension to vision and commitment [to user involvement] was clarity about who the organisation was for and therefore who is was trying to involve. (Robson et al 2003,1)

Bennis puts this very elegantly when he says that 'effective leaders put words to the formless longings and deeply felt needs of others.... creat[ing] communities out of words' (Bennis, 1996). For many users and members of voluntary organisations greater involvement in decision making, and with it increased power may indeed be a

---

8   Gabriel also reminds us that in Martin et al's study of organisation story 'types' (1983) five out of seven of the basic narratives concerned leaders.

'deeply felt need'. The founding story reinforces that clarity 'about who the organisation was for' emphasised by Robson et al (above) as critical to participative leadership.

This section explored the metaphor of leading as storytelling. Chief executives make use of stories to create their own interpretations of organisational reality and to communicate those interpretations to others. Smircich and Morgan (1995) defined leadership as the 'management of meaning', emphasising the symbiotic relationship between the consent of the workers to accept the definition of reality that is proposed by the leaders and the obligations of the leaders to create those definitions, to construct a plausible story that will 'co-ordinate flows of things and people towards collective action' (Czarniawska-Joerges and Wolff 1995, 349). The appeal to the authority of the founding vision is an important element in winning that consent.

Storytelling as a function of leadership

Throughout this book I have given examples of the use of storytelling to achieve certain ends (for example, to create relationships with funders and to reinforce campaigning activities, as described in chapter four). This section explores some of the ways in which leaders use storytelling to create meaning within the organisation.

Managing meaning by linking the individual, the world and the cosmos

A key task of leadership is to create a story that interprets and makes sense of experience and that creates meaning for the audience. Sievers is another theorist (along with Smircich and Morgan 1995 and Pondy 1978) who develops the idea of leadership as the management of meaning. He identifies various dimensions of meaning of which the fifth dimension 'is the link between the individual, the world and the cosmos' (Sievers 1994, 242), without which work is essentially meaningless. So the leader's stories must be about the exploration and interpretation of those links (which we have seen may be constructed differently in different cultures) if they are able to rescue workers from meaninglessness.

> *We started with day long workshops. The team who were running the workshops they'd bring in their lunch with them and they'd take lunch separately and they'd think about how the morning had gone and plan. And that caused more ripples amongst our staff...*

This story ended with a shared lunch break. This leader saw the significance of sharing lunch in creating a sense of connectedness between the participants in the workshops (parents of small children) and the team who were running them (paid professionals).

The metaphors which emerged strongly from both sets of interviews that emphasise the interconnectedness between the individual, the world and the cosmos are these metaphors of relatedness demonstrated most symbolically by story of the road which the founder and the other villagers made, and also by the fishermen whose story opens this book.

A conference in Chennai in 1993 organised by a voluntary organisation brought together environmentalists, scientists and philosophers to explore the urgent problems of the environment in a way that would highlight this interconnectedness.

> It is the people whose livelihoods are destroyed who ...are the kind of people who come into the slums and who create "social problems". I think the relevance of the debate today is not only in bringing back the question of ecology, but also the philosophical question of survival, and which is really a question of livelihoods. (Surendra 1996, 49)

Sustainability is a concept not only used by environmental groups. In another context an article in an Indian daily newspaper suggests that 'sustainability is the ultimate challenge to the energy and creativity of the human race', and goes on to link this concept with education, saying,

> *If education is to promote sustainable living, it needs to become a liberating and emancipative force...Poor countries which achieved political freedom need to seriously rethink their current educational practices and introduce a change in their educational endeavours.*[9]

Sustainability is invoked as a way of expressing the interconnectedness that I have referred to above, Wallace's research (2004) demonstrated that the way in which sustainability was interpreted by a small group of local activists (referred to in her work as social entrepreneurs) was profoundly different to the interpretations of policy makers. The 'community-defined' concept of sustainability focussed on collaboration and co-operation while the policy discourse, Wallace refers to this as the 'meta-narrative of sustainability' (Wallace 2005, 4), demonstrates a much narrower understanding that is primarily economic, focussed on whether or not an organisation can achieve financial independence through economic activity.

The metaphor of stuffing envelopes, cited in the example below, also conveys some sense of this interconnectedness. The envelopes are sent out bearing the organisation's visions and aspirations and returned with the funding and goodwill of an ever increasing (hopefully) and interconnected web of supporters.

> *I do think I set a very good example and I think they know that if there's work to be done I will always shoulder, you know, I'll go and stuff envelopes as well...*

'Stuffing envelopes' is a powerful metaphor. Envelopes are usually stuffed by volunteers – the metaphor reinforces the spirit of voluntarism that is at the heart of the sector. Stuffing envelopes is work that just about anyone can do, it requires little professional skill except manual dexterity. And it serves the cause because the envelopes are containers in which the organisation's dreams and aspirations are conveyed, often with the hope that they will be returned with funding and good will.

---

9   Mammen, K. (1998) 'The Sustainability Connection', in *The Hindu*, 1 March, 1998, Kochi.

These examples show some of the ways in which the stories create meaning in the sense that Sievers (1994) suggests, in which work is made meaningful by being located in a narrative of interconnectedness. However, the example below demonstrates another way in which storytelling plays an important function of leadership: legitimising the leader's management style.

Legitimising the leader's management style

Previously I exposed a tension between the invocation of the founding values to emphasise the centrality of the users, or beneficiaries of the organisation, those people for whom the organisation was founded on the one hand, and on the other, the invocation of those values to invest the leaders with a mantle of sacred authority.

One way in which leaders can legitimate their position is by recourse to the founding story to justify their particular management style by demonstrating its congruence with the founding values. For example, the leader quoted below is making an explicit link between the founding values of empowerment and his management style.

> *See I am the founder of this organisation but I have no problem for managing because I am giving power to the people. I am just the driver, guiding them from the back.*

The people he manages might have a different view, but here again, Smircich and Morgan's (1995) point about the provisional nature of the consent on which leadership is based, is important. The story has to be plausible and convincing or it will not be compelling. In the example below these links between founding values and leadership style are also explicit:

> *...If we believe in de-centralisation and if we believe in participation and of collective leadership system – we have not created a CEO in this organisation. We don't have a chief executive officer or an executive director who is the head of this organisation. We believe in collective leadership and we have translated it into operation.*

Many managers talked about their leadership style in terms of the decentralisation of power and decision making, and as in the above examples, saw this as a way of putting the founding values into practise. This doesn't just hold true for founder leaders but for successor leaders as well who can use these stories as a way of reinforcing their own position as against that of their predecessor, as in this example:

> *She [the founder] has seen the success of her model and is therefore convinced of it and is therefore motivated to ensure it survives. That provides support to her, you know the key people, the founder group, founder supporters, support her and say, 'stick with it, because it's too good to lose'. Okay? So they do feed off each other. But only so far. The myth takes it so far...*

Here the leader is emphasising both his understanding and valuing of the founding vision but also his belief that the values need to be reinterpreted in a changing context.

In talking about a year when she had to take a leave of absence one leader said:

> *I think it has taught us many lessons because it actually demonstrated that the organisation was not dependant on me.... it also increased the clarity of the role that I play in the organisation which is that of one who seeks new directions, explores new possibilities, opens new possibilities....It's a personal trait which has now become a professional capacity of not staying in the routine, of constantly exploring new ways of doing things, exploring new areas of setting alliances, of new ways of doing things. And 90% of the time when I bring that new idea in, everybody rejects it. And what we learned over time is that I have to manage that, that I have the responsibility of managing that sensitively, that I haven't failed them yet. That somehow at the end of the day something wonderful emerges.*

Here she is invoking not only the founding values but also appealing to the continuing history – 'I haven't failed them yet' – to reinforce her particular leadership style. However, when she says 'something wonderful emerges' she is not only reinforcing her position but also theirs, because what emerges is dependent on shared participation.

> ...managers, in particular, have the task of experiencing as directly as possible, the business as-a-series-of-events-in-its-environment through participating in bringing them into being and interpreting the resultant experiences mutatively. (Lawrence 2000, 9)

'Participating in bringing them into being' seems to be a description of both of narrative construction but also of the process in which the relationship between leaders and followers is created and sustained and given form as consent. Yeats, in a poem, posed the question, 'how can we know the dancer from the dance?' (Yeats 1965, 130). Perhaps the dancer expresses, through the dance, the storyteller through their story and the leader through their leadership their interconnectedness with the world around them.

Concluding thoughts

This chapter has concentrated on one aspect of the leadership of voluntary organisations; leadership as constructed and carried out through storytelling. The stories suggest that the values of leadership include the idea of sacrifice for the achievement of a perceived good. They also suggest that for an individual leader to have some legitimacy they must, in some sense embody the values of the organisation, although there was an interesting distinction here between a more objectified embodiment as a symbolic representative of the organisation (more likely to be expressed by the UK storytellers) on the one hand, and the ongoing adoption of a way of life that was true to its values (as described by the Indian storytellers).

The metaphor of leading as storytelling focuses on the ways in which leaders and followers, or storytellers and audience participate in developing a shared interpretation of organisational events that each can accept, if only provisionally. As there can be no story without an audience this focuses our attention on one of the most significant (but often neglected) aspects of leadership – no-one, individually or as part of a collectivity, can exercise leadership without there being some element of shared understanding between them and those they seek to lead. If a leader is not understood they will not be able to accomplish anything at all (Gergan, 1992). This is equally relevant whether the leaders are formal or informal, users, stakeholders or members of an organisation or community; they must share their understanding with others. Furthermore, it is arguable that if a leader cannot lead if they have no understanding of the stories of followers.

Storytelling is also one way in which a leader (whether that person is occupying a formal or informal leadership role) can reinforce their position; by demonstrating their commitment to the founding values of the organisation, by presenting themselves as people who are able to wield some measure of control over destiny (Czarwiawska Joerges and Wolff, 1995) and, as a corollary to this, by subtly invoking a resonance of sacred authority. Clearly this is a use of storytelling which is very open to misuse. Stories in this sense mediate power.

If leadership resides in the ability to create an interpretation of lived experience that makes sense to the audience, that demonstrates how the organisation's values are to be applied to that interpretation then it follows that there can be no leadership without shared understanding.

This sounds fairly uncontentious, perhaps even boring. However, my experiences of initiatives designed to encourage participation, consultation, involvement of communities, users, members is that shared understanding is remarkably hard to come by. Writing about the Labour Party Conference in autumn 2005 Simon Callow noted the impenetrability and lack of meaning in much of the political rhetoric, 'effortless extrusion of all-purpose blether'. He writes 'the political class defends itself very strongly against outsiders by this kind of language'. 'If you can't understand it you're out of the argument.'[10]

The research by Robson et al into user involvement concluded that 'inequalities in knowledge, resources and power were undeniable but conscious efforts to put these one one side to enable an honest exchange of views were crucial for enabling change' (Robson et al 2003, 2). For people to be able to exercise real leadership institutional and policy processes need to be made sufficiently transparent that real understanding of the issues and dilemmas can be shared. The workings of organisations, the ways in which values are translated into actions and, perhaps most significantly, how and where organisations manage the tensions and contradictions that threaten to throw them off course, all these have to be made visible, understandable and mutable.

Storytelling offers some possibilities. Many organisations pride themselves on their ability to make marginal voices heard – although this activity is usually directed outwards, towards public policy makers. I am a trustee of an organisation that works

---

10   We can't understand them and they don't want us to', by Simon Carr in *The Independent*, 28 September, 2005, .2.

with people with learning difficulties (some of whose stories I have used in previous chapters). In the past two years the organisation has developed a national forum of people it supports which has elected two people, both with learning difficulties, onto the governing board. (I carefully did not say that the forum has elected them to represent it because it is not clear if they are there to represent themselves and their experiences as people with disabilities, as consumer representatives who share the use of a particular model of service provision or as the subaltern members of a marginalised group).

This organisation relies heavily on storytelling as a means of communication, The stories of members of the Forum are relied upon as one of the principle means thorough which the trustees without learning disabilities can develop some understanding of the experiences of the service users. Interpreting those stories is regarded as an important part of exercising governance.

This is the story of a trustee of the Scottish Consortium for Learning Disability:

> I now represent Key Housing as vice-convenor of the Learning Disability Alliance Scotland and as a Trustee on the board of the Scottish Consortium for Learning Disabilities. It is great that I look around the table at Trustee meetings and see people with learning disabilities debating, discussing and sharing decision-making with professionals. The reason why I am actively involved in campaigning is to change things for the better. I want to see a better future for people with learning disabilities. A future where people can not only live in communities but be a part of them… There's no magic to being a disabled champion or advocate. Two things need to happen: you need the confidence to say what you feel and what is in your heart [and] the people you are talking to need to hand over power and be prepared to welcome you and change the way they work. This isn't easy and involves some pain – handing over power is never easy. (Lewis 2004)[11]

Diniz and Hamdy researched a rural NGO in India that prides itself on having encouraged the development of 'non-traditional' participatory governance. They conclude that 'the model depends very highly on the organisation's ability to foster a culture where all participants acquire leadership and facilitation skills complemented by a sense of solidarity' and that further, 'these factors cannot be achieved if the organisation does not make strenuous efforts to ensure consensus building and foster a culture of mutual trust among all members (Diniz and Hamdy 2004, 29). A sense of solidarity, consensus building and a culture of trust are things which cannot be achieved by individuals alone. These requirements, as with Lewis's two recommendations, the confidence to say what you feel and the willingness on the part of others to share power and responsibility, require an understanding of leadership as a process that is constructed through developing and negotiating shared meaning.

---

11 SCLD Launch, Hampden Park, October 2001: speech given by Idem Lewis, Trustee, Scottish Consortium for Learning Disability (SCLD). Source; www.scld.org, downloaded 27 September. 2005.

Chapter 7

Swimming Sharks: Storytelling and Managing Change

Actually the metaphor that I use most is that [the organisation] *has got to be like a shark. Always moving forward. Apparently a shark never stops moving. When it stops moving it dies...so that's why I use it...but I suppose I was thinking, a shark has a very menacing image. Teeth. But we're not in the business of gobbling everybody up. It's just that we have to be moving forward. A lone shark. Perhaps a dolphin would be better. A basking shark. I use that a lot. We must be like a shark.*

Introduction

This quote comes from an interview with the chief executive of a voluntary organisation that was formed from a merger of two older organisations, both working in a similar field. To me it conveys a number of the dilemmas not only of managing change but of conceptualising change within voluntary organisations. The metaphor suggests that change is constant and essential for the organisation's health and also suggests some of the restlessness that may characterise founders, entrepreneurs and those who are strongly motivated by a desire to achieve positive social change. Since there can never be a point at which that desired state is reached the organisation can never stop looking for the next campaign, the next service, the next battle.

But change can be exhausting and provoke anxiety, a constantly changing organisation can be an uncomfortable place to work. Some people may lose their jobs, their status, long standing volunteers may feel alienated, the organisation may risk its reputation and funding. Change in the form of growth also tends to come at the expense of other organisations if it is dependant on limited sources of funding or winning contracts. Someone else has lost the tender, had their funding proposal rejected. This can be uncomfortable to live with because success is not dependant on having a more worthy cause or a greater need, but more often on professional skills of fundraising, lobbying, networking. This is one of the ambiguities with which voluntary organisations struggle, and another example of the dilemmas thrown up by the increasing professionalisation of the sector. The most critical emerging needs, the most marginalised and isolated communities are often those that are least well equipped to succeed in the networking game (it's hard to network if you are isolated).

In the quote above the chief executive seems to demonstrate some of this ambiguity in regard to the teeth of the shark. She says 'we're not in the business of gobbling everyone up' and yet the organisation was formed from a merger which swallowed two organisations to produce one. She touches on a more gentle metaphor, the dolphin, but then goes back to the shark – the dolphin does not seem to resonate so well for her. How to reconcile the competing emotional demands of competition and compassion is one of the great challenges for managers.

This chapter explores various aspects of the role that storytelling plays in facilitating change and specifically in managing ambiguity. Often the impetus for change comes from a crisis and myths may be of particular potency in such times. My own experience of working in voluntary organisations undergoing change is that it is not unusual to find an appeal to the founder as an element of thinking through, or 'checking out' a particular strategic direction. 'What would Elfrida say?'[1] Barnardo's (a long established, UK based organisation working with children) are reputed to have justified a change in activity from running orphanages to family centres by saying that Dr. Barnardo was concerned with the welfare of children and while the best way of providing for needy children in the 19th century was by running orphanages, now it was not. In other words they were still being true to his vision.[2] Defining the future strategic direction of the organisation is an important function of leadership.

Exploring the way in which the founding story is interpreted may provide some indicators of the ways in which each particular organisation approaches this wider task of interpretation. If stories are seen as 'generative processes that yield and shape meaning' (Schon, 1979) we can begin to suggest that these stories may be a powerful heuristic in sensemaking, perhaps especially in times of crisis.

A very brief overview of theory on storytelling and organisational change

Stories can play many roles in managing change. Amongst these are creating a link between the organisation's past and future so that the desired change is presented as consistent with the history and culture. Greiner (1972) comments that problems of mismanaged change are 'rooted more in past decisions that in present events or outside market dynamics' Greiner 1972, 38).

The organisation's history and 'past decisions' are often communicated through the stories that are told about the events that surrounded them. Sometimes these can assume mythic proportions. Pondy says that a myth is 'a timeless pattern which explains the present and the past as well as the future' (Pondy 1983, 159). A myth juxtaposes the past and the present in order to show both how the present resembles

---

1   The organisation I worked for at the time was founded by Elfrida Rathbone, whose bust sat in my office overlooking the desk.

2   I discussed this observation at the NCVO *Researching the Voluntary Sector* conference in 1999 with colleagues from the voluntary sector and many of them gave more examples of this reference to the founder being cited in times of change as a justification for the new proposals.

the past and also how it differs from it. In this sense myths facilitate the management of change by emphasising both the continuities and discontinuities with the past.

> Myth relates to events that happened at the beginning of time which have the purpose of providing grounds for the ritual actions of man (sic) today. (Ricoeur1991b, 482)

Schon's (1983) article on 'generative' metaphors demonstrated how the different root metaphors that underlie the conceptualisation of social problems generate quite different perceived solutions. And even the same metaphor can inspire quite different responses.

For example, Elfrida Rathbone worked with children who had been excluded from school because they had learning disabilities. Is the organisation now being more 'true' to its founder if it continues to work with people with learning disabilities (who are no longer excluded from school but may find themselves excluded from other activities and services)? Or should it take on work with children who are currently being excluded from school, almost always because of aggressive behaviour? The stories can give rise to multiple and conflicting interpretations. There may be an infinite number of ways in which a myth can be interpreted and an interpretation of the founding story may be invoked to support either renewal or stagnation. But is this process of interpretation always benign? Are these stories only used as clarion calls for action which reinterpret, and thereby renew, the founding impulse and values, keeping them fresh and relevant?

Mehta (1992) commented on the way in which religious observances can become sterile and ritualised.

> ... it happens, as so often in history, especially in religious and intellectual history, that one possibility latent at the beginning was actualised historically by the immediate recipients of the founding event, who understood it, interpreted it and transmitted it in one way rather than another thus creating a tradition that rested on incomplete 'otherwise' understanding and misprision and inability to hold the original vision in its purity and starkness. (Mehta 1992, 103)

Ricoeur (1991b) describes myth as the 'bearer of possible worlds' because of the productive capacity of myth to inspire the imagination. Gardner says that successful leaders 'told stories...about themselves and their groups, about where they were coming from and where they were headed, and about what was to be feared, struggled against and dreamed about' (Gardner 1995, 14). These stories play a role in facilitating change because they 'help[ing] their audience think through who they are' (Gardner 1995, 14).

However, Ricoeur (1991b) also distinguishes between those interpretations that leads to liberation and those that lead to exclusion, nationalism, racism, which he termed 'a perversion of myth'. Distinguishing between these interpretations requires approaching myth from a critical, not a naive perspective. Loyalty to the organisation's history can produce stasis as well as change.

Another important role of storytelling is in its contribution to sustaining organisational culture. In previous chapters I have explored the role of storytelling in defining the way an organisation understands creativity and leadership within its own cultural context, both of which are highly significant to the ways in which change is conceptualised. Stories contribute to the creating and sustaining of the culture of the organisation through the transmission of information, coded symbolically, about what values, norms, standards and beliefs the organisation holds.

Culture can be a significant determinant of whether or not people feel comfortable with change. Wilkins (1983) and Weick (1995) suggest that stories maintain 'third order' controls – the 'assumptions or definitions of the situation which can be taken as "given" by participants' (Wilkins, 1983).[3]

Weick describes this process by saying that 'stories enable people to hold a data base of experience from which they can infer how things work' (Weick 1995 p129). And this information 'tells' the individual 'how things are done (and not-done) here'. But Wilkins and Ouchi (1983) suggest that this function of control may not be equally important in all organisations. For a local culture to develop it requires a fairly stable membership over time, and also regular opportunities for organisational members to interact with each other. They also concluded that the circumstances in which culture is likely to play a major role in efficiency and control are those of high complexity and ambiguity.

Wilkins and Ouchi (1983) suggest that culture is most relevant in the establishment of third order controls in organisations where the 'transaction costs' incurred in establishing equity between what an individual gives and receives from the organisation cannot easily be costed. The market establishes equity through competitive pricing but this mechanism will fail in conditions of uncertainty and ambiguity, where it is difficult, or impossible to establish a price. 'Markets', say Wilkins and Ouchi, 'are inherently incapable of valuing and controlling all social exchange' (Wilkins and Ouchi 1983, 480). Bureaucracy reduces the ambiguity by establishing a contract of employment in which the terms of the transaction are clearly established, but this too fails if ambiguity increases. The 'clan' organisation establishes equity through 'goal congruence' and a sharing of moral assumptions and values, and they conclude that this form of organisational control will be most efficient in conditions either of high ambiguity and complexity, or where the organisation is involved in activities which cannot be adequately priced. This suggestion is of particular importance to voluntary organisations which generally operate in conditions of high uncertainty and ambiguity and with 'products' such as social change that cannot be priced.

So, storytelling contributes to the creation of organisational culture, and culture may play a particularly significant role in facilitating change in voluntary organisations. In this, the final chapter on the internal management of voluntary organisations, I explore stories about change. In the following section I use the

---

3   As contrasted with first order controls which are direct orders or rules, and second order controls, such as procedural manuals and standards of good practice.

content of stories to uncover the underlying metaphors that structure the storytellers' imaginative conceptualisations of organisations. These foundational metaphors, according to Schon (1983) 'generate' different ways of responding to change and different ideas about what those desired changes might be. I then go on to look at how narrating an interpretation of organisational events contributes to decision making and how organising itself can be seen as a constant process of interpreting and re-interpreting experience. Finally, I explore the functions of stories in providing leaders and managers with a source of inspiration and guidance, and consolation in times of hardship. Stories can frame the ways in which success and failure are both understood and managed. These functions of storytelling can play an important role in managing the countervailing tensions of compassion and competition.

Stories about change in organisations

Schon's (1979) and Morgan's (1986) work on metaphors alert us to the importance of exploring the underlying images that structure the thinking of organisational actors involved in change, because of the ways in which those images influence and also limit the range of future possibilities. In my interviews with managers, staff and beneficiaries of voluntary organisations I asked them to tell me stories about times when the organisation had gone through significant changes or crises. Through exploring the content of these stories it is possible to make some tentative suggestions about the underlying metaphors, or assumptions about the nature of organisations, that structure the tellers' imagination and of the ways in which the processes involved in organisational change are conceptualised.

Metaphors of change

Organisations as organisms   The organic metaphor of organisations was very prominent in the stories, as exemplified by phrases such as 'grass roots' 'life cycles of organisations', 'growing new projects' (as described in more detail in chapter five). In India the growing concern about environmental degradation and the reliance of the majority of people on agriculture for their livelihood, all contribute to an organic conceptualisation of organisations and of organising.[4]   For example, in an article specifically about collaboration and partnership in the sector Tandon comments on 'the notion of environment and the *essential balance between humanity and its natural habitat*' (Tandon 1991a,1).

---

4   An awareness of environmental issues figured in the majority of the interviews I did in India, even in organisations not directly involved with environmental work. Concern about environmental degradation led to a symposium in Chennai, in 1993, bringing together scientists, philosophers and environmentalists, to share perspectives and to 'look at the human predicament vis-à-vis nature's resources and the ruthless plunder of those resources that a technocratic civilisation cynically promotes' (Surendra 1996, 2).

The metaphor is not always invoked positively; one person described a project that had been mismanaged as 'bleeding at the jugular'. This manager made a distinction between opportunistic and strategic growth with opportunistic growth being described in more organic (and less favourable) terms. The organisation she worked for had grown rapidly in its early years, developing new services initially for children with a medical condition and then, as the children grew up, services for adults as well. This was one of two organisations I visited where the development of new services had grown alongside the growth of the original cohort of service users. However this organic approach to growth was not without problems:

> *We've got a school in* [a remote rural area] *which to this day is in the most God-awful place, you know if you were starting from here you'd never put it there, you can't recruit staff, no-one can get to it but it's there because* [a previous manager] *wanted to live there.*

This is an interesting example of the ways in which metaphors can be limiting. Organisational growth, in this interview was described as being an almost unconscious process of following opportunities wherever they arose, a very powerful illustration of Schon's (1979) point that while the generative metaphor is 'taken-for-granted' the alternatives it suggests can be accepted and acted upon without question. Yet when the situation is reframed and the underlying metaphor is challenged earlier solutions can seem strange. 'Metaphor', Morgan writes, 'frames our understanding in a distinct, yet partial way' producing 'one sided insight' (Morgan 1986, 13).

Organisation as sacred space   The organisation as organism metaphor featured in both Indian and UK stories. However, one metaphor that was suggested only in the Indian stories was the metaphor of organisation as sacred space. For example, the Jabalpur branch of the Shri Mahila Griha Udyag, Lijjat Pappad is a small scale, income generating women's project. In its brochure it says that 'our organisation is a revered place of worship.' (Cited by Smith-Sreen 1995). In another example Chakravarty, the founder of the Institute for Human Values Research at the Kolkata Indian Institute of Management, uses the phrase 'business ashram' to convey the idea that organisations are sacred space and that work is a sacred activity, that the workplace is a locus for spiritual growth and fulfilment.[5]

In my experience this is not a common metaphor for voluntary organisations in the UK[6] and in India religious communalism is seen as a major social ill that voluntary organisations should actively oppose.[7] But the concept of sacred space goes beyond specific religious affiliations. A daily newspaper column in the *Times of India* is called *Sacred Space*. Rickshaws, offices, banks, most public spaces and

---

5   We discussed his ideas about the sacred nature of work in a meeting at the Institute in Kolkata in March, 2001.

6   However, the 'resacralisation of work' is the subject of a current research project in the UK (see Bell and Taylor 2001).

7   See brochures and pamphlets from VANI and PRIA, for example.

many domestic houses will contain some specially designated area, often containing statues of gods and often garlanded daily. Also, the Gandhian ideal of service through constructive action, the 'sacralising' of work, is an idea that still seems to find resonance.

Shah writes:

> One wonders if there is any word in Sanskrit which corresponds exactly to the concept of the sacred or the holy as the polar opposite of the profane. Sanskrit with its rich ambiguities seems to have developed right from the beginning, in-built correctives against that representational and objectifying tendency which it might have shared with European languages...Indian sensibility can be seen to operate on both planes - the empirical and the transcendental, the sacred and the profane dimensions of existence simultaneously. (Shah 1997, 2)

In the UK we distinguish between 'political' and 'Political', the distinction being between certain kinds of activities that influence public policy versus affiliation to a specific party. Perhaps in India there is a similar sense of a distinction between 'sacred' and 'Sacred', with the later referring to membership of a particular religion.

Organisation as family   The metaphor of organisation-as family featured strongly in many interviews. The Shri Mahila Griha Udyag, Lijjat Pappad, describes itself as; '...a synthesis of three different concepts including 1) the concept of business, 2) the concept of family, and 3) the concept of devotion...Our organisation is like a family and the sisters run it as if they all belong to the same family' (Lijjat brochure cited by Smith-Sreen 1995).

However, the metaphor was used in different ways. Below are two examples where the concept of 'family' is of a bounded entity and its usage derives from the need to express an emotional response. The metaphor is being invoked to capture some sense of the emotional experience of working in the organisation.

> *It* [the organisation[*just becomes a kind of womb, doesn't it?*

> *It was always run by this one woman who was a complete sort of matriarch.*

Whereas in the following example the metaphor is used to describe the culture and the values of the organisation:

> *...here there is a kind of group life in the sense that we are trying to imitate certain things from the family culture...gradually the Western philosophy or Western culture is entering into our lives, in our culture. So that is why the families are breaking very easily now. And we want to practice a kind of group life like a family, like a joint family to experience what are the problems and how to overcome that.*

I think that the following example is different again. Here the metaphor of organisation as family is being used as an underlying organising principle. This chief executive is describing their organisation as if it were a family that gives birth and nurtures new organisations which then may grow away as they have lessened their needs of the parents. And yet the involvement of the parent, and of the family members with each other, goes on.

> *We have about 15 people who are full time staff and now we begin to take on people for projects... and now the number will go down, because we had a rural section and that's grown and expanded so much that we registered that as a separate* [organisation] *... so I'm on the board... but it's a separate organisation. In fact that's another interesting thing that we do. In 1986 we started a whole study to look at drug abuse... and then the research began to expand so much that we registered that* [also] *as another organisation.*

Tandon et al (1991) describe organisations such as SEWA[8] as 'mother' organisations that encourage people who work for them to move out and create new organisations which will apply the same ideology. Another example of such an organisation is the Association of the Rural Poor in Chennai, which has strongly encouraged and supported the founding of many, smaller organisations by its staff. [9] In the Indian stories the metaphor of organisation as family seemed to be less used as a referent of emotion and more a metaphor for structuring relationships.

The relevance of this discussion on metaphor to the management of change is that if Schon's (1979) and Morgan's (1997) suggestion is valid then we would expect the ways change is conceptualised in these organisations to be, at least to some extent, influenced by these underlying metaphors. Certainly several managers who described their organisations in terms of the family metaphor were engaged in a process of developing new organisations that was described in terms that were resonant of a growing family where some members break away, others move out but still retain their links with home, and still see themselves as part of the extended family. This metaphor seems to structure the range of possibilities of organisational relationships.

> *We have built enough centres, community development centres, and training centres in different parts where we worked. Among the fisherfolk in Mahaballipuram we have a centre, and that centre is being given to* [our] *ex-staff, there's a lady now staying there, with a few ex-staff who have become part and parcel of this lady's organisation... My linkage is to go and see whenever they call us...*

Good parents make themselves available if their children need them.

---

8   The Self Employed Women's Association, founded by Ela Bhatt in Ahmedabad, Gujerat.

9   From the brochure of the Association of Rural Poor, 1998.

Evaluating change

Similarly, the values that inspired the original founders, as communicated through the founding stories can be used to provide a litmus test against which the organisation can evaluate its work. Here is one such example:

> *... So we are saying, 'we will reinvent ways by which we should be evaluated and assessed, because we don't fit into a norm of efficient service delivery'.*

Campbell (1988a) said that myths link values and actions by showing how everything that is, is the vehicle of the transcendent. This is the most explicit example:

> *...we remain an organisation that's prepared to take risks and confront institutional arrangements which challenge people's rights to do that. <u>And that's how we started in '84, and that's the basis on which we evaluate ourselves</u>, not on how many people have been helped, how successful, we say 'how many institutions have we developed? How strong is their capability? How confident are they to negotiate?'. (*my emphasis)

Here is another explicit statement of the link between the beliefs and the actions of this organisation founded to work with parents needing support in this excerpt (which I have cited before, in Chapter 4):

> *I think the key issue must have been the therapeutic input that Anne* [the founder] *wished to bring to the issue of why women were not doing well in those circumstances.... where do the causes of poor parenting lie? They lie in the parent as child, in their history. And what can you do about it to secure permanent change in that condition... And so it* [the organisation] *transmuted, quite substantially, within really quite a short period, I'd say up to about 1984 it moved away from being an ancillary support service towards a model of securing permanent change in the cycle of destructive behaviour within families.*

These links serve a number of functions. They reinforce the sense of identity and uniqueness in that while the values and beliefs may be similar they will find expression in as many different ways as there are organisations. But they also provide a yardstick against which the actions of the organisation can be measured and a means for interpreting what is defined as success or failure.

Defining success

Critical to managing change is recognising success and these stories can provide a benchmark against which successes can be defined. The sense of achievement and confidence that comes with success is crucial to morale and yet defining what constitutes success for each organisation is an interpretive process. For organisations that seek to make the world a better place or to right a social wrong the task is very daunting and consolation may come from identifying small successes along the way.

You need to win a few battles. You have to parcel up what you're doing to try to achieve it in bite-sized pieces.

I asked the managers to give me examples of successes in order to discover how they defined it within their own context. In many cases the themes or metaphors of the founding stories were also manifested in the stories of success. For example, this quote comes from a founder for whom the struggle against oppression provided a frame for the founding story.

When we organised the wages struggles to raise the wages of the labourers with whom we had been working for quite some time, in five or six instances we were successful, you know the government fixes the wages, it's called the Minimum Wages Act, according to the Act every labourer who works in the field, different kinds of activities like you know, transplanting is an activity, harvesting is an activity, for each activity there's a particular wage. But nobody pays. So using that legal loophole, we used to organise the people and demand the landed, upper class gentry to offer the right wages, the just wages to the people. They wouldn't easily give. But you know we had to send letters to all the other villages... and at the same time to bring all the people to come together and continue the struggle, the strike for maybe three or four days, until the landless and the landlords come together and the wages raised. So in five or six instances we did it.

The organisation in the following example is a co-operative, founded because of a belief that fishermen have the right to organise their own affairs collectively.

Well, I think that the functioning of the primary societies is a very big success. Mr Anton, he comes from Vilna, a village where middlemen control is so strong. Here we now have something like a hundred boats, which are completely free from the middlemen, marketing their fish, managing their own business, so it is a very big success.

While for an orphanage, founded on ideals of service and sacrifice, success is seen when these values have been inculcated in grateful recipients. This organisation has a profoundly different value base than the two cited above and therefore defines success very differently.

We are meant for service. So success for us is measured in the amount of service we put it for others. And since we are dealing with children that are young and we measure success in the way, when we look at them we like to see doing well in their lives, being good people. And being in turn, able to do service to others... See a girl grows up here... And finally she gets married. Then she's married, she's at home, and we tried to get a job for her husband or for her, so that they live- they live as poor people, but okay. And they also serve the other poor. Which they very often do. Which is very enriching.

There can be a temptation for managers to borrow ready made models of change management and indicators of success rather than to draw on the wealth of experience and cultural knowledge that each organisation creates for itself. But if an organisation can draw on, and value, its own resources of knowledge and experience perhaps it can own and be empowered by them in a way that outside expertise can never achieve. At the same time, an organisation that draws from within rather than looking outside does risk becoming insular. The examples given here show how a combined process of drawing on the organisation's values and culture, while simultaneously re-interpreting those values against the demands of the current situation may offer an interesting alternative.

In all of the above examples success is defined differently and yet for each manager their definition of success was congruent with the founding values. These brief excerpts from the stories show that the underlying images that structure the manager's thinking are profoundly influential to the ways in which change is conceptualised how success is defined and evaluated. In the following section I go on to explore how that process unfolds.

Storying and decision making

Boje (1998, 2001) uses the word 'storying' in order to distinguish research that looked the ongoing praxis of unrolling events. Storying, in this sense is something in which we are all participating and any attempt to draw boundaries around particular events or circumstances is, therefore, artificial.

I have found this quite a difficult concept to work with but I do remember when I was a manager being frustrated when staff, perfectly reasonably, would ask 'but how *do* decisions get made around here?'. My frustration was because I didn't know myself. I could recite the standing orders and terms of reference for all sorts of meetings and committees in which, in theory, decisions get made. But there was another kind of decision making altogether whose processes are harder to capture, and this, I think, is what Boje refers to as storying. Events unfold, one leads to another; perhaps they are following underlying narrative patterns, but these patterns may be indiscernible at the time.

Decisions are clearly being made because certain roads are taken, and others rejected. This kind of decision making is determined by an underlying logic that is not only hard to discern at the time, it is also hard to make transparent and thereby open to influence. The organisation's repository of stories and myths, (particularly the founding myth) and the interpretations made of those stories, may often contribute to the making of that underlying pattern.

Beach (1992), in analysing the processes by which metaphors influence decision making identified three different kinds of images that influence decision making including organisational value images; the values, standards and ethics that are the imperatives of the organisation and can therefore provide criteria for the rightness of a decision or course of action. These values generate new ideas about appropriate goals and ways of working for the organisation and also act as a yardstick by which alternatives are chosen or rejected. The decisions thereby embody the values that the organisation holds dear.[10] The task of an organisation is to construct or enact a reasonable interpretation of events and experiences that 'makes previous action sensible and suggests some next steps' (Daft and Weick 1994, 69-87). To the extent that the founding stories (as interpreted by the chief executive) are repositories of the organisation's values, they provide an available yardstick.

In all of the examples cited so far the influence of the founding story could be said to be at least benign, and often the inspiration for creative decision making. There was one example however, in which the chief executive described her organisation as being shackled by its history.

Basically it was tied up a lot with the founders. The founders were very actively involved until the late 60s, early 70s....That's why the organisation is incredibly difficult and misleading; difficult to manage and misleading in its remit.

I asked her how much of the history she had been aware of when she started.

I think if I'd known more about the organisation I wouldn't have been so disappointed with it. I was disappointed that it's like a big white elephant.

As she told it the founding story was based on the values of philanthropy and service, which she saw as signifying a 'top-down' approach. More than one hundred years on she sees the organisation's future in becoming much more of a community resource with de-centralised decision making. Yet despite the efforts of four chief executives it has proved very difficult to enact this cultural shift. Here is an excerpt from my interview with her:

... I think in some ways the organisation is tired and that's reflected in the feel of it at the moment. ...The thing about [the organisation's] *staff is that a lot of them... have been there for a long time and they feel like they need to be looked after...To be candid really, it's a little bit top heavy... in terms of what the organisation is, and what it really is – we have all these big establishment costs, finance, admin, directors, you know, massive really. ... And don't forget, those people who did the first bit lived up on the hill, they didn't live down in the bottom, so it's kind of trying to be less paternalistic....*

Her use of the phrase 'they... need to be looked after' is interesting to contrast with her aims of 'being less paternalistic' in an organisation that was started by Victorian, philanthropic women who 'lived up on the hill, they didn't live down in the bottom'.

This manager regards the founding story as a millstone around the neck of the organisation because it contained values and assumptions that to her have little current relevance. Yet although she could conceive, in the abstract, of a new story for

---

10   Beach's other two 'images' are organisational trajectory images and organisational strategic images – essentially shared, but not always articulated views about where the organisation is going.

the organisation's future she was struggling to carry it through. The contradictions between the values and assumptions of its history, which were critical to its identity, made her new vision very difficult to implement.

Why was this so? One could say that if organisations 'are' stories the next chapter that she wanted to write didn't 'fit the plot'. This leads me to wonder whether we have some underlying, pre-existing sense of what does, or does not make a good story. Are the next chapters of the story there to be discovered or can they be created, re-written even ? What limitations do the stories place on future storytellers? If the stories can confer legitimisation on future actions can they also render actions illegitimate? Are there bad plots? Are organisations that fail organisations without compelling plots?

There was one such example. All but one of the organisations that were featured in this research had been founded by individuals or groups that were motivated by passion. But some voluntary organisations come into being for administrative convenience; to manage contracts, for instance, to split off from others for operational reasons or to come together as a result of a merger. One might speculate that if the founding stories are so significant in the creation of identity and meaning, then an organisation whose founding story was devoid of passion, as in these examples, might struggle to find a sense of identity. This was, indeed, the case with the only such organisation in the sample. This organisation had previously been run as a semi-autonomous programme within a larger organisation but concerns about mismanagement of funds led them to become independent.

> *...a decision was taken to set up an independent organisation, which was because there was a bit of argy bargy I think, because they felt that* [the organisation that originally managed this programme] *was hiving off some of the money, some of the core costs.*

The new manager is struggling to define a clear sense of purpose and direction. These are not provided by the founding story. The influence of the founding event is felt more by default.

> *.... so it* [becoming independent] *wasn't a strategic decision, it was more of an operational decision..... so the organisation became an independent charity and a company. Strangely, in a way... A lot of decisions feel, I feel are made like that, you know it's what's good for bureaucracy and their decision making and cycles of decision making as opposed to what's good for community development and the work that we're doing.*

The 'struggle to find meaning' is reinforced in the following quote:

> *Well, my primary concern, when I came in, was does it make sense? This organisation. Does it make sense? Because it seemed to me that it made more sense for it to be part of another organisation, like the* [organisation that had previously housed it]*...Well I suppose this does make sense in that it has a job to do, there's definitely work to do and we do it, but....it seems to me a healthy organisation is about much more complex needs, to have come out of that needs base so that it's doing a variety of things and sort of addressing a variety of needs and issue...*

This is of some importance as more and more organisations (in the UK especially), such as consortia are being created to manage public service contracts and registered as charities but whose founding stories are not rooted in passion. If there is no passion can there be authority? In the example above, the organisation has found it difficult to 'name' the vision that underpins its work and the chief executive recognises that she cannot search for the vision in the founding story, it has to be found elsewhere. The story does not confer sacred authority. Its influence is a negative influence; the absence of passion has left the staff struggling to find meaning.

Organisational change, in this sense, is not something that can be isolated and objectified, it is an on-going process of reality creation. In the next section I turn to the functions of stories and how managers make use of them as a source of inspiration, guidance and consolation.

The functions of stories in the management of change

In one interview, cited earlier, the chief executive described the story of the founding of the organisation as 'still something of the fount we draw upon'. This is one of the clearest examples of the ways in which organisational stories can be a source of inspiration and solace. Czarniawska-Joerges and Wolff suggest that leadership expresses 'the hope of control over destiny' (Czarniawska-Joerges and Wolff 1995, 349). Stories in which hope has triumphed serve to reinforce this not only for followers, but also for the leaders themselves, particularly in times of crisis and change.

> There are certain boundary situations such as war, suffering, guilt and death in which the individual or community experience a fundamental, existential crisis. At such moments the whole community is put into question. For it is only when it is threatened with destruction from without or within that a society is compelled to return to the very roots of its identity; the mythical nucleus which ultimately grounds and determines it. The solution to the immediate crisis is no longer a purely political or technical matter but demands that we ask ourselves the ultimate questions concerning our origins and ending. (Ricoeur 1991b, 484)

In this section I explore the ways in which reference to the 'mythical nucleus' of an organisation can provide a heuristic though which organisational actors can find renewed energy and inspiration in such times of crisis.

Founding stories as sources of inspiration

> *I've read his stuff* [the founder's] *and it's, I find it inspiring. I often quote him in speeches and things....*

There were many examples in the interviews of chief executives consciously using the founding stories for inspiration. Creation myths, and indeed, according to Campbell (1988b) all myths, can provide inspiration through the depiction of heroic figures who undergo trials, often including rejection and ridicule, before undergoing an experience of initiation. This depiction of heroism becomes an inspiration for others. Some stories had clearly identifiable 'heroic' characters. For an individual leader, on their own journey of self transformation, these stories can provide moral and ethical exemplars.

> *...I certainly think it would be useful for the new staff to know where we come from, cause out of where you come from, usually your values arise.*

There is an important distinction between founding chief executives (19 out of the sample of 35) and non-founders. Non-founders were likely to see the founders as heroic figures, while founders located their source of inspiration elsewhere.[11] Some of the stories depict the hero's journey (Campbell, 1988b) from trials (of oppression and ridicule) through to transformation as in this example:

> *I am from a very poor family, fisherman family. So I suffered a lot, as a member of a backward family, community, so all this helped me to come up with instituting this type of organisation.... why I came into this work.*[12]

Ricoeur suggests that creation myths depict the successful resistance to 'those forces hostile to a well ordered and beneficial creation for human beings' (LaCocque and Ricoeur,1998, p. 69). Heroism, in these creation myths, sets out the ways in which that resistance occurs and how it leads to social change. In these stories destiny has been controlled and tamed.

Some chief executives conceptualise their organisation's mission within a metaphor of warfare. They see their organisations as involved in a struggle of good against evil. Some derive inspiration from the founding story as an energising battle cry:

> *I just sit in this office here and if I feel I'm getting a bit stale I'll make sure I spend a lot of time going to see what actually happens, and it's that which keeps me going. We've got a team that's working to protect children from paedophiles and if I feel my anger level dropping I pop down and see them and I can come back raging.*

Working with marginalised people who may be experiencing profound injustices, confronting and trying to ameliorate intractable social problems must, at times, seem fairly hopeless. Maintaining anger may help to do the job well.

---

11 Saul Alinsky, Gandhi and Paolo Freire, were specifically mentioned while others referred to their families as sources of inspiration.

12 By 'backward' this founder is referring to his family's place in the Indian caste system where lower castes are referred to as 'backward' or 'scheduled' (see Baker 1990, 37-58 for a brief overview of caste).

Fundamentally the [founding] *story's about people not settling for crap, and people giving a damn. That's the story. So it's all relevant. It's all about passion and commitment and not letting go, and ambition, yes, but grounded in reality.*

These examples show that the founding stories can provide a source of inspiration to future managers by 'rekindling' the founders' anger and passion, and through the implicit suggestion that the organisation is involved in a battle against evil which is not yet won.

Founding stories as a source of guidance

I have previously mentioned that when facing with difficult decisions in my job as chief executive I often used the organisation's founding story as a source of guidance by asking myself what Elfrida would have done. I believe that when the Puritan colonisers in New England wanted guidance they would open the Bible and let it fall to a random page and then look for suggestions in the text. The founding stories can play the same role, representing the sacred texts of the organisation.

Re-focusing on the founding values and vision   Perhaps the most overt connections were demonstrated in the stories of organisations where a serious crisis had led them to 'refocus' on their original mission. Here, a regional fishermen's co-operative society was originally founded to support local, 'primary' societies:

> *... the first thing was to unite all the fishermen who had developed some kind of internal divisions. Because when things go wrong, you are often not very clear why they are going wrong, then you think that someone else is at fault, and so that leads to kind of breakdown. So uniting, that was the first thing, and I think that has been accomplished. The other was to refocus the organisation attention on the primary societies and their functioning.*

Another organisation which had diversified its activities said:

> *... we have issued a re-visionary statement. Because one day we woke up, a few years ago to find we are doing everything.... you know, we are doing it all! And I said, 'People come to us for expertise in malnutrition and paediatrics'. So then we had to redefine our statement... So that's how we brought our focus, sharpened our focus a little.*

These examples show that the leader's preferred course of action is strongly influenced by the founding vision, even if that vision needed to be re-interpreted to suit the different circumstances. Here the influence of the founding story is overt. By holding elements of a vision, however cryptic, the stories provide a source of sacred authority.

Legitimising change and diversification   In contrast to the examples above, the following organisations are involved in an increasingly diverse range of activities. But, just as the founding vision was evoked by the previous managers to re-focus, in these stories it is diversification that is justified by suggesting that there is an organic process of evolution in which each new activity can be seen to be linked, in a great chain of being, to the founding impulse.

> *...This is the way I started the projects...education was started, literacy is going on, health education is going on, and the leadership vocational training is started, then I feel ...problem is another thing. Because they are not touching the food production.... soil health will not improve. Soil health. ... better sanitation for the poor people, drinking water scheme, small scale way, now there are already over 2,000 houses we made for the poor, 4,000 sanitary latrines we made, tow or three villages pukka [good quality] drinking water scheme we introduced... Then after 1979 to '80... our health programme is large in various villages...through that survey we find a lot of addicts, drug, alcoholic people. They require treatment. See, actually this drinking alcoholism is a disease. That disease requires treatment. That time I started a counselling centre...then after one year I started a de-addiction treatment.*

The way in which he describes one development leading to another was consistent with the idea of connectedness which was the dominant metaphor in his founding story as symbolised by the building of the road which made it possible for the villagers to be more connected to the outside world, to education, to new ideas, opportunities. The decisions he has made about the growth and diversification of the organisation are portrayed as entirely consistent with this vision.

For the following organisation, a campaigning organisation, the critical issue in the diversification of its activities is how to maintain the radical edge while making the transition from a new to a mature campaign. The chief executive describes this in terms of a reinterpretation of the founding vision.

> *... Some people say that we've lost our radical edge, our cutting edge, I don't think that's true, I think what we're doing is we're actually fighting the same fight but in a different way. [my emphasis] And I think we spend much more time actually lobbying and talking to senior people... we're actually reaching people who influence policy and set policy.... so we are very, very active, and what we say is just as strident as it was, but we do it differently, we do it in a way which I feel is more productive because we're aiming it at people who can actually change things.... And I think that the other thing also is that the difference between what we say and what a lot of other organisations say, that difference is less, not because [we have] changed but because the world has changed and become closer to [our] argument.*

Pondy (1983) says that metaphors enable change to be acceptable because the strange is made to seem familiar. Chief executives can create legitimacy for their decisions by reference to the founding stories even when, as in the case of two organisations, the story is 'woolly' and 'vague' enough to sanction many conflicting interpretations.

> *So in a sense it's [the founding story] allowed us to have two very different missions and founding myths, or continuing myths within the organisation, and with this very, very woolly 'we believe in education and assisting people in conflict zones' it's the key to development as well as the settlement of refugees in the UK. So we had to end up with*

a strap line that was, in a way, very, very vague, just to be able to encompass the whole organisation.

Gouldner (1969) concluded that the rapid growth of the YMCA in American was due to its having such vague mission that it was possible to justify expanding into just about any area of work it wanted to do. Similarly, these chief executives said that the founding story was sufficiently flexible to sanction all sorts of things.

We had a long discussion about the mission statement last year, we decided to keep it because it allows us to be specific and yet vague, because what does 'at risk' mean?

Two things are particularly interesting here. One is that although the myth is vague that vision is still seen as having the authority to sanction what the organisation does. The other is that, again, this flies in the face of much management orthodoxy that emphases the importance of having very clear aims. The suggestion that emerges from these comments, as with the stories on creativity, that having a strong sense of identity is important rather than a clear sense of direction.

Founding stories as a source of consolation

I suppose the myth is a sort of teddy bear...

I have already touched on the challenges for management that accompany high aspirations for social change. People who work in voluntary organisations are very ambitious. They want to change the world and right injustice. They are likely to experience some frustrations along the way.

Invoking the miraculous Miraculous stories can be a source of consolation because they imply that 'all will be well', that 'God is on our side' when a less optimistic assessment of the circumstances would suggest that times are very rocky indeed. Some stories contained elements of the miraculous with the miracle being the unexpected arrival of money, described in almost mystical terms.

The myth is, somehow money comes to you because you're good. That's part of the myth.

Here is an example in which one founder describes how the organisation received a very substantial windfall through the involvement of a colleague who was a Loretto nun:

...And after we had been running about three four months, she had access to a big amount of money – by my estimates in those days – from the Loretto nuns in the US, who had a lot of pension funds. They said, 'Look, we don't need the pension funds, we want to give it to the Loretto nuns worldwide'. So she got a chunk of $100,000. And she said, 'Look, can you use the money?' I still remember drawing up the proposal in just about two hours!... I got about $50,000, but anyway even $50,000 for a guy who was working with $200 was

a lot of money! So, we drew up the proposals, sent it up, and the money came. My God, now what do we do? So then I realised it had to grow, I had to run it....

Chatterjee (1998) points out that through the trials they undergo the heroic figures of mythology acquire greater spiritual or moral strength. Stories that show the organisation overcoming adversity or as an object of grace as in the following example, can provide solace by the implication that the present difficulties are merely transient.

Now is a little bit problem [financial] *for us! We are looking some agency for getting this support. This grace of God... God will help somehow.*

Do they also imply that the organisation itself has achieved a transformation and is in a state of grace?

I think something happens in you and you want to do something, and that's how the thing grows. Otherwise if you just are not really being pushed from somewhere, from where one doesn't know... these kind of things never really sustain for a very long time...

The implication is that for an organisation to be sustainable there must be some source of transcendental legitimacy.

Making sense of tragedy, mediating despair Another way in which myths offer consolation is by providing a schema by which we can ascribe some sort of meaning to the tragic things that happen to us. Here are two examples in which the organisation went through a very difficult period. In each of these examples the founding values provide an interpretive framework.

I think the other very, very big juncture, that was very traumatic for the organisation was anti-racism. It was actually a major programme of change to go from an organisation with a staff that were 98% white to now, an organisation whose staff is 40% black. And a comparable change in users, as I said.... It was an amazing change to the organisation... enormous levels of distress and hurt and upset.

This organisation was founded by conscientious objectors. They faced immense opprobrium by refusing to fight in the Second World War. Instead, they put their energies into re-building damaged communities. Within this story are themes of moral courage and a commitment to construction rather than destruction which are also present in the way in which its current leader discussed the turmoil that the anti-racism programme brought.

The following organisation faced a serious crisis when a negative evaluation report threatened their very existence. The report projected an image of the organisation and their work which they did not recognise. The funders then offered a final grant to help them in closing down the organisation. But they rejected it, choosing to undergo considerable hardship rather than accept a description of their work that they did not believe. Where the founding story resonates in this example is that the poor evaluation report partly stemmed from the evaluator's lack of understanding about the nature of the 'people's theatre' they were trying to create.

Then the evaluation was over and when we got the report of 24 pages we saw that we were being betrayed.... There are sentence [that are] self contradictory...against such plays which have made us famous... they have really said very, very negative sentences about us, and very vague. So we said our stand against this report with another 24 pages report. But the person in charge... he is a very arrogant. And when we said that the evaluators were not doing their job well, then he became blamed in a way.... So it went to such extent that we had to negotiate with the head office even, but nobody could help the process, and they came up with a decision to give us the last grant...a withdrawal grant. And we said, 'We are sorry, we will not accept this. If we accept this then we will agree to your evaluation report...Rather let us struggle for some time, so that people may be kind sometime, looking at our sufferings they may give us money.' So we opted for a stand against this report as a group decision. So within the last two years we couldn't manage to get alternative funding...

CS: How were you living?

It was very, very difficult. We lived in two houses, we squeezed ourselves into two buildings.... And we invited people who can run without money. Just little bit place to sleep, a little bit food.... Nothing more.... Eight people they left. ... So we could manage to survive but it was very, very difficult..... But somehow in January the Norwegian embassy they decided to give us a cultural fund ...

Here is another example:

Some of us have been arrested, and put in prison for no reason, and some of us have been beaten up by the upper castes, because we are involved deeply with the peoples' problems, and there was a time when the oppressors organised a strike against us and wanted to send us away from the area, and there was a lot of misunderstanding between us and the government, at that stage.

The oppression they have experienced is explained by reference to their 'involvement with the peoples' problems'. In each of these examples people faced real pain and hardship. Suggesting that these struggles are necessary and not meaningless might make them easier to bear.

My suggestion is that the founding stories provide a source of sacred authority within the organisation; 'sacred' in the sense of transcending the mundane through the exemplification of the organisation's most deeply held beliefs. These stories provide a powerful reference point for the interpretation of experience, for the legitimization of future directions, for winning consent and maintaining hope in times of hardship.

Concluding thoughts

The stories that people tell about organisational experience can be revelatory of the foundational metaphors that the storytellers are using. These metaphors, as Morgan (1986) and Ibrahim (2005) suggest, influence not only the ways in which we interpret current events but also future choices. They influence the way we determine what is to be regarded as success or failure. They propose new possibilities but also put limitations on the ways in which future action can be imagined. In this chapter I have shown that some of the ways in which managers and leaders interpreted their organisation and its future development were profoundly influenced by the symbolic meanings embedded in the stories.

Stories can create and reveal the 'perceptual frames' (Ebrahim 2005) through which current experience is interpreted. They provide a means to structure our thinking so that our interpretation can be located in an on-going narrative in which there is some underlying logic, rationale or plot to link events. They 'facilitate change' (Pondy, 1983) by mediating between past and future, and most crucially, by presenting the future directions as congruent with the organisation's most deeply held values.

Although I have proposed several specific metaphors that seem to be particularly dominant; the metaphors of organisations as organisms, as families and as sacred space[13] what is more important are the ways in which stories can be used to bring these metaphors to light.

Decision making, and in particular decisions that lead to organisational change can be seen as falling into two categories; decision making as ongoing action, where one thing follows seamlessly from another, and decision making as an event. The first is likely to be much less conscious than the second. Ongoing, processual decision making strongly influences the way in which an individual organisation's culture is created and sustained. Here, becoming more aware of the ways in which we create our stories, both as individuals and in groups, can offer a means of reframing our interpretations, of consciously changing our metaphors and creating new plots.

The second type of decision making, which I am calling decision making as an event, is more likely to be used in times of crisis when groups of organisational actors, whether they be staff, members, users or trustees, come together in a formalised setting to decide how the organisation will respond or to plan its future direction. Here, as I have shown in the previous section, the use of organisational stories, particularly those of significant events can be a powerful tool in providing inspiration and guidance but also in winning consent for the proposed course of action. I have shown that an appeal to the founding stories and the founding values they preserve, can be used to legitimise all sorts of actions; diversifying, consolidating, changing tactics, maintaining momentum. Perhaps the power of these stories can only be challenged with competing narratives.

---

13 I have also written about metaphors of movement (Chapter 5) and alchemy (Chapter 2).

For many leaders their use of stories and storytelling is deliberate, and even, on occasion, deliberately misleading. Ebrahim comments that 'NGOs resist funder attempts to structure their behaviour through a series of strategies including the "symbolic" generation of information in order to satisfy funder needs, the selective sharing of information in order to protect their core activities from unwanted interference' (Ebrahim 2005, 78). Storytelling can be a form of resistance. Stories of success are desirable commodities to provide to funders; stories that conceal can protect not only vulnerable people, but also vulnerable ideas and values.

Just as the shark must keep swimming, whose very life depends on being in a state of perpetual motion, must kep swimming so organisational stories, as sensemaking heuristics, must be reinterpreted over and over again as circumstances change. This requires managers to be continually learning from their experiences.

Ebrahim regards organisational learning as 'a key process of change in NGOs' (Ebrahim 2005, 107). Among the factors that can constrain or enable learning he identifies; 'cognitive capabilities, relationships of power and perceptual fames' (Ebrahim 2005, 110). Ebrahim's 'perceptual frames' are 'the basic infrastructure through which situations are organised, defined and given meaning' (Ebrahim 2005, 113). These frames would appear to be close relatives of Morgan's metaphors. They have a dialectical relationship with learning; 'the frame guides learning and behaviour but learning and behaviour constantly modify the frame' (Ebrahim, 2005 114).

One Indian founder told me that when she started the organisations she spent the first six months just talking to people. I was somewhat astonished that she could devote so much time at the beginning to thinking and listening and studying rather than doing – and that funders would allow that to happen. But I later discovered that the Indian organisations often had built in formal systems for reflection and learning and in particular, for documenting how they worked. These managers described a reflective approach to their work that is consistent with the emphasis on on-going learning and reflection that categorises participatory research. While reflective learning is an idea has captured the imagination of managers in both countries (at the university where I currently teach there is a whole postgraduate course on reflective learning) this idea seems to have been refined to a greater degree of sophistication in the Indian sector.

Some of these organisations described their activities in very hermeneutic terms. Consider these two examples:

So, a discussion needed to be held. Then a study had to be conducted. So each of our groups were asked to do a quick, spot survey and study on how religion impacts on the lives of women, impacts on the lives of people. And then see what are the areas where they have impacted... So as we moved from one to the other we were able to establish a common position. So this is necessary. Constantly necessary to arrive at the root cause.

And:

> *... And when they come back the whole performers group, sit together. So then the people who have not gone* [on tour] *they start questioning. And the people who have gone, they start answering. And by that it's a kind of process of identifying the correct problems and the proposed kind of pattern of script.*

Several of the Indian managers related the story of the organisation's creation and development as if it followed a process of realisations rather than a procession of events.[14] These stories followed an underlying structure; 'first we realised this, then we learned that, then after that we learned something else'. Here is one such example:

> *The second thing that we realised was that in this process, because India is bound by a cultural, religious heritage, which considers the woman second class, until men are partners with women in changing these values and attitudes, women would not achieve anything. And therefore men also came to be involved in the whole work of the* [organisation].

Each new stage of development follows a realisation.[15]

It is worth mentioning that all of these examples come from the interviews with Indian managers. Ebrahim also observed that 'many Northern NGOs have invested very little in their own learning and self reflection systems' in 'marked contrast and odd contrast with their willingness to build up the same capacities in their Southern counterparts' (Ebrahim, 2005, 150 citing Smillie and Hailey, 2001). This matched my observations.

Apart from the demands of funders what factors might go some way towards explaining this contrast? I offer two tentative possibilities. One is that a predisposition towards a philosophical orientation that assumes a more mutable and subjectively created reality rather than a more objectified one may support a more reflective approach, in that what we perceive as reality is then assumed to be more open to exploration and reinvention. Another possible factor may be that remnants of colonialist thinking, carrying with it a foundational assumption that 'we' in the first world have achieved a greater sophistication in our management practices than those in the South may also, if only at a subliminal level, play some role.

The tasks of managing and leading voluntary organisations require engagement with passion and altruism, but also with pain, anger and disappointment. The stories we tell to ourselves and each other can be powerful ways of managing these tensions.

---

14 I should say that one of the Indians I discussed my findings with was very wary of the word 'realisation' in this context, as to him realisations are of a more transcendent order altogether.

15 It is hard to give good examples of this process without quoting at very great length. What these interviews demonstrate, of which these are only tiny examples, is that the connecting verbs which link one section to another are all verbs of thought.

In each of these three chapters on the management of voluntary organisations I have given examples of managers' theories-in-use about manageament that are inspirational and also, in many ways, a challenge to the hegemony of functionalist management orthodoxy. However, I have also shown that these practices can be problematic in themselves. Managers tell stories to foster creativity, participation and change. The stories can also reinforce their own position and impose limits on the range of perceptible possibilities. In the final chapter I make some proposals about managing these tensions.

Chapter 8

A Vehicle for Exploring:
Concluding Thoughts

It's a vehicle that explores it but it's not an end in itself.

Introduction

In the opening chapter I set out a number of questions that I suggested are critical to people involved in voluntary organisations whatever their role. These were: how do voluntary organisations contribute to social change? Is their role is distinct to that played by public or private organisations? Does the plurality and diversity represented by the voluntary sector hold intrinsic worth?

How do voluntary organisations assist people in marginalised positions to take up power?

And, last but not least, what are their implications for management and leadership?

At the beginning of this book I suggested that voluntary organisations have been neglected by researchers who study organisations from a social constructionist or a critical perspective. Similarly, researchers of voluntary organisations tend to write about them from the perspective of political theory. They are more likely to concentrate on voluntary organisations as players on the political scene, rather than as a distinct type of organisation.

The central proposition of this book is that using a social constructionist perspective to explore the ways in which reality and meaning are created within organisations offers new and important insights. Therefore, having made this claim I have a responsibility to draw out some conclusions that demonstrate that my approach has provided some new answers, or ways of thinking about these questions.

However, drawing conclusions is difficult to do without generalising from the specific. Stories capture the singular, the personal, the individual. Chakrabarty asks:

> Can we imagine another moment of subaltern history where we stay – permanently and not just as a matter of political tactics – with what is fragmentary and episodic, precisely because that which is fragmentary and episodic does not, cannot dream of the whole called the state and therefore must be suggestive of knowledge forms that are not tied to the will that produces the state? This is precisely where we, the middle classes, children of the state, go to the subaltern to learn to imagine what knowledge might look like if it were to serve histories that were fragmentary and episodic. (Chakrabarty 2000a, 274)

This is a significant challenge: how to develop some conclusions without falling into the danger of generalising, which risks obscuring the different experiences of individual voices. To stay with the fragmentary, as Chakrabarty extols us to do, is profoundly difficult for the fragmentary is also provisional, tentative, unfinished. Ricoeur talked about 'mourning for certainties that have had to be abandoned' (Ricoeur 1992a). We seek order and intellectual tidiness that is challenged and subverted by the fragmentary, the particular and the messy. So, the challenge is to frame some concluding remarks that shed light on the contributions of voluntary organisations to social change in such a way that respects the complexity and the diversity of the individual stories, while also offering some fresh insights into current debates within the sector.

I opened this chapter with a quote from an interview with an Indian manager who said:

It's a vehicle that explores it but it's not an end in itself

This manager was applying the vehicle metaphor to her organisation; the organisation was the vehicle. The 'it' that was being explored in the context of the interview was oppression and the experience of poverty and she was making the point that the organisation had legitimacy only insofar as it remained true to its vision.

This use of the metaphor of the vehicle is interesting; vehicles are an important aspect of the Hindu cosmology. All deities have vehicles, usually animals or birds. These vehicles are usually included in statues and iconography, for example Ganesh, the elephant headed god, is depicted with a rat at his feet and Vishnu travels with a garuda, or eagle. The choice of the vehicle is important: they carry the gods but also the meanings that the gods represent.

Organisations can be seen as vehicles of the imagination, bearing the values of the founders and participants involved. In the fourth chapter I described the ways in which different ways of imagining society and social change led people to imagine different roles for organisations.

Stories are also the vehicles of the imagination; vehicles for an exploration of the unknown. Stories are fragmented histories. Stories disrupt the certainties of the universal and the generalised. Stories can be quietly subversive. Stories imply multiple voices, a plurality of histories, a multi-textured, 'polyphony' (Czarniawska 1997a).

Organisations are stories, too. Good stories don't reveal all their secrets immediately, if ever. The stories that I have used in this book could be interpreted in many ways; regarded as myths their potential to generate new insights is limited only by the perspectives of their audience.

In this book I have been using the stories as vehicles to explore some of the ways in which our understandings, of voluntary organisations are constructed and the meanings of the roles they play. But I have also been using the idea of a story as a metaphor *for* organisations, and of storying for organising.

When I was working as a voluntary sector manager I was very interested in the implications of the idea that organisations were vehicles for answering questions; in the case of the organisation I was working for questions about the limits of the possibilities of empowerment for people with learning difficulties and the best ways of supporting them in pushing those limits ever further. Kay (1991) wrote that the metaphor of the journey might be particularly relevant to voluntary organisations. The idea of a journey of exploration carries with it a sense of the unknown and of risk and of an uncertain destination. When applied to organisations, this suggests that voluntary organisations are engaged in a journey into the unknown; an implications that carries with it a sense of risk and uncertainty, but also of the hope of new discoveries.

In the rest of this chapter I will briefly review what has been discovered through these explorations of stories and storytelling. I have divided these observations into three sections. The following section looks at the role of voluntary organisations in contributing to change at a societal level. The next section looks at the empowerment of individuals and the third section explores the implications for management and leadership.

If organisations can be read as stories, then it follows that they must be coherent because good stories require coherent plots. My proposal is that this coherence is demonstrated by the relationship between utopian visions that inspired the founders and the values of the organisation as expressed by the actions the organisation takes. It is this coherence that the organisation's legitimacy is located; therefore leadership requires hermeneutic engagement with the dialectic between vision and values.

Visions, voluntary organisations and social change

Ricoeur (1986) suggests that social imagination is constitutive of social reality. A social constructionist perspective focuses our attention on the ways in which we conceptualise society and social change. I have attempted to apply Ricoeur's idea of the social imaginary by using the stories of founding and managing voluntary organisations as a vehicle for uncovering the underlying images of society and of the roles of the various institutions within it that structure the storytellers' visions.

How do voluntary organisations contribute to social change?

Firstly, the very creation of an organisation changes the social landscape. People create voluntary organisations because they perceive some social ill, injustice or need that an organisation can meet. The organisation both emerges from its context and changes that context – and becomes part of the context it seeks to change.

In what ways do voluntary organisations change their contexts? Voluntary organisations change the way we think. They change out perceptions of ourselves and of each other.

Voluntary organisations create different ways of constructing the social world through manifesting and giving form to alternative ways of organising, alternative approaches to social problems and alternative identities to their participants.

In the second chapter I explored the ways in which the organisation can be seen as a representation of the issue, or problem that it seeks to address. One example that I gave to illustrate this was the instances where the name of the organisation, such as the National Association for the Prevention of Cruelty to Children (a representation of a problem) or Participatory Research in Asia (a solution) immediately draws attention to that problem or solution. These issues have become objectified through the very existence of the organisation and the social context altered through our heightened awareness.

Their creation also involves a re-negotiation of boundaries; the boundaries between sectors but also between sacred and secular (as suggested by the metaphors of business ashrams and organisations as sacred space discussed in chapter seven) between the individual and the community and between personal and professional.

Secondly, voluntary organisations are catalysts. This role was captured by the storytellers' invocation of the metaphor of the journey, supported with phrases such as giving local societies 'a bus ticket to re-affiliate' (described in chapter five) and the story of construction of the road (in chapter two) that made it possible to the residents of an isolated Indian village to 'become connected'. That these connections are metaphorical as well as physical was strongly implied in the stories that told of the isolation of urban labourers cut off from their families, and the pride of the fishermen that 'we are now able to come to Trivandrum City, meet people, explain our point of view, something we would not even imagined or dared to do before'. The metaphor of 'walking alongside' (chapter four) extends this idea, according the organisation a supportive, but not overly directive role.

Voluntary organisations create 'space'. Ideas about space seem to influence the way we imagine society. The metaphors of centre and periphery, of edges and margins and the ways in which we locate ourselves in relation to each other and to the institutions of society are highly significant.

We want to create space, both geographical and social space for poor communities to collectivise their experiences, strengthen their ability to find solutions to their own problems.

One way of conceptualising this space is as a place where people concretise, and thereby construct their contingent conceptions of ethical behaviour. The subject of all the stories is the taking of ethical action. I read a book in India while I was carrying out my field work that gave weight to this suggestion.

...unless the social virtues of care and concern inform the process of economic growth the dangerous divide between unsustainable lifestyles and unacceptable poverty will remain....Can the Indian middle class take the right fork in this historic crossroads before it?....What can be done to resurrect the citizen who cares?....The answer appears to be a conscious and quantum increase in voluntary activities outside the government, particularly in the areas of education, poverty eradication and health. (Varma 1999, 193, 202, 204)

Varma is arguing for voluntary organisations to take an increased role in the provision of services but I think the quote implies more than just that. He is arguing for a change in thinking, a transformation of the ways in which we imagine our social world, and a future in which 'the social virtues of care and concern' are central to our thinking. This suggests that there is a need for voluntary organisations to lead, and to be seen to be leading the debate about the nature of ethical action within our current environment and failing to engage in this task runs the risk of an increase in distrust, of cynicism and dislocation.   I am not suggesting that voluntary organisations can provide the answers which would be an impossible expectation. However, speaking out, raising issues, challenging the ethics of the corporate and public sectors is a responsibility that perhaps is critical.   If our notions of the just society and ethical action are culturally contingent rather than absolute, then the locus of debate has to focus on the underlying structures of the imagination that influence those notions. The sector can give voice and form to beliefs but it cannot be their resolution

One example of how voluntary organisations can carry out this role is a conference that I attended in Delhi, organised by the Voluntary Associations' Network India (VANI) on corruption. Speakers were invited to talk about corruption in government, corruption in the private sector, the media and in the voluntary sector as well. The organisers were creating the opportunity for the issues to be raised and debated, creating a space where the idea of corruption could be constructed and challenged as much as providing solutions.

Do voluntary organisations make a distinctive contribution to social change?

My second question is whether the roles that voluntary organisations play in contributing to social change are inherently distinct. Are they intrinsically different from public or private organisations? This is an important question. We saw in chapter four that the ways in which we imagine and conceptualise the roles of state and market influence the roles that we ascribe to voluntary organisations – but also that voluntary organisations challenge and change our perceptions of state and market.

When Varma locates the 'citizen who cares' in voluntary organisations he is providing his answer to this question about the distinctiveness of the sector, and also the high expectations he has projected onto it. Putting aside for a moment the question of whether or not the voluntary sector is capable of shouldering the burden of rescuing the world from the negative consequences of globalisation this may shed some light on why issues such as the definition of the sector; its 'boundary patrol' (Perri 6 1995) and the perceived dangers of the sector 'morphing' (Rosenman 2000) into other sectors cause such anxiety.[1]   If we 'need' voluntary organisations to create

---

1   Evidence for this comes from such examples as the furore that greeted the publication of the Centris report (Knight 1993) and the relatively high proportion of papers that dominate

a space where we construct our conception of ethical behaviour then perhaps we also need them to remain quite distinct from other organisations.

Some indicators that support this notion that we have such high expectations of voluntary organisations (and anxieties that they may not be fulfilled) are the increased emphasis on transparency and accountability[2] and perhaps also the debates about the administrative and fundraising costs of charities. These indicators suggest that the expectations of ethical behaviour are far higher of voluntary organisations than they are of the corporate sector. In India too voluntary organisations attract much negative publicity. For example:

> One senior trade diplomat in Geneva quite rightly points out that NGOs often display none of the transparency they seek in others, hide the sources of their funding and represent only narrow special interests, not the wider public. Some of the more aggressive NGOs are more interested in confrontation than consensus and are out to kill rational debate through biased, if not erroneous scare-mongering. Their holier-than thou tactics are often clearly undemocratic. But they are not going to go away. (from the *Indian Express* 6 March, 1999)

This was from an article about the influence of NGOs on a global economic summit. It might be suggested that the corporate interests that are also represented at such summits are not noticeably more ethical in their operations (Enron comes to mind) but this display of righteous indignation is reserved for voluntary organisations from whom, presumably much higher standards of behaviour are expected.

The stories about creativity and innovation suggested that it is in the space that voluntary organisations make that there is the potential for creativity to emerge. I noted earlier in Chapter 5 that while all of the people I interviewed for the study on creativity said that creativity was extremely important, the 'life blood of the sector' as one said, there were different views about how important it was that creativity was specifically located in voluntary organisations rather than others. This raises an interesting question about whether it is important for society as a whole that we can 'locate' creativity in particular places or institutions. I noted then Bion's (1971) tentative proposal that societies establish institutions to manage certain anxieties and projections on behalf of that society as a whole (such as church, army, criminal justice system).

---

academic conferences about the independence of the sector, its increasing adoption of corporate culture, and in India, articles about the 'purity' of the sector.

2   The American based website GuideStar is a data base designed to help individual donors, governments and businesses decide whether an organisation is using its funding well and providing value for money. Guidestar was established in the UK in 2003. Guidestar describes its aims as 'promot(ing) voluntary self-regulation through an easy-to-use platform that helps nonprofits demonstrate transparency and accountability by providing information about their finances and programs to the public'. They describe themselves as 'a powerful regulatory tool'. 'Using GuideStar, government regulators can assess the most complete picture of an organization's operations and its financial status.' www.guidestar.org.

He [Bion] postulated that society hives off specialist work groups to deal on its behalf with basic assumption emotions that would otherwise obstruct the work group activity of the whole. The well known examples he offered were church (dependency), army (fight/ flight) and aristocracy (pairing). (Khaleelee and Miller 1992, 356)

Bion evidently did not develop these ideas further and I only mention them because of the suggestion that institutions may play particular roles within our imaginative constructions of society that go beyond the purely instrumental. If this is so then to answer the question of the distinctiveness of voluntary organisations may require us to look beyond their immediate functions.

Ricoeur writes that 'the particular relationship between political institutions, nature and the individual is rarely if ever the same in any two cultures' and is 'determined by some hidden but 'mytho-poetic nucleus' (Ricoeur 1991b, 483).

These myths include the stories and traditions that are created, perpetuated and reinterpreted within cultures and it is therefore not surprising that some analogies can be drawn between the philosophical traditions of the two cultures and these different imaginative conceptions of society. My interpretations of the stories told by activists, founders, volunteers and managers in voluntary organisations in the UK and in India suggested that there were some differences between the two groups of stories that could be related to the differing, underlying philosophical traditions with the Indian storytellers tending towards a notion of society as more fluid and mutable than those of the UK storytellers. Similarly, notions of the process of social change differed with the British favouring incremental change aimed at the inclusion of marginalised people into society and the Indians favouring a more radical restructuring of society itself.

The nature of the activities of voluntary organisations vary greatly in counties with different assumptions about the role of state and market (whether all powerful or impotent), the size of the space between them and about what can legitimately occupy that space. In this sense their stories need to be read hermeneutically in relation to their context. I am not offering these observations as generalisations about the voluntary sector in India or the voluntary sector in the UK and in any case there are undoubtedly organisations in both countries whose stories could be invoked to illustrate very different conclusions. What I think is more interesting is that using the stories hermeneutically to explore the different ways in which people imagine the social world creates new opportunities for us to re-imagine our own contexts. In this sense such an analysis creates the possibility of new possibilities.

In the opening chapter of this book I alluded to the increasing expectations of voluntary organisations play, some of which included the guarantor of democratic society, the means to include the excluded, the way to restore or preserve our sense of communality with others, the best hope for the regeneration of deprived and despairing neighbourhoods and, as above, the enemy of corrupt and self serving government. I also said that with such expectations inevitably comes failure. Managing these competing and conflicting expectations is an important challenge for leadership.

Voluntary organisations can be seen as representations of differing (and competing) visions and aspirations. This implies that we need to be more aware of the ways in which the very existence of an organisation creates social change.

Is the plurality represented by voluntary organisations intrinsically important?

If voluntary organisations represent differing perspectives and aspirations then the plurality of the sector is clearly inherent. Consistency is widely regarded as synonymous with quality; note for example the production of league tables in the UK for education and health to allow comparisons of performance to be made across very different communities and circumstances and the emphasis on the replicability of models of good practice that underpins much development policy. In this context of the hegemony of the universal is there any intrinsic value in plurality?

This tension is apparent in the emphasis on managerialism and capacity building which assumes that there is only one true approach to management. The discourse of funders and policy makers about voluntary organisations, particularly small organisations and those run by people from minority ethnic, religious or refugee groups is redolent with the discourse of colonialism; small, community based organisations, especially those run entirely by volunteers are often described as chaotic, lacking in leadership, indisciplined and, at their worst, corrupt. The response of many funders and policy makers veers between the provision of 'capacity building' services, ultimately designed to remake these organisations in the image of the funders or imposed competition for funds, a competition where the imperialist tactic of divide and rule can be discerned in the background.

A recurring theme in postcolonial theory is the 'colonisation of the imagination' (Said, 2004). Perhaps it is not overly fanciful to cast donors and policy makers as the new imperialists, the new colonisers of the imagination. While governments all over the world are pulling back from direct involvement in the provision of services this is not to say that they want to relinquish control. In fact, the growth of the industry of regulation may be seen as a direct response to this need to continue to exert power over the kinds of services that are delivered and the ways in which this is done. These methods for wielding control are not, on the part of many of the power brokers, done without good will – after all missionaries are usually quite convinced of the righteousness of their mission. The evangelists of the new managerialism, with their commitment to the values of accountability, transparency and efficiency are often equally convinced of the essential goodness of their endeavours. The receivers of the largesse of capacity building may not see them in so wholly a positive light.

Or perhaps they do. Postcolonial writers, in their attempts to build theory from the perspectives of the subalterns, those who have been colonised, offer a useful metaphorical framework for exploring the experiences of people who are located in marginalised positions more generally. They concentrate on the experiences of colonisation, the dynamics of oppression and resistance and the collusion of subalterns in their own marginalisation. When Bhabha (1994) writes of the mimicry of the colonisers by the colonised and the resultant hybridity he captures some of this sense that the colonised, to some extent, accept the judgement of the colonisers, the image of self offered to them by others. So too, do voluntary organisations often seem to accept the judgement of funders and policy makers, and collude in the assessment of their management practices as inferior. Resisting the judgments of others is another critical challenge for leadership.

Nandy suggests that to bring utopias into dialogue with each other represents a powerful challenge to the hegemony of the 'grand narrative' 'the One World which nineteenth century Europe visualised' (Nandy 1987, 4). A dialogue between differing world views admits the possibility of transcending any individual one. This dialogue, he cautions, should not attempt their integration – this would be the creation of a new grand narrative with all its inherent oppressive capabilities - but rather their interrogation. This prescription offers the possibility of creating a technology of diversity, a way of working within different imaginations and world views without seeking to create a synthesis which would do violence to that which could not be absorbed. Within the tension that is created between differing visions, as between the actual and the ideal there is the space for new possibilities to emerge. The importance of this is hard to underestimate as people all over the world struggle to find ways of managing the dialectic between difference and commonality.

To sum up so far: voluntary organisations contribute to social change by their very existence. They create representations of differing world aspirations and visions. They change way we imagine society. They create opportunities for people to pursue those visions and a space in which new understandings of ethical action and the just society, including the different roles ascribed to the actors within it can be constructed, debated and enacted. This suggests that we must pay attention to the ways in which these constructions are made and the meanings they propose. The significance of a voluntary organisation is therefore not only in what it *does* but also in what it *is*. The significance of a road is not only that it has a function but that it is there. As a symbol, it plays a role in representing the unknown, new journeys, new possibilities.

Voluntary organisations and empowerment

How do voluntary organisations assist people in marginalised positions to take up power? The stories suggested that people conceptualise power in terms of the location they give themselves within society as they imagine it and whether they see themselves as having the agency to change, or renegotiate that position. When people change the ways they perceive themselves then society itself is changed.

The metaphor of the road captures the sense that voluntary organisations can create the possibility for change but that people themselves must chose whether to take the journey.

However, the stories also suggest that taking up power is not something that people can do alone. Given that people imagine power (and powerlessness) in relational terms it is not surprising that the quality of the relationships that voluntary organisations build between themselves and the people, institutions, sectors and cultures with whom they work are highly significant. In chapter three I showed that the storytellers believed that these relationships must be based on mutual respect to be empowering.

Mutual respect also implies mutual humility, that no single individual, whether that is a person, an institution, a sector or a culture can provide a solution on their own. Voluntary organisations can play a catalytic role in gaining access to the voices and experiences of those who are not traditionally seen as occupying powerful roles in society and bringing them together in new configurations. Diniz and Hamdy's (2004) research emphasised the importance of a sense of solidarity, consensus building and a culture of trust and these are things which cannot be achieved by individuals alone but by developing and negotiating shared meaning.

The needs of marginalised communities to create a space where their culture and identity is reinforced and valued is a compelling reason for creating new organisations. But participation also requires developing dialogue across different experiences, cultures, social positions and across differing understandings of reality. Such dialogue requires, first and foremost, the *desire* to achieve shared understanding (as demonstrated in the quote below) which is not always evident in many of the initiatives that are developed to promote consultation and transparency.

> *And when it comes to changing the status of the woman in her home and in her small locality you needed the participation of men. Otherwise, a woman getting sensitized and the man not recognising it, he is going to beat her up for it. So conflict situations would increase. So we have to take note of that.*

Creating space also makes possible the disrupting of certainties and the imagining of alternatives. The stories also suggested that the creativity of the sector is still strongly defined as being about the changing of thinking and attitudes, the challenging of orthodoxy and developing new approaches to social problems. Creativity is located in the seeing of new possibilities, new opportunities and retaining the capacity to be surprised.

What are some of the challenges to orthodoxy and new ways of understanding the processes of empowerment that were suggested by the stories?

> *We have a lot of things that we strongly believe which go against what we think is traditionally written. Like you have this thing that says 'don't re-invent the wheel'. We say if you want to be empowered you have to re-invent the wheel.... I can say that you are doing something successfully and so why should I reinvent it? But until I reinvent it and when I say that I reinvent it that means I begin to explore what actually makes that system work, only then can I come to looking at how I can fiddle with it. Until then I am a consumer of that system.*

This quote represents such a challenge. This Indian manager is saying that the importance of reinventing the wheel is that it is through this reinvention (and presumably, through 'fiddling' with it, also reinterpreting and adapting it to current circumstances) that people can take power and move from the role of consumer to participant. Although no-one would suggest that the best way to teach people to read is to read to them in social policy, as I have mentioned earlier in this chapter, there is a strong emphasis on replicability and consistency, that a model that has been seen to work in one situation will be equally successful in others.

However challenging to conventional orthodoxy the value of reinventing the wheel may be, there is evidence that suggests that this notion is indeed deeply embedded within the voluntary sector. One piece of evidence is the fecundity of the sector mentioned in the second chapter, which implies both a striving for new answers and a rejection of existing ones. People don't want to simply adopt a tested model. They want to create their own.

Another is that voluntary organisations have a strong resistance to franchises and, to a lesser degree, to mergers. Although there are some highly successful examples of mergers between voluntary organisations and partnerships across different organisations and sectors are extremely common, there are few, if any examples of organisations adopting a franchising model.[3]

This drive to create new organisations acts as a powerful counterbalance to the hegemony of the universal model. People simply refuse to accept imposed solutions, services, even imposed notions of identity if they feel they can create something better.

Janeway (1981) writes that one of the 'powers of the weak' is that of disbelief and doubt (and also the power of disdain as Rosy demonstrated in chapter three). Although many of the stories are not overtly about resistance some do contain this notion of refusal, refusal to accede to hegemonic assumptions and interpretations and resistance to limiting assumptions.

The metaphor of reinventing the wheel also implies an uncertainty and uncontrollability of outcome. This is probably the hardest challenge for funders and policy makers and also for managers beset by the high expectations and anxieties of others. The implications that I have drawn for these stories are not particularly comfortable for managers. If people have to chose whether or not to take up the opportunities for empowerment and reinventions that are offered to them, if those opportunities arise from mutuality, if outcomes are uncertain and empowerment resides in learning and experimenting (and failing and risking) then the implications are that sometimes managers have to wait and see. This requires the good manager or leader to take up what Keats called negative capability, 'when man (sic) is capable

---

3   This assertion is based on my own observations and some attentive reader may correct me on this. However, over the years that I was involved in voluntary organisations as a manager I remember many times in which discussions about the value of franchising as a model would come up, and yet I am aware of no organisation anywhere that has actually developed it within the voluntary sector. Even if there are some examples that I have not come across, which is perfectly possible, franchising is certainly very much less common in the voluntary sector than in the private sector.

of being in uncertainties, mysteries, doubts, without any irritable reaching after fact and reason'.[4] It is hard to resist the irritable reaching after fact and reason.

Values: implications for leadership and management

Many of the tasks of management and leadership are shared across organisations of all sectors. However, this book has been specifically concerned with the roles that voluntary organisations play in contributing to social change and whether their role is in any way distinct. So far in this chapter I have been suggesting some answers to those questions. In this section I explore the implications for management that have arisen from them. I am going to concentrate on three areas; managing the congruence between vision and values, managing the emergent paradoxes and the managing 'negative capability'.

Managing the coherence between vision and values

> The metaphor of the text (Ricoeur 1971) suggests that the organisation theorist should view organisational activity as a symbolic document and, employing hermeneutic methods of analysis, as a means of unravelling its nature and significance. (Morgan 1980, 617)

In Hindu cosmogony the vehicle that carries the god also symbolises their particular role within the pantheon. Similarly, if one role that voluntary organisations play in contributing to social change is to create new meanings of ethical action then the organisations themselves can be read as stories that represent those meanings in terms of the visions they pursue and the ways they chose for achieving them. Regarding an organisation as a symbolic document means that the way it is managed is intrinsic to it. Stories create meaning symbolically; they encode, through narrative devices such as plot, characterisation and sequencing the visions and the values of the storytellers. Similarly, organisations can be regarded as texts that encode beliefs about the futures they aspire to achieve and the most appropriate ways of achieving them.

Good stories require good plots. Therefore, one implication of reading voluntary organisations as stories, is that their legitimacy is at least partly based on the extent to which they maintain some congruence between their visions and their values as expressed through the ways they work. It matters what kind of road is being created; wide or narrow, smooth or rocky, straight or winding. This implies that one leadership role is that of engaging hermeneutically with the dialectic between visions and values, or between ends and means. Good plots are coherent and plausible. Similarly (to push the metaphor perhaps to its limits) for organisations to be good stories there needs to be narrative coherence between their actions, the methods they chose and the values inherent in their visions of a better world.

---

4   The poet, John Keats, writing on Shakespeare in a letter to his brothers, George and Thomas Keats dated 21 December, 1817, also cited in Chapter 5.

In the discussion on leadership (in Chapter 6) I cited the metaphor used by one manager of 'stuffing envelopes' to describe her management style. Stuffing envelopes is one of the most traditional occupations that organisations give to volunteers. This metaphor symbolises voluntary endeavour; work that does not require professional skills, only time and commitment. The envelopes themselves usually contain documents that communicate the organisation's vision. They are sent out to win support for the organisation's work through donations of money and also through more active forms of involvement; signing petitions, writing letters on behalf of the organisation or its members (as, for example, in Amnesty International's letter writing campaigns) lobbying politicians, giving time as a volunteer. This metaphor captures much of the essence of voluntary organisations' endeavours to raise ethical issues and influence public opinion.

But stuffing envelopes also conveys a sense of the importance of linking the organisation's purpose with its methods. Voluntary organisations are engaged in the task of developing this shared meaning and it is necessary to do this by both outside and inside the organisation, in both the vision *and* the values.

> Traditional boundaries between what is inside and outside the organisation begin to dissolve when it becomes clear that organisational survival depends on a shared meaning with those in the surrounding ethos of understanding. (Gergan 1997, no page given)

The internal debates about the nature and meaning of ethical management are as essential as the external debates. The more traditional understanding of storytelling, as a function of management rather than as a metaphor for organisations, is equally relevant in the management of the dialectic between vision and values. Storytelling provides one way of pursuing shared understanding. Stories can function as extended metaphors (Pondy 1983), suggesting that one event can be understood in terms of another. The story of how a particular policy or decision has affected an individual, a story about how things might be in the future once a proposed change has been put in place, these are powerful tools in negotiating shared meaning.

Storytelling is also one way in which a leader (whether that person is occupying a formal or informal leadership role) can reinforce their position; by demonstrating their commitment to the founding values of the organisation, by presenting themselves as people who are able to wield some measure of control over destiny (Czarwiawska Joerges and Wolf, 1995) and, as a corollary to this, by subtly invoking a resonance of sacred authority. Here again, this applies as much to subaltern leadership as to leadership carried out by people in traditionally powerful positions. Stories of experience can be used to legitimise authority. It is hard to argue against some one telling their own story and stories of experiences of pain, oppression, hardship or alternatively, of courage, sacrifice and idealism are very powerful indeed.

However, stories contain 'tricksters', sub-plots, subterfuges, characters who are not what they seem. Similarly, the conviction that we understand another's story can be profoundly misleading. The tasks of managing and leading voluntary organisations require engagement with passion and altruism, but also with pain, anger and disappointment. The stories we tell ourselves and each other can be powerful ways of managing these tensions.

The necessity of mutual respect of others requires an awareness of self in order to manage the tension between the submersion and the dominance of the individual (person, organisation, sector or culture). The anxieties that are generated by the fears of both of these can be profoundly inimical to the sharing of mutual horizons and the developing of shared understanding. Vaill (1996) makes the point that acceptance does not necessarily require agreement but this is a hard distinction to apply.

Creating a story involves bringing together disparate elements, looking for opportunities in unusual places and the constant interpreting and re-interpreting of experience. While the leader does not always have to carry out those roles s/he has to make it possible for that leadership to emerge and thrive. The social environment, its attitudes, rituals beliefs and practices are constantly changing, constantly being re-imagined and recreated in the light of current experience. Our notions about what we regard as ethical action will differ enormously over time and place. These need to be congruent for the organisation to represent a 'good' story. Their meaning also needs to be shared with those in the 'surrounding ethos of understanding' (Gergan 1997). This is a critical task for managers because organisations that fail in these tasks risk a loss of legitimacy.

But meanings are not fixed; they must be constantly interpreted and re-interpreted and in this sense leadership *is* hermeneutic. Organisational change is not something that can be isolated and objectified, it is an on-going process of meaning creation. Leading requires managing that process hermeneutically. Here is one such example of a manager talking about the importance of reinterpreting the organisation's founding story:

> *It's necessary* [the story of the founding of the organisation] *as I said, but not sufficient. The myth... it's ever present, and it informs, and supplies and is the main part of what* [the organisation] *is about in terms of its core focus, but it's not quite enough on its own to make it last forever. And, like all good myths, it transmutes, into other things... At some point, it will transmute into it, into a whole new set of responses which are not premised on the woman in the domestic role per se ... and the transmutation is an important part of the myth. It departs. The* [organisation's] *myth itself will not be so personalised.*

Such reinterpretation is essential for the organisation to grow and remain relevant. There are dangers in an overly respectful approach to the past that sets those visions in aspic.

> In narrating a myth one re-actualises, in some sense, the sacred time in which the events narrated took place.... From the mere fact of the narrative of a myth profane time is, at least symbolically, abolished; the narrator and his (sic) hearers are rapt into sacred and mythical time' (Eliade 1961, 57, 58)

The power of metaphor and myth to inspire acts which have not led to positive social change or the shared participation in ethical issues has been more than amply demonstrated by such examples as the evocation of Chinese mythology by the Red Guards during the Cultural Revolution (Cheng 1995), the Aryan and Viking mythologies that inspired the Nazis (Jung 1947) and the references to the Hindu gods Ram and Agni which appeared in Indian newspapers in summer 1998 following the nuclear tests in Pohkran.

How can managers avoid this risk? While I have mentioned before that ascribing to people roles other than those of dependent or victim is, in itself, both a responsibility and a contribution to a different kind of social imaginary (Ricoeur 1986), in the examples above show that there are also dangers in an overly heroic interpretation of tradition.

The following is an interesting example in which a manager of a voluntary organisation reinterpreted the story of Sita[5] in order to create the possibility of imagining alternative roles for women:

> *I am asked occasionally to speak on women's rights, and crimes against women and things like that. Recently I was at the National Institute Of Public Co-operation in Child Development... and I started with the story of Sita. And I said that Sita is our role model. For every Hindu woman, Sita, the sacrificing wife, the obedient wife is the role model. Why is Sita, the protesting model not used? So naturally everybody started saying, 'She never protested...' I said, 'She did. She said I've had enough.'... she told Mother Earth, 'Mother Earth, I've had enough! Open your bosom and take me in!' She made a choice. Why don't you take up this aspect of Sita and tell your wives about it? So these men started saying, 'This is your interpretation...' I said, 'No. I am only telling you the story which you have read. She didn't decide to live with Ram until she died, she said, 'I don't want to live with him any more.' So then naturally they then said afterwards, ' thank you very much, we didn't think of this story, we only had half the story'. So I think you have to reinterpret, just like I have reinterpreted the stories from the Bible related to women, I am also now trying to reinterpret the stories from the Hindu shastras. So to see which of these could be used positively. Because we now need to use them positively, and if we throw them away, then we are supposed to be feminists! And anti-Indian. And anti-Indian culture.*

This is a fascinating example of the hermeneutic reinterpretation of tradition in the light of current experience. For a reinterpretation to be empowering, for it to support renewal and liberation, as in this example, there must also be an emphasis on the positive, on that which is of value, as this storyteller has done in presenting new ways in which Sita can be re-interpreted as an icon of strength.

The process through which an organisation is made and remade through the interpretation and re-interpretation of the founding story is itself a hermeneutic process. If we regard organising as storytelling it becomes clear that the creating and

---

5   The story of Sita is told in the Ramayana, first written by Valmiki but possibly dating back to as early as 500BCE. Sita is often presented to Indian girls as a model of womanhood. She is married to Rama who doubts her faithfulness and she undergoes many trials to demonstrate her purity. (Werner 1994, Richman 2001)

ongoing developing of organisational activity is hermeneutic – as is demonstrated in these excerpts from the interviews:

> *...In 1990 I did three training programme here in Kerala.... That was in English... Then there further emerged a demand from the participants saying we need this type of support in our parochial language. In our Malayalum language. Otherwise we are not in a position to assimilate our distinction, get it utilised.*

Here the organisation developed its programmes in response to the emergent demand that the organisation create the circumstances in which the participants can engage for themselves in a reconstruction of their identity and create new roles for themselves within new stories. I have quoted from both to of the stories below already but they are worth repeating because they capture this process of interpreting, or storying so well:

> *...although they* [villagers in rural India] *had good experiences of sharing their own stories of struggle, and so on, yet they were all stories of defeats, stories of failures. So we thought we should certainly help them to see life with a different perspective.*

And:

> *...So we use this research of participating as a group, not the questionnaire thing... with the grass roots people it is participatory. It has to be a group discussion. Because we have a third intention, which is not a part of the study. Which is merely to clarify their viewpoint for themselves. So while they discuss, and questions are thrown to them, answers are sought, new questions are asked. And each one responds. Their own vision is cleared.*

These are all descriptions of the hermeneutic process, these managers are using hermeneutic methodologies.

Stories of defeat do not engender a spirit of hopefulness. The emphasis on strengths comes across strongly in the stories about creativity, as well as celebrating successes, having high expectations of staff and allowing them sufficient responsibility to be able to develop their potential.

But while this is a logical implication of valuing creativity it also challenges the orthodoxy of the centrality of needs and problems.

Leading as managing paradox

My second suggestion is that leading involves managing paradoxes. Throughout this book I have generally described the work of voluntary organisations in quite idealistic terms, even while noting here and there that sometimes the picture isn't quite so rosy. Clearly there are times when organisations are not empowering, when the interests of elites come to dominate those of subalterns, when organisations find themselves reinforcing the status quo rather than challenging it, when they become corrupt, overweening or just plain dull. Things do go wrong.

Anarchistic utopias are… distinctive in their defence of the priority of diversity, difference and voluntarism over collective norms and orthodoxies. (Reedy 2001, 3)

Such utopias pose challenges to management. I have described a number of paradoxes in some detail in earlier chapters that are I believe are inherent in the roles that voluntary organisations play in contributing to social change. My proposition here is that leadership has to involve managing these contradictions, or paradoxes creatively so that new possibilities can emerge. I believe that it is when these tensions are not engaged with dynamically and creatively that organisations can lose their way. However, managing paradox is difficult.

One of these paradoxes is that although the creating of a new organisation can be regarded as subversive, a radical critique of the status quo, the remedy is the creation of another institution. Organisations are systems in which power is wielded and manipulated and in which the individual good is usually subjugated to the shared purpose. Organisations have a tendency to act to maintain the status quo rather than to subvert it.[6]

The more reverent you become to your institutional identity the less risks you will take, the less you will hold yourself accountable to the basics. And you can play all the games that institutions play to survive. But you cannot answer the question of whether you are fulfilling the obligation for which you were set up.

Secondly, while the founding events can be seen as inherently subversive activities in many of the interviews chief executives gave examples of using the stories about them to legitimate their own authority. The very act of telling these stories contains this tension between the questioning and legitimising of authority.

Another paradox that I explored in some length in the second chapter is that while organisations are often created to remedy a perceived problem, perhaps one which had not been hitherto regarded as such, the very naming of something as a social ill can increase our awareness of it and perhaps even its very existence. This was reflected in the comment by the manager working in the field of child protection who said that there seems to be more child abuse now than there was a hundred years ago when the organisation was founded.

Organisations can become complicit in maintaining the very problems they are trying to overcome. The expression of solidarity with others in an organisational form, while intoxicating and potentially subversive simultaneously creates a new boundary and a new privileging of outsiders and insiders. This is one of the dynamics at play that Ludema et al (2001) note when they say that we bring into being that on which we concentrate. The constitutive power of the imagination may not only produce utopias but also dystopias.

---

6   See, for example, Morgan's (1986) discussion of the flux and transformation metaphor as a description of the processes by which organisations seek to maintain stability and Di Maggio and Powell (1983) on institutional isomorphism caused by coercive mimetic and normative pressures.

A fourth paradox is that alongside a belief in the intrinsic importance of voluntarism and non-professionalism, there seems to be an almost inexorable drive towards professionalisation. This increasing professionalisation is, of course, an issue that has occasioned a great deal of debate and not a little soul searching. Ebrahim (2005) notes its significance as one of a series of influences that have affected the way in which development activity itself is understood, noting that increasing involvement with large funding bodies brings with it not only the need to be able to be accountable for the funds received, but even prior to that, the ability to present the organisation's work in a way that makes it seem worthy of funding. He notes the increasing reliance on professional staff and consultants (on relatively good salaries), the attractiveness of careers in the voluntary sector to young, highly qualified and idealistic graduates and the increasingly public role and political role that organisations play

In this context one possible explanation for the process, alluded to in some of the stories, whereby informal, non-professional activities became professionalised is the increasing importance of the expert against which the values of informality and non-professionalism may seem inadequate. When professional expertise and competence seem to be more highly valued than other forms of activity, the informal, the neighbourly and sisterly offer of help and support can seem fairly humble. It is hardly surprising then, that organisations seek to surround their activities with the aura and panoply of professionalism in order to demonstrate their worth.

Finally, as I have noted previously although the stories about founding voluntary organisations tell how concerned individuals took action against injustice the subject of the story is rarely the subject of the action. These are not subalterns' stories even if they are stories *about* subalterns: they are the stories of the concerned citizen, the citizen who cares. And, while they tell of people expressing their concern for others they may inadvertently capture the 'other' within the constructs of the needy, the underprivileged or the victim.

If society is made and remade hermeneutically it follows that these paradoxes cannot simply be resolved. My suggestion is that the task of leading voluntary organisations in their fulfilment of the role of creating space for the construction of contemporary notions of ethical behaviour is to expose and manage these and other such contradictions and paradoxes so that in this space new possibilities and new imaginaries can emerge.

How is this to be done? By now it is probably obvious that the prescriptions of performance management do not hold much appeal to me. I strongly suspect that they are not only unhelpful, they are counterproductive. They do not provide even the language to name and learn the skills needed for the tasks of leadership that I have defined. And in the very absence of such vocabulary it becomes much harder to debate them and to support individual leaders or groups of leaders in their struggles to fulfil them.

But what surpasses language is imagination, and storytelling, while it relies on words, also enlists the imagination. In stories we can be presented with images that are incongruous with our notion of lived experience and it is this incongruity that opens up the possibilities for a new way of seeing. The task of the leader is to allow this space to exist and to attend to what emerges. This requires leaders to develop Keats' negative capability; the capacity to wait and to be.

Managing negative capability: revelation and refusal

Throughout this book I have made various references to the importance of the dynamics of emergence. This was particularly highlighted by the stories about creativity (in which creative ideas 'emerged') and also my use of the alchemical metaphor (in chapter five) to capture the idea that some organisations were founded to be the crucible in which new thinking, new solutions, new configurations could emerge. I suggested that in our attempts to focus on what organisations do we tend to lose sight of what they are.

Lawrence (2000) defines revelations as the unthought thoughts that emerge from attention and awareness and says that 'it is through this kind of thinking that innovation is more likely to happen,' (Lawrence 2000, 178). Revelation relies on mutuality, because it is in the space between individuals that such innovatory thoughts emergé. It also empowering because the power to create is dependent on people coming together rather than being reliant on another, whether that is an individual, an organisation or a sector. He terms his work 'the politics of revelation' because he contrasts revelation with salvation, the idea that some one else has the answers. The desire for salvation, in this sense, is disempowering.

One task for the manager of a voluntary organisation is, therefore, to create the conditions for the emergence of the unthought thought, to develop within themselves their capacity for entering into Keats' 'negative capability'.[7]

Voluntary organisations cannot provide salvation, regardless of the high expectations that are placed on them. These expectations are not only unrealistic, they imply that the voluntary sector can be the salvation of the other institutions of society, an implication which is profoundly disempowering. However, organisations must engage, and sometimes lead the debates about the critical ethical issues facing the societies in which they are located.

Furthermore, one implication of plurality is disagreement. The importance of disagreement is foundational: organisations are founded because people disagree with the way things are. They disagree with the visions of the good society presented to them by the state, by the market and by each other. Without that disagreement there would be no need for voluntary organisations. We must retain that capacity to disagree.

---

7   A colleague, in talking about a time when the organisation she worked for was going through enormously traumatic times was impressed by one of the trustees who said that although she could do very little to resolve the circumstances she knew that it was very important to just 'be' there for people. This sense of being is similar to the idea of providing a container for anxiety (Sievers 1996) but goes a little further in that it emphasise the productive as well as the consoling power of attentiveness.

I would argue that it is in the dialectical debates between different visions that new ideas and new ways of imagining an ethical society emerge. Success, for a voluntary organisation should be evaluated not only by the extent to which it achieves it own vision but also by whether or not it engages with the contradictions inherent within that vision.

Perriton and Reynolds suggest that Memmi, who wrote about the colonisation of North Africa, offers a useful construct in the idea of the 'colonizer that refuses', the 'individuals who worked within the colonial state apparatus *despite* being politically uncomfortable with the idea and reality of colonial rule' (Perriton and Reynolds 2004, 72). They suggest an interesting parallel with critical management educators who 'live with, and desire the capitalist society in which they seek to bring about change' (Perriton and Reynolds 2004, 74). A similar parallel could be drawn with the manager of a voluntary organisation. The dilemmas that organisations find themselves in when the government of the day seeks to work with them (or co-opt them) as willing partners in a shared endeavour are heartfelt and well documented (see Rosenmann 2000 for example). It takes great skill and a fairly heightened awareness to walk the tightrope between challenge and collusion. Memmi's 'manager who refuses' may capture something of that nature of this tension. Another metaphor I have used elsewhere (Schwabenland 2001) to describe this relationship is that of the 'holy fool': traditionally the role of the fool, the only one who could speak truth to power, was to keep the king honest. The fool also, by the very act of making something into a joke, refuses to accept its power.

Earlier I referred to the need, felt at times by all of us whether working in the state, public or voluntary sectors, to believe that someone else has a solution. But this need captures us within someone else's narrative. Neither the fool nor the refuser are quite so captured. We need to be able to distinguish between the consoling power of a story to reinforce old certainties and the disruptive and revelatory power of the story, in which the storyteller becomes aware of latent knowledge they have held within them.

These particular challenges for management; the need to engage hermeneutically with the dialectic between vision and values, the ability to hold paradoxes in creative tension and to develop the capacity of negative capability sound very daunting. However, the stories gave countless examples of people engaging in just these tasks. What is most important, I suggest, is to retain our awareness of them as critical to the capacity of voluntary organisations to contribute to positive social change.

Final concluding thoughts

The work of hermeneutics is not limited to a thorough understanding of the structure of another religious tradition. It is at the same time a matter of recognising the shape and the power of our own – its shape being revealed in the sudden light thrown on it by other traditions, its power manifesting itself in providing vital resources in places where we had not expected life. (Bolle 1967, 106)

Hermeneutics is not simply a methodology; it is a way of thinking about meaning which brings with it a particular set of fundamental assumptions about the nature of reality. The choice of a particular methodology for a research project is, therefore, not value-free, but involves, at least for the duration of the project, allying oneself with a particular set of philosophical assumptions, because behind all methodologies there must be some assumptions about the nature of reality, the nature of knowledge and of the process by which we come to know. So, choosing a constructionist perspective for a cross cultural research project makes certain assumptions about the nature of what is being researched and what will be discovered.

When I began the research that led to this book I was employed as a chief executive of a voluntary organisation. In my encounters with colleagues in India, running organisations that were superficially similar to my own, I was impressed by the more radical orientation of many of these managers, their ability to reflect critically and analytically on their work and to perceive the connections between their organisations and the wider contexts in which they were located. These qualities seemed to me to be much more well developed and integrated into the management of Indian organisations than in the UK. This may have been idealistic, it probably is. But for me, as a manager, these observations were inspiring and allowed me to perceive some of the paradoxes and tensions described above more clearly and, in my often used phrase, see the possibility of new possibilities in my own work.

This is a testimony to the power of a hermeneutic enquiry to make us aware of our own, unquestioned assumptions (in my case, about the limits that I had placed on radical possibilities) which Mehta terms 'the core of our peculiarity' (Mehta 1992, 249). While it is clearly not feasible for every manager to spend time travelling around the world in pursuit of new insights, the opportunities to share 'horizons' (Mehta, 1992) with colleagues across traditional boundaries are there for everyone.

Bibliography

Abravanel, H. (1983), 'Mediatory Myths in the Service of Organisational Ideology', in Pondy (ed).

Adams, G.B. and Ingersoll, V.H. (1991) 'Painting Over Old Works, the culture of organisation in an age of technical rationality' in Turner (ed).

Adams, T. (1998) 'The Twenties Roared, the Sixties Swung...' in *The Observer,* 24 May, 1998.

Adirondack, S. and Sinclair Taylor, J. (1996) *The Voluntary Sector Legal Handbook* (London: Directory of Social Change).

Aktouf, O. (1991) 'Corporate Culture, the Catholic Ethic and the Spirit of Capitalism in Quebec' in Turner (ed).

Alcoff, L.M. (2003) 'Whose Afraid of Identity Politics?' in Moya and Hames-Garcia (ed).

Alcoff, L.M. (2000) 'What Should White People Do?' in Narayan and Harding (eds).

Alinsky, S. (1989a) *Reveille for Radical,* (New York: Vintage).

Alinsky, S. (1989b) *Rules for Radicals* (New York: Vintage).

All India Council for Mass Education and Development (eds.) (1998) *Rural Development:Panchayat-Volags Interface* (Kolkata: Vision).

Alvesson, M. (1993) 'The Play of Metaphors' in Hassard and Parker (eds.).

Amabile, T. (1995) 'The Unknowable and the Unimaginable' in Ford and Gioia (eds.).

Anderson, J. (1996) 'Yes, But IS it Empowerment? Initiation, implementation and outcomes of community action' in Humphries (ed).

Arendt, H. (1973) *Crises of the Republic* (London: Penguin).

Argyris, C. (1992) *On Organizational Learning* (Cambridge, MA: Blackwell).

Armistead, C. (ed.) (1994) *Managing Service Provision* (Herts: Cranfield University Publications).

Armstrong, D. (1991) *Thinking Aloud: contributions to three dialogues* (London: The Grubb Institute).

Austin, J.L. (1975) *How To Do Things With Words* (Cambridge: Clarendon Press).

Badrinath, C. (1996) transcription of dialogue following a lecture by K.M.Meyer-Abich 'Towards a Physio-centric Philosophy of Nature' in Surendra et al (eds).

Bailey J. (2000) *Customer Perceptions of WRVS* unpublished MBA Dissertation (Oxford: Oxford Brooks University).

Baker, S. (1990) *Caste: at home in Hindu India* (London: Jonathon Cape).

Ball, C. and L. Dunn (1996) *Non-Governmental Organisations: guidelines for good practice* (New Delhi: VANI and London: The Commonwealth Foundation).

Bandyopadhyay, D. (1998) 'Rural Development; panchayat-volags interface' in All

India Council for Mass Education and Development (ed.).

Bartel, D. (1997) 'The Role of "Fictions" in the Redefinition of Mission', *Nonprofit and Voluntary Sector Quarterly* Vol 26:4, 399- 420.

Bate, P. (1994) *Strategies for Cultural Change* (Oxford: Butterworth Heineman).

Bava, N. (1997) 'Towards an Integrated Theory of Peoples Participation', in Bava (ed).

Bava, N. (ed.) 1997 *Non Governmental Organisations and Development* (New Delhi: Kanishka).

Beach, L. (1992) 'Formal Image Theory' in Heller (ed).

Beazley, M., Griggs, S. and Smith, M. (2004) *Rethinking Approaches to Capacity Building* (Birmingham: INLOGOV).

Bell, E. and Taylor, S. (2001) 'The Re-sacralisation of Work' *,Proceedings of the Critical Management Studies Conference* 11 – 13 July, Manchester.

Bennis, W. (1996) 'The Leader as Storyteller', *Harvard Business Review* 1, 154-160.

Beveridge, L. (1948) *Voluntary Action; a report on methods of social advance* (London: George Allen and Unwin).

Bhabha, H. (1994) *The Location Of Culture* (London: Routledge).

Bharathi, K.S. (1991) *The Social Philosophy of Mahatma Gandhi* (New Delhi: Concept Books).

Bhattacharya, M. (1998) 'Whither "Development"!' in All India Council for Mass Education and Development (eds).

Bilimoria, P. and Mohanty, J.N. (eds.) (1997) *Relativism, Suffering and Beyond* (New Delhi: Oxford University Press).

Bion, W.R. (1961) *Experiences in Groups* (London: Tavistock).

Bloch, E. (2000) *The Spirit of Utopia* (CA: Stanford University Press).

Boal, A. (1998) *Theatre of the Oppressed* (London: Pluto).

Bogan, M. (1997) 'The New Corporate Culture', *Charity World,* July/Aug. 97, 29-31

Boje, D. (2001) *Narrative Methods for Organizational and Communication Research* (Sage: London).

Boje, D. (1998) 'The postmodern turn from stories-as-objects to stories-in-context methods', *1998 Research Methods Forum No. 3*, Fall, available online: <http://www.aompace.rmd/1998_forum_postmodern_stories.html,> accessed 05/09/2004

Boje, D., Alvarez, R. and Schooling, B. (2001) 'Reclaiming Story in Organization: narratologies and action sciences' in Westwood and Linstead (eds.).

Boje, D., Brewis, J., Linstead, S and O'Shea, A. (eds.) (2006) *The Passion of Organizing* (Malmo: Liber/Copenhagen Business School Press).

Boland, R.J. and Greenberg, R.H. (1988) 'Metaphorical Structuring of Organisational Ambiguity', in Pondy, Boland and Thomas (eds).

Bolle, K.W. (1969) 'Speaking of a Place', in Kitagawe and Lang (eds.).

Bolle, K.W. (1967) 'History of Religions with a Hermeneutic Orientated Toward Christian Theology?' in Kitagawe (ed.).

Bowens, R. (1997) 'Multi-voiced Organising: polyphony as a pommunity of practice' *Proceedings of the Conference: Organising in a Multi-Voiced World* 4-6 June, Leuven: European Institute for Advanced Studies in Management (EIASM).

Brandon, D. (1999) 'The Trick of Being Ordinary' in Schwabenland (ed.)

Brockington, J. (1997) 'Bhagavadgita: text and content' in Lipner (ed).

Broms, H. and Gahmberg, H. (1983) 'Communication to Self in Organisations and Cultures', in *Administrative Science Quarterly,* 28, 482-495.

Brown, L.D. (2004) 'Building Civil Society Legitimacy and Accountability with Domain Accountability System', *Proceedings of the Conference; Contesting Citizenship and Civil Society in a Divided World,* 11-14 July, Toronto, ISTR.

Bruns, G. (1992) *Hermeneutics Ancient and Modern* (CT: Yale University Press).

Budhananda, S. (1994) *The Ramakrishna Movement* (Kolkata: Advaita Ashram).

Burrell, G. (1997) 'Linearity, Text and Death' in *Proceedings of the Conference: Organising in a Multi-Voiced World* 4-6 June, Leuven: European Institute for Advanced Studies in Management (EIASM).

Burrell, G. (1992) 'Back to the Future' in Reed and Hughes (eds.)

Burrell, G. and Morgan, G. (1979) *Sociological Paradigms and Organisational Analysis* (London: Heinemann).

Bushrui, S. (2000) *A Defence of Poetry* (London: The Temenos Academy).

Butler, J. (1997) *Excitable Speech: The Politics of the Performative* (New York: Routledge).

Cairns, T. (2001) *Basic Skills for Adults with Learning Difficulties* unpublished report for the Elfrida Society (London: The Learning From Experience Trust).

Calas, M.B. and Smircich, L., (1992) 'Re-writing Gender into Organisational Theorizing: directions from feminist perspectives', in Reed and Hughes (eds).

Campbell, J. (1989) *The Power of Myth* (New York: Doubleday).

Campbell, J. (ed.) (1988a) *Myths, Dreams and Religion* (Dallas: Spring).

Campbell, J. (1988b) *The Hero With a Thousand Faces* (London: Paladin).

Campbell, J. (1982) *The Masks of God II: occidental mythology* (Harmondsworth: Penguin).

Campbell, J. (1978) *The Masks of God IV: creative mythology* (Harmondsworth: Penguin).

Carter, J. (1998a) 'Preludes, Introductions and Meaning' in Carter (ed).

Carter J. (1998b) 'Studying Social Policy After Modernity' in Carter (ed.

Carter, J. (ed) (1988c) *Postmodernity and the Fragmentation of Welfare* (London: Routledge).

Chadha, P. (1995) *Development Management; the need for capacity building in community based NGOs* (New Delhi: PRIA)

Chakrabarty, D. (2000a) 'Radical Histories and the Question of Enlightenment' in Chaturvedi (ed.).

Chakrabarty D. (2000b) 'Postcoloniality and the Artifice of History: who speaks for Indian pasts?' in Guha (ed.).

Chakraborty, S.K. (1998) *Values and Ethics for Organisations* (New Delhi: Oxford University Press).

Chakraborty, S.K. (1993) *Managerial Transformation by Values* (New Delhi: Sage).

Chakraborty, S.K. and Battacharya. P. (eds. and trans.) (1999) *Human Values: the Tagorean panorama* (New Delhi: New Age International).

Chakravarty, A. (1996) *The Geeta and the Art of Successful Management* (New Delhi: Indus/ Harper Collins).

Chamberlayne, P., Bornot, J. and Wengraf, T. (eds) (2000) *The Turn to Biographical Methods in Social Science* (London: Routledge).

Chambers, R. (1997) *Whose Reality Counts? putting the first last* (London: Intermediate Technology Publications).

Chaterjee, P. and Jeganathan, P. (eds.). (2003) *Community, Gender and Violence* Subaltern Studies XI, (New Delhi: Permanent Black).

Chaterjee, S. (1998) 'Voluntary Action in Development and its Challenges' in All India Council for Mass Education and Development (ed.).

Chatterjee, D. (1998) *Leading Consciously* (India: Viva / Butterworth Heinemann).

Chatterjee, P. (1997) '"Dynastic" Democracy in a Sea of Poverty', in *Development and Co-operation,* 6/1997 14-16 (Bonn: InWEnt).

Chatterjee, S.R (2001) 'Relevance of Traditional Value Frameworks in Contemporary Chinese Work Organisations: implications for managerial transition', in *Journal for Human Values* 7:1 21-31: (New Delhi: Sage).

Chaturvedi, V. (ed.) (2000) *Mapping Subaltern Studies and the Postcolonial* London: Verso).

Cheng, N. (1995) *Life and Death in Shanghai* (London: Flamingo).

Chia, R. and S. Morgan, (1996) 'Educating the Philosopher Manager: de-signing the times', in *Management Learning* Vol. 27/1 37-65.

Clarke, B. (1972) 'Organisational Sagas in Higher Education', in *Administrative Science Quarterly,* 17 178-184 (NY: Cornell University).

Clarke, J.J. (1997) *Oriental Enlightenment: the encounter between Asian and Western Thought* London: Routledge).

Clegg, S. and Dunkerly, D. (1984) *Organization, Class and Control* (London: Routledge and Kegan Paul).

Collingwood, R.G. (1973) *The Idea of History* (London: Oxford University Press).

Commission on the Future of the Voluntary Sector (1996) *Meeting the Challenge of Change: voluntary action in the 21st century,* (London: NCVO).

Cooke, B. and Kothari, U. (eds.) (2001) *Participation: the new tyranny?* (London: Zed Books).

Cooper, R. (1990) 'Organisation / Disorganisation' in Hassard and Pym (eds).

Cross, S. (1997) *Ex Oriente Lux: how the Upanishads came to Europe* unpublished lecture given at the Temenos Academy, London.

Crowther, D. and Green, M. (2004) *Organisation Theory* (London: CIPD).

Czarniawska, B. (1999) *Writing Management: organisation theory as a literary genre* (Oxford: Oxford University Press).

Czarniawska, B. (1998) *A Narrative Approach to Organisation Studies* (Thousand Oaks: Sage).

Czarniawska, B. (1997a) 'On the Imperative and the Impossibility of Polyphony in Organisation Studies' in *Proceedings of the Conference: Organising in a Multi-Voiced World* 4-6 June, Leuven: European Institute for Advanced Studies in Management (EIASM).

Czarniawska, B. (1997b) 'A Four Times Told Tale: combining narrative and scientific knowledge', in *Organisation* 4/1: 7-30 (London: Sage).

Czarniawska-Joerges, B. (1992) *Exploring Complex Organisations* (Thousand Oaks: Sage).

Czarniawska-Joerges, B., and Wolff, R. (1995) 'Leaders, Managers, Entrepreneurs: on and off the organisational stage' in Smircich and Calas (eds.).

Dachler, P. and Hosking, D.M. (1995) 'The Primacy of Relations in Socially Constructing Organisational Realities' in Hosking et al (eds.).

Daft, R.L. and Weick, K.F. (1994) 'Towards a Model of Organisations as Interpretation Systems' in Tsoukas (ed.).

Damanpour, F. (1995) 'Is Your Creative Organisation Innovative?' in Ford and Gioia (eds.).

Dantwala, M.L. (1998) 'Promises to Keep' in Dantwalla et al (eds.).

Dantwala, M.L., Sethi, H, and Visaria, P. (eds.) (1998) *Social Change Through Voluntary Action* (New Delhi: Sage).

Das, V. (1989) 'Subaltern as Perspective' in Guha (ed.).

Davidson, S. (2005) 'A Demographic Time Bomb? the politics of aging and the British media' *Proceedings of the 55th Political Studies Association Annual Conference,* April, Leeds.

Deakin, N. (2001) *In Search of Civil Society* (Basingstoke: Palgrave).

Deakin, N. and Scully, J. (1999) 'Reflections on Civil Society' *Proceedings of the Conference on Researching the Voluntary Sector* 7-8 September, London, NCVO.

de Gourdon, C.C. (1997) *Mytha, Mythos, and Mythal: myth and symbol in the Semitic and Indo-European traditions* unpublished lecture (London: the Temenos Academy).

Dees, J.G. (1998) 'Enterprising Non-Profits', in *Harvard Business Review,* 76/1 54-67.

Di Maggio, P.J. and Powell, W.W. (1983) 'The Iron Cage Re-visited: institutionalisomorphism and collective rationality in organisational fields' in *American Sociological Review* 48/147-160.

Dinez, L. and Hamdy, F. (2004) 'The Changing Face of Non-traditional NGO Governance: the case of the Chinmaya Rural Primary Health Care and Training Centre, India' *Proceedings of the Conference: Contesting Citizenship and Civil Society in a Divided World* 11-14 July, Toronto. ISTR.

Douglas, M. (1976) *Purity and Danger* (London: Routledge and Kegan Paul).

Dutta, K. and Robinson, A. (2000) *Rabindranath Tagore, The Myriad Minded Man* (New Delhi: Rupa and Co).

Eastwood, M. (1998) 'Purpose and Values', in *NCVO News,* April, 1998, (London: NCVO).

Eade, D. (ed.) (2005) *Development NGOs and Civil Society* (Jaipur: Rajwat).

Ebrahim, A. (2005) *NGOs and Organizational Change: discourse, reporting and learning* (Cambridge: Cambridge University Press).

Edgren, L.P. (1991) 'The "Commando" Model: a way to gather and interpret cultural data' in Turner (ed.).

Eliade, M. (1961) *Images and Symbols* (London: Harvill Press).

Eliot, T.S. (1943) *Four Quartets* (NY: Harcourt, Brace and Co.).

Erel, U. and Tomlinson, F. (2005) 'Refugee Women: from volunteers to employees – a case study' paper presented at a seminar organised by the Working Lives Research Institute, London Metropolitan University.

Etzioni, A. (1969) 'Dual Leadership in Complex Settings' in Gibb (ed.).

Feldman, M.S. (1991) 'The Meanings of Ambiguity; learning from stories and metaphors' in Frost et al (eds).

Fernandes, W. (ed.) (1986) *Voluntary Action and Government Control* (New Delhi: India Institute of Social Sciences).

Fineman, S. and Gabriel, Y. (1996) *Experiencing Organisation* (London: Sage).

Fletcher, C. and Kay, R. (1994) 'From Managers to Leaders: The journey metaphors of voluntary sector chief executives' in Armistead (ed.).

Flowerdew, J. (1997) 'The Discourse of Colonial Withdrawal; a case study in the creation of mythic discourse, in *Discourse and Society* 8(4) 453-477.

Ford, C. and Gioia, D. (eds.) (1995) *Creative Action in Organisations* (Thousand Oaks: Sage).

Foucault, M. (1979) *Discipline and Punish* (Harmondsworth: Penguin).

Freire, P. (1996) *Pedagogy of the Oppressed,* trans: M.B. Ramos, (London: Penguin).

Frost, P., Moore, L. F., Laws, M. R., Lundberg, C.C and Martin, J. (eds.) (1991) *Reframing Organisational Culture* (Thousand Oaks: Sage).

Gabriel, Y. (ed) (2004) *Myths, Stories and Organisations: pre-modern narratives for our times* (Oxford: Oxford University Press).

Gabriel, Y. (2000) *Storytelling in Organisations: facts, fictions and fantasies* (Oxford: Oxford University Press).

Gabriel, Y. (1998) 'Same Old Story or Changing Stories? folkloric, modern and postmodern mutations' in Grant et al (eds.).

Gabriel, Y. (1997) 'Meeting God: when organisation members come face to face with the supreme leader', in *Human Relations* 50/4: 315-342

Gabriel, Y. (1991) 'Turning Facts into Stories and Stories into Facts: a hermeneutic exploration of organisational folklore', in *Human Relations* 44/8: 857-877.

Gadamer, H. (1975) *Truth and Method* (London: Sheed & Ward).

Gahmberg, H. (1992) 'Metaphor Management; on the semiotics of strategic leadership' in Turner (ed.).

Gandhi, L. (1998) *Postcolonial Theory: a critical introduction* (New Delhi: Oxford University Press).

Gardner, H. (ed.) (1995) *Leading Minds: an anatomy of leadership* (London: Harper Collins).

Gergan, K. (1997) 'Voices, Vistas and Values: rationality versus relationship in the emerging organisation' *Proceedings of the Conference Organising in a Multi-Voiced World* 4-6 June, Leuven: European Institute for Advanced Studies in Management (EIASM).

Gergan, K. (1992) 'Organisation Theory in the Postmodern Era' in Reed and Hughes (eds.)

Gersie, A. (1992) *Story Telling in Times of Change* (London: Merlin Press).

Ghosal, J.K. (1998) 'The Role of NGO's Vis-a-vis Panchayati Raj in the Context of Rural Development: a different view' in All India Council for Mass Education and Development (eds.).

Gibb, C.A. (ed.) (1969) *Leadership* (Harmondsworth: Penguin).

Gioia, D.A. (1995) 'Contrasts and Convergence in Creativity' in Ford and Gioia (eds.).

Gioia, D.A. and Thomas, J.B. (1996)' Identity, Image and Issue Interpretation During Strategic Change in Academia' in *Administrative Science Quarterly,* 41:370-403.

Gold, J. (1997) 'Story Telling, Organising and Learning' in *Proceedings of the Conference:Organising in a Multi-Voiced World* 4-6 June, Leuven: European Institute for Advanced Studies in Management (EIASM).

Gouldner, A. (1969) 'The Secrets of Organisations' in Kramer and Specht (eds.).

Grant, D., Keenoy, T. and Oswick, C. (eds.) (1998) *Discourse in Organisations* (London: Sage).

Greiner, L. (1972) 'Evolution and Revolution as Organisations Grow', in *Harvard Business Review* 6: 37-46.

Gribben,C., Robb, C. and Wilding, K. (2002) *The Third Sector: vision for the future* (London: NCVO).

Grove, N. (2004) 'It's My Story', in *Community Living* Vol. 17/3: 16-18 (Minehead: Hexagon).

Guha, R. (ed). (1989) *Subaltern Studies VI: writings in South Asian history and society* (New Delhi: Oxford University Press).

Guha, R (ed.) (2000) *A Subaltern Studies Reader, 1986-1995* (New Delhi: Oxford University Press).

Gulhati, R., Gulhati, K., Nagar, V. and Subramanian, S. (1995) *Improving Voluntary Work in India* (New Delhi: Centre for Policy Research).

Hacking, I. (1999) *The Social Construction of What?* (Cambridge, MA: Harvard University Press).

Hall, S. (1983) 'The Great Moving Right Show' in Hall and Jacques (eds.).

Hall, S. and Jacques, M. (eds.) (1983) *The Politics of Thatcherism* (London: Wishart).

Hallberg, P. and Lund, J. (2005) 'The Business of Apocalypse: Robert Putnam and diversity', in *Race and Class* Vol. 46(4) 53-67 (London: Sage).

Harris, M. (1998) *Organizing God's Work: challenges for churches and synagogues* (Houndmills Macmillan).

Hassard, J. and Pym, D. (eds.) (1990) *The Theory and Philosophy of Organisations*

(London: Routledge).

Hassard, J. and Parker, M. (eds.) (1993) *Postmodernism and Organisations,* (London: Sage).

Hatch, M.J. (1997) *Organisation Theory: modern, symbolic and postmodern perspectives* (Oxford: Oxford University Press).

Hatch, M.J., Kostera, M. and Kozminski, A.K. (2005) *The Three Faces of Leadership* (Maldon, MA: Blackwells).

Heidegger, M. (1996) *Holderlin's Hymn 'The Istr'* McNeill. W. and Davis, J. (trans.) (Bloomington: Indiana University Press).

Heidegger, M, (1971) *Poetry, Language and Thought* Hofstadter, A. (trans.) (NY: Harper and Row).

Heidegger, M. (1949) *Existence and Being* (London: Vision).

Heller, F. (ed.) (1992 *Leadership and Decision Making* (London: Tavistock).

Herbert, J. (2001) *The German Tradition: uniting the opposites: Goethe, Jung and Rilke* (London: Temenos Academy).

Herman, R.D. and Renz, D.O. (1999) 'Theses on Nonprofit Organisational Effectiveness', in *Nonprofit and Voluntary Sector Quarterly,* Vol. 28 /2 (Sage: Thousand Oaks).

Heron, J. (1981) 'Philosophical Basis for a New Paradigm' in Reason and Rowan (eds.).

Hofstede, G. (1994) *Cultures and Organisations* (London: Harpers Collins).

Hofstede, G. (1980) *Culture's Consequences* (London: Sage).

Holroyd, S. (1997) *The Elements of Gnosticism* (Dorset: Element).

Hopper, G.R. (1988) 'Myth, Dream and Imagination' in Campbell (ed.).

Hosking, D.M. (2004) 'Social Constructionism Comes to its Senses' *Proceedings of the Conference of the Standing Conference on Organisational Symbolism (SCOS)* 8-10 July, Halifax: Nova Scotia.

Hosking, D.M., Dachler, P. and Gergan, K. (eds.) (1995) *Management and Organisations: relational alternatives to individualism* (Aldershot: Avebury).

Hosking, D.M. and Anderson, N. (1992) *Organising Change and Innovation* (London: Routledge).

Hudson, M. (1999) *Managing Without Profit* (London: Penguin).

Humphries, B. (1996) 'Contradictions in the Culture of Empowerment' in Humphries (ed.).

Humphries, B. (ed) (1995) *Critical Perspectives on Empowerment* (Birmingham: Venture Press).

Huntingdon, S. (1997) 'Why the West Has Not Won', in *Prospect* February: 40- 42 (London: Prospect).

Hutton, W. (1995) *The Shape We're In* (London: Jonathon Cape).

Ihde, D. (1971) *Hermeneutic Phenomenology; the philosophy of Paul Ricoeur* (Evanston IL: Northwestern University Press).

Inns, D. (1996) 'Organisational Development as a Journey' in Oswick and Grant (eds.).

Isherwood, C. (ed.) (1945) *Vedanta for the Western World* (California: Vedanta

Press).

Jackson, W.J. (ed.) (1992) *J.L. Mehta on Heidegger, Hermeneutics and the Indian Tradition* (Leiden: Brill).

Jaeger, A.F. (1990) 'The Applicability of Western Management Techniques in the Management of Organisations in Developing Countries' in Kanungo and Jaeger (eds.).

Jain, L.C. (1986) 'Debates in the Voluntary Sector; some reflections' in Fernandez (ed.)

Janeway, E. (1980) *Powers of the Weak* (New York: Morrow Quill Paperbacks).

Jochum, V. (2003) *Social Capital: beyond the theory* (London: NCVO).

Jung, C.G. (1968) *Analytical Psychology: its theory and practice* (London: Routledge and Kegan Paul).

Jung, C.G. (1947) *Essays in Contemporary Events,* trans. Welsh, E., Hannah, B. and Briner, M. (London: Kegan Paul).

Kafka, F. (1976) *Collected Writings* (London: Martin Secker and Warburg Ltd.).

Kakar, S. (1997) *Culture and Psyche* (New Delhi: Oxford University Press).

Kaker, S. (1996) *The Indian Psyche* (New Delhi: Viking/Penguin).

Kahane, B. (1997) 'Narrative Paradigm: how to mix fiction and demonstrative rationality in a single-story action' *Proceedings of the Conference: Organising in a Multi- Voiced World* 4-6 June, Leuven: European Institute for Advanced Studies in Management (EIASM).

Kanungo, R.N. and Mendonca. M. (1998) 'Ethical Leadership in Three Dimensions', in *Journal for Human Values,* Vol. 4/2 (New Delhi: Sage).

Kanungo R.N., and Jaeger, A.M. (1992) 'The Need for Indigenous Management in Developing Countries' in Kanungo and Jaeger (eds) Kanungo, R.N. and Jaeger, A.F. (eds.) (1992) *Management in Developing Countries* (London: Routledge).

Kavanaugh, D., O'Leary, M. and O Giollain, D. (2002) 'Stories of the Subaltern' *Proceedings of the Seminar on Subaltern Storytelling* 28-29 June, Cork.

Kay, R. (1991) *An Analysis of the Use of Metaphor in Voluntary Organisations,* unpublished PhD thesis (Bedford: Cranfield University).

Kelly, G. (1996) 'Understanding Occupational Therapy: a hermeneutic approach', in *British Journal of Occupational Therapy,* 59/5.

Kearney, R. and Rainwater, M. (eds.) (1970) *The Continental Philosophy Reader* (London: Routledge).

Kendall, J. and Knapp, M. (1993) *Defining the Nonprofit Sector: The United Kingdom,* Working Paper #5, Johns Hopkins Comparative Nonprofit Sector Project (MD: Johns Hopkins University).

Kenner, C. (1986) *Whose Needs Count? community action for health* (London: Bedford Square Press).

Kets de Vries, M.F.R. and Miller, D. (1987) 'Interpreting Organisational Texts', in *Journal of Management Studies* 24:3 234-247.

Khaleelee, O. and Miller. E. (1992) 'Beyond the Small Group: society as an intelligible field of study' in Pines (ed.).

Khan, A.M. (1997) *Shaping Policy: Do NGO's Matter? lessons from India* (New

Delhi: PRIA).

Khilnani, S. (1997) *The Idea of India* (London: Hamish Hamilton).

Kitagawe, J, and Lang, C, (eds) (1969) *Myths and Symbols* (Chicago: University of Chicago Press).

Kitagawe, J. (ed.) (1967) *The History of Religions* (Chicago: University of Chicago Press).

Knight, B. (1993) *Voluntary Action* (London and Northumberland: Centris).

King, R. (1999) *Indian Philosophy* (Edinburgh: Edinburgh University Press).

Kline Taylor, M. (1986) *Beyond Explanation* (Macon GA: Mercer University Press).

Kosambi, D.D. (1998) *Myth and Reality*, (Bombay: Popular Prakashan).

Kramer, R. and Specht, H. (eds.) (1969) *Readings in Community Organisation Practice* (NJ: Prentice Hall).

Kretzmann, J.P. and McKnight, J. (1993) *Building Communities From the Inside Out: a path towards finding and mobilizing a community's assets,* (Evanston IL: Center for Urban Affairs and Policy Research).

Kurtz, C,F. and Snowdon, D. (2003) 'The New Dynamics of Strategy: sensemaking in a complex and complicated world', in *IBM Systems Journal* 42/ 3 <http://www.research.ibm.com/journals/sj/423/kurtz.html> accessed 31/10/04.

Kwek, D. (2003) 'Decolonising and *Re*-Presenting Culture's Consequences: a postcolonial critique of cross cultural studies in management in Prasad (ed.).

LaCocque,A. and Ricoeur,P. (1998) *Thinking Biblically: exegetical and hermeneutical studies,* trans. D. Pellauer (Chicago: University of Chicago Press).

Lakoff, G. and Johnson, M. (1980) *Metaphors We Live By* (Chicago: University of Chicago Press).

Landry, D. and MacLean, G. (eds.) (1996) *The Spivak Reader* (New York: Routledge).

Lannoy, R. (1974) *The Speaking Tree, a study of Indian culture and society* (New York: Oxford University Press).

Lawrence, W.G. (2000) *Tongued with Fire: groups in experience* (London: Karnac).

Lawrence, W.G. (1991) *Thoughts Bound and Thoughts Free* (London: The Grubb Institute).

Lawrence, W.G. (1982) *Some Psychic and Political Dimensions of Work Experience* (London: Tavistock Institute).

Leat, D. (1995) *Challenging Management* (London: VOLPROF).

Leonard, R. and Onyx, J. (2003) 'Networking Through Strong and Loose Ties: an Australian qualitative study' in Voluntas 12/2 189-204.

Levitas, R. (1990) *The Concept of Utopia* (New York: Phillip Allan).

Levi Strauss, C (1970a) *The Raw and the Cooked* trans. Weightman, J. and Weightman, D. (London: Jonathon Cape).

Levi Strauss, C. (1970b) 'The Structural Study of Myth', in Kearney and Rainwater (eds.).

Lewis, C.S. (1975) *The Allegory of Love* (London: Oxford University Press).

Lewis, C.S. (1964) *The Discarded Image* (London: Cambridge University Press).

Linstead, S. (2005) 'No Time for Love if They Come in the Morning' *Proceedings of the Conference on Gender, Work and Organisations,* 21-23 June, Keele.

Linstead, S. (ed.) (2004) *Organization Theory and Postmodern Thought* (London: Sage).

Lipman-Bluman, J. (1994) 'The Existential Bases of Power Relationships: the gender role case' in Radtke and Stam (eds.).

Lipner, J. (1999) *Hindus: their religious beliefs and practices* (London: Routledge).

Lipner, J. (1997a) Sankara on *Satyam Jnanam Anantam Brahma,* in Bilimoria and Mohanty (eds.).

Lipner, J. (ed.) (1997b) *The Fruits of our Desiring* (Calgary: Bayeaux Arts Press).

Lovejoy, A.O. (1974) *The Great Chain of Being* (Cambridge, USA: Harvard University Press).

Loveridge, R. (1997) 'Social Science as Social Reconstruction: a celebration of discontinuity or a test of the resilience of belief?' in *Human Relations* 50/8 879-884.

Ludema, J.D., Cooperrider, D.L. and Barrett, F.J. (2001) 'Appreciative Inquiry: the power of the unconditional positive question' in Reason and Bradbury (eds.)

Ludema, J.D., Wilmot, T.D. and Srivasta, S. (1997) 'Organisational Hope: reaffirming the constructive task of social and organisational inquiry', in *Human Relations* 50/8: 1015-1052

Lukka, P., Locke, M. and Soteri-Proctor, A. (2003) *Faith and Voluntary Action: community values and resources* (London: Institute of Volunteering research).

Lyotard, J.F. (1981) 'What is Postmodernism?' in Kearney and Rainwater (eds.).

Mahajan, G. (1997) *Explanation and Understanding in the Human Sciences* (New Delhi: Oxford University Press).

Mammen, K. (1998) 'The Sustainability Connection', in *The Hindu,* 1 March, 1998, Kochi.

Mangham, I. and Overington, M. (1987) *Organisations as Theatre* (Chichester: John Wiley).

Mannheim, K. (1960) *Ideology and Utopia*: an introduction to the sociology of knowledge (London: Routledge and Kegan Paul).

Marriott, M. (ed.) (1990)) *India Through Hindu Categories* (New Delhi: Sage).

Martin, J. and Powers, M. E. (1983) 'Truth or Corporate Propaganda; the value of a good war story' in Pondy, Frost and Morgan (eds.).

Martin J., Feldman, M., Hatch, M.J. and Sitkin, S. B. (1983) 'The Uniqueness Paradox in Organisational Stories', *Administrative Science Quarterly,* 28: 438-453.

Massey, L. (1994) *Women, Philanthropy and the Infant Welfare Movement: a study of the north Islington maternity centre and school for mothers 1913-1923* unpublished MA thesis (Canterbury: University of Kent).

McAuley, J. (1997) 'Book Review: Work, Death and Life Itself: essays in management in organisations', by Seivers, B. in *Human Relations* 50/4 469-482.

McCall, M.W. and Lombardo, M.M. (1978) 'Leadership' in McCall and Lombardo (eds.).

McCall, M.W. and Lombardo, M.M. (eds.) (1978) *Leadership: where else can we go?* (NC: Duke University Press).

McSweeney, B. (2002) 'Hofstede's Model of National Cultural Differences and Consequences: a triumph of faith a failure of analysis', in *Human Relations* 55/1: 89-118.

Mead, G. (2001) *Unlatching the Gate: realising my scholarship of living enquiry,* PhD thesis available on http://www.bath.ac.uk/~edsaj/mead.html> accessed 28/01/06.

Mehta, J.L. (1992) J.L. 'Mehta on Heidegger, Hermeneutics and the Indian Tradition' in Jackson (ed.).

Mei, T. (1996) *Hermeneutics and the Unity of Truth* paper given to the Temenos Academy, London.

Menski, W. (1996) 'Hinduism' in Morgan and Lawton (eds.).

Merrifield, J. (2003) 'Learning and Citizenship' in Schwabenland (ed).

Miller, D. (ed.) (1995) *Popper Selections* (NJ: Princeton University Press).

Miller, D.L. (1988) 'Orestes: myth and dream as catharsis' in Campbell (ed.).

Miller, D.F. (1999) *Neighbours and Strangers,* (New Delhi: Rainbow).

Miller, D.F. (1990) *The Reason of Metaphor,* (New Delhi: Sage).

Miller, E. (1993) *From Dependency to Autonomy* (London: Free Association Books).

Milne. J. (2001) *Thought and Reality in Nagarjuna,* lecture delivered to theTemenos Academy, London.

Mintzberg, H. (2004) *Managers Not MBAs* (London: Prentice Hall).

Mintzberg, H. (1989) *Mintzberg on Management* (London: Macmillan).

Mintzberg, H. (1987) 'Crafting Strategy', in *Harvard Business Review,* 7: 66-75

Mody, N. (1996) 'Ecology and Underdevelopment' in Surendra et al (eds.).

Mohanty, C.T. (2003) *Feminism Without Borders*: *decolonizing borders, practicing Solidarity* (New Delhi: Zubaan).

Mohanty, C.T. (1991a) 'Cartographies of Struggle: third world women and the politics of feminism' in Mohanty et al (eds.).

Mohanty, C.T. (1991b) 'Under Western Eyes: feminist scholarship and colonial discourses' in Mohanty et al (eds.).

Mohanty, C.T.,Russo, A. and Torres, L. (eds.) (1991) *Third World Women and the Politics of Feminism* (Bloomington and Indianapolis: Indiana University Press).

Morgan, G. (1993) *Imaginization: the art of creative management* (Thousand Oaks: Sage).

Morgan, G. (1988) *Riding the Waves of Change* (San Francisco: Jossey Bass).

Morgan, G. (1986) *Images of Organization* (London: Sage).

Morgan, G. (1983a) 'More on Metaphor: why we cannot control tropes', in *Administrative Science Quarterly,* 28/4: 601-607.

Morgan, G. (1980) 'Paradigms, Metaphors and Puzzle Solving', in *Administrative Science Quarterly,* 25: 605-622.

Morgan, G., Frost, P.J. and Pondy, L.R. (1983) 'Organisational Symbolism' in Pondy et al (eds.).

Morgan, P. and Lawton, C. (eds.) (1996) *Ethical Issues in Six Religious Traditions* (Edinburgh: Edinburgh University Press).

Morris, M.B. (1977) *An Excursion into Creative Sociology* (Oxford: Basil Blackwells).

Moya, P.M.L. and Hames-Garcia, M.R. (eds.) (2003) *Reclaiming Identity: realist theory and the predicament of postmodernism,* (Hyderabad: Orient Longman).

Murthy, P.N. (1998) 'Leadership: a comparative study of Indian ethos and western Concepts', in *Journal of Human Values* 4 /2: 155-165 (New Delhi: Sage).

Nadkarni, M.V. (1996) 'Politics of Environment: issues and responsibilities' in Surendra et al (eds.).

Nandy, A. (2002) *Time Warps: silent and evasive pasts in Indian politics and religion* (London: Hurst and Co.).

Nandy, A. (2001) *An Ambiguous Journey to the City* (New Delhi: Oxford University Press).

Nandy, A. (1999) *Traditions, Tyranny and Utopias: essays in the politics of awareness* (New Delhi: Oxford India Paperbacks).

Nandy, A (1995) *The Savage Freud and other essays on possible and retrievable selves* (NJ: Princeton University Press).

Nandy, A. (1983) *The Intimate Enemy: loss and recovery of self under colonialism* (New Delhi: OUP).

Narayan, S. (ed.) (1995) *State Panchayat Acts: a critical review* (New Delhi: VANI).

Narayan, U. (2000) 'Essence of Culture and a Sense of History: a feminist critique of cultural essentialism, in Narayan and Harding (eds.).

Narayan, U. and Harding, S. (eds.) *De-centering the Center: philosophy for a multicultural, postcolonial, and feminist world* (Indiana: Bloomington University Press).

Naydlor, J. (1997) *The Divine Origin of the World: Creation Myth as Imaginative Metaphysics,* unpublished lectured delivered to the Temenos Academy, London.

NCVO, (1998) *Research Quarterly,* 1 (London: NCVO).

Nelson, C. and Grossberg, L. (eds.) (1988) *Marxism and the Interpretation of Cultures* (Houndsmill: Macmillan).

Norton, M. (1997) 'What's Due South?', in *Trust Monitor* summer (London: Directory of Social Change).

Norton, M. (1996) *The Not-for-Profit Sector in India* (Kent: Charities Aid Foundation).

Norton, M. (1995) *The Voluntary Sector in India: issues and ideas for its future* (London: Centre for Innovation in Voluntary Action).

Nystrom, H. (1995) 'Creativity and Entrepreneurship' in Ford and Gioia (eds.).

Okin, S.M. (2000) 'Feminism, Women's Rights and Cultural Differences' in Narayan and Harding (eds.).

Ortony, A. (ed.) (1979) *Metaphor and Thought* (Cambridge: Cambridge University Press).

Osborne, S. (1994) *The Once and Future Pioneers* (York: Joseph Rowntree Foundation and Birmingham: Aston Business School).

Oswick, C. and Grant, D. (eds.) (1996) *Organisational Development: metaphorical explorations* (London: Pitman).

Pandey, G. (2000) 'Voices From the Edge: the struggle to write subaltern histories' in Chaturvedi (ed.).

Pandey, S.R. (1991) *Community Action for Social Justice* (New Delhi: Sage).

Pareek, V. and Rao, T.V. (1981) *Learning From Action* (Ahmedabad: Ahmedabad Public Systems Group).

Parikh, I. (1990) 'Indian Value Dilemmas in Management Roles' in Kanungo and Jaeger (eds.).

Parvada, V. (1996) *Interpreting Corruption: elite perspectives in India* (New Delhi: Sage).

Patel, R. (1998) 'Voluntary organizations in India: motivations and roles' in Dantwala et al (eds.).

Paton, R. (2003) *Managing and Measuring Social Enterprises* (London: Sage).

Pattanaik, S. (2000) *Use of Theatre for Trauma Counselling: with special reference to super cyclone, 1999* (Orissa: Natya Chetana).

Perri 6 (1994) 'The Question of Independence': working paper 3: *The Future of Charities and the Voluntary Sector* (London: Demos).

Perriton, L. and Reynolds, M. (2004) 'Critical Management Education: from pedagogy of possibility to pedagogy of refusal?' in *Management Learning* 35/1: 61-77.

Pines, M. (ed.) (1992) *Bion and Group Psychotherapy* (London: Routledge).

Pintchman, T. (1994) *The Rise of the Goddess in the Hindu Tradition* (NY: SUNY Press).

Poll, C. (2003) 'Putting the Humanity Back Into Human Services' in *Community Living* 17/1: 24-25.

Pondy, L.R., Boland, R. and Thoman, H. (eds.) (1988) *Managing Ambiguity and Change* (NY: John Wiley and Sons).

Pondy, L.R. (1983) 'The Role of Metaphors and Myths in Organisation and in the Facilitation of Change' In Pondy et al (eds.).

Pondy, L.R., Frost, P.J. and Morgan, G. (eds.) (1983) *Organisational Symbolism* (CT: JAI).

Pondy, L.R. (1978) 'Leadership is a Language Game' in McCall and Lombardo (eds.).

Popper, K. (1995) *Popper Selections* Miller in (ed.).

Post, V. and Preuss, H.J. (1997) 'No Miracle Weapon for Development: the challenges facing NGOs in the 21st century', in *Development and Co-operation:* 6.

Parish, S. (1996) *Hierarchy and its Discontents* (PA: University of Pennsylvania Press).

Power, M. (1990) 'Modernism, Postmodernism and Organisation' in Hassard and Pym (eds.).

Prasad, A. (2003) 'The Gaze of the Other: postcolonial theory and organizational analysis in Prasad (ed.).

Prasad, A. (ed.) (2003) *Postcolonial Theory and Organizational Analysis* (New York: Palgrave).

Pratt, J., Locke, M. and Burgess, T. (1994) *Popper and Problems, Problems with Popper* (London: Centre for Institutional Studies (CIS), University of East London).

Putnam, R.D. (2000) *Bowling Alone: the collapse and revival of American community* (NY: Simon and Schuster).

Putnam, R.D. (1993) *Making Democracy Work* (NJ: Princeton University Press).

Putnam, R.D. and Feldstein, L.M. (2003) *Better Together: restoring the American community* (NY: Simon and Schuster).

Radtke, H.L. and Stam, H.J. (eds.) (1994) *Power/Gender: social relationships in theory and practice* (London: Sage).

Raine, K. (1985) *Defending Ancient Springs* (Ipswich: Golgonooza Press).

Ramanujan, A.K. (1990) 'Is There an Indian Way of Thinking?' in Marriott (ed.).

Ramchandran, V. (1998) 'Voluntary Organisations: professional agency or sub-contractor' in Dantwala et al (eds.).

Ranganathanda, S. (1996) *The Essence of Indian Culture* (Kolkata: Advaita Ashram).

Rathna Reddy, A.V. (1997) *The Political Philosophy of the Bhagavad Gita* (New Delhi: Sterling).

Rawlinson, H.G. (1952) *India: a short cultural history* (London: Cresset).

Reason, P. and Bradbury, H. (eds.) (2001) *Handbook of Action Research* (London: Sage).

Reason, P. and Rowan, J. (eds.) (1981) *Human Enquiry in Action; developments in new paradigm research* (London: Sage).

Reed, B. (1995) *The Psychodynamics of Life and Worship* (London: The Grubb Institute).

Reed, B. (1991) *Professional Management* (London: The Grubb Institute).

Reed, M. and Hughes, M. (eds.) (1992) *Rethinking Organisations* (London: Sage).

Reedy, P. (2001) 'Keeping the Black Flag Flying: anarchy, utopia and the politics of nostalgia' *Proceedings of the Conference on Critical Management Studies* 11-13 July, Manchester.

Richman, P. (ed.) 2001) *Questioning Ramayanas* (Berkeley: University of California Press).

Ricoeur, P. (1992a) *An Interview with Jonathon Kee,* Talking Liberties Series: London: Channel 4, broadcast on 27/7/92.

Ricoeur, P. (1992b) *Hermeneutics and the Human Sciences* in Thompson, J. (ed. and trans.) (Cambridge: Cambridge University Press).

Ricoeur, P. (1991a) *From Text to Action: essays in hermeneutics* in Blamey, K and Thompson, J (ed. and trans.) (London: Athlone Press).

Ricoeur, P. (1991b) *A Ricoeur Reader: reflection and imagination* Valdes, M. (ed. and trans.) (Hemel Hempstead: Harvester Wheatsheaf).

Ricoeur, R. (1988) *Time and Narrative:* Vol. 3 Blaney, K. and Pellaur, D. (eds. and trans.) (Chicago: University of Chicago Press).

Ricoeur, P. (1986) *Lectures on Ideology and Utopia* Taylor, G.H. (ed.) (NY: Columbia University Press).

Ricoeur, P. (1978) *The Rule of Metaphor* (London: Routledge and Keegan Paul).

Ricoeur, P. (1976) *Interpretation Theory: discourse and the surplus of meaning* (Fort Worth: Texas Christian University Press).

Ricoeur, P. (1974) *Social and Political Essays* Stewart, D. and Bien, J. (eds.) (Athlone: Ohio University Press).

Ricoeur, P. (1965) *History and Truth* Kelbley, C. (trans.) (Evanston: Northwestern University Press).

Robinson, A. (1997) *Contrasting Visions: Tagore, Nehru and the West* lecture given at Gresham College, 24/11, London.

Robinson, C. (1998) 'Sita and Savitri: traditional role models and the Indian women's movement' ,*Proceedings of the Conference of the Dharam Hinduja Institute of Indic Research,* 3-4 July: Cambridge.

Robson, P., Begum, N. and Locke, M, (2003) *Working Towards User-Centred Practice in Voluntary Organisations* summary version available on http://www,publicnet. co.uk/publicnet/fe031007.htm accessed on 20/03/-6 (Policy Press: Bristol).

Robson P., Dawson, J. and Locke, M. (1997) 'User Involvement in the Control of Voluntary Organisations' in *Findings* 93/ May (York: Joseph Rowntree Foundation).

Ros, E. and Visscher, K. (1997) 'An Arena of Storytelling; narrative analysis of the Fokker crisis'in *Proceedings of the Conference: Organising in a Multi- Voiced World* 4-6 June, Leuven: European Institute for Advanced Studies in Management (EIASM).

Rose, K. (1995) *Where Women are Leaders: the SEWA movement in India* (London: Zed Books).

Rosen, S. (1987) *Hermeneutics as Politics* (NY: Oxford University Press).

Rosenman, M. (2004) 'Human Services and Civic Engagement' *Proceedings of the Conference on Researching the Voluntary Sector* September, Sheffield, NCVO.

Rosenman, M. (2000) 'Morphing into the Market: the danger of missing mission' *Proceedings of the Conference on Researching the Voluntary Sector* September, Birmingham, NCVO.

Rowan, J. and Reason, P. (1988) *Human Enquiry in Action: developments in new paradigm research* (London: Sage).

Sackmann, S.A. (1991) *Cultural Knowledge in Organisations* (Thousand Oaks: Sage).

Said, E. (2004) *Power, Politics and Culture: interviews with Edward Said* in Viswanathan (ed.).

Said, E. (1993) *Culture and Imperialism* (London: Chatto and Windus).

Sainath, P. (1997) 'In Kerala They Never Stopped Fighting' in *Lifelong Learning in Europe,* 4: 242-244.

Salamon, L.M. and Anheier, H.K. (1996) *The Social Origins of Civil Society; explaining the nonprofit sector cross nationally)* Working Paper of the

Johns Hopkins Comparative Nonprofit Sector Project (MD: Johns Hopkins University).

Salamon L.M. and Anheier, H.K. (1992a) *Towards an Understanding of the International Nonprofit Sector* Working Paper #1, Johns Hopkins Comparative Nonprofit Sector Project (MD: Johns Hopkins University).

Salamon L.M. and Anheier. H.K. (1992b) *In Search of the Nonprofit Sector: the question of definitions* Working Paper #2, Johns Hopkins Comparative Nonprofit Sector Project (MD: Johns Hopkins University).

Sassoon, A.S. (1996) 'Complexity, Contradictions, Creativity: transitions in the voluntary sector' in *Soundings* 4:183-194.

Satterthwaite, J., Martin, W. and Roberts, J. (eds.) (2006) *Discourse, Resistance and Identity Formation* (London: Trentham).

Saunders, S. (1998) 'What Does the Term "Voluntary Sector" Mean?' in *Third Sector* 2 April, 1998

Schein, E. (1991) 'The Role of the Founder in the Creation of Organisational Culture' in Frost et al (eds.).

Schein, E. (1986) *Organisational Culture and Leadership* (San Francisco: Jossey Bass).

Scheurich, J.J. (1997) *Research Methods in the Postmodern* (London: Falmer Press).

Schon, D. (1979) 'Generative Metaphor: a perspective on problem solving' in Ortony (ed.).

Schwabenland, C. (2006a) 'Leaders' founding stories as creation myths' in Boje et al (eds.).

Schwabenland, C. (2006b) 'Stories, Mythmaking and the Consolation of Success' in Satterthwaite et al (eds.).

Schwabenland, C. (ed.) (2003) *Participation North and South* (London: The Elfrida Press).

Schwabenland, C. (2001) *Creation Mythology in Voluntary Organisations in the UK and India* unpublished PhD thesis (London: University of East London).

Schwabenland, C. (ed.) (1999) *Relationships in the Lives of People with Learning Difficulties* (London: The Elfrida Press).

Schwabenland, C. (1996) *Metaphors of Creativity in the Voluntary Sector,* unpublished MA dissertation (London: University of East London).

Schwabenland, C. (1995) 'Breaking Creative Deadlock' in *VOICE* June (Harrow: Association of Chief Executives of National Voluntary Organisations).

Scott, D. and Usher, R. (eds.) (1996) *Understanding Educational Research* (London: Routledge).

Scott, J.W (1991) 'The Evidence of Experience' in *Critical Inquiry* Vol. 17: 773-797.

Seabrook, J. (1996) *Notes From Another India,* (East Haven: Pluto).

Sen, J. and Tandon, R. (1992) 'The Role of Voluntary Action: response to structural adjustment and re-colonisation' *Report of a National Seminar in Thiruvananthapuram*, 21-22 April, (New Delhi: VANI).

Sen, A. (2005) *The Argumentative Indian: writings on Indian history, culture and identity* (London: Allen Lane).

Sen, A. (2003) *On Ethics and Economics* (New Delhi: Oxford India Paperbacks).

Sen, S. (1997) 'Voluntary Organisations in India: historical development and institutional genesis' in *Institutional Development* IV/ii: 29-40.

Sen, S. (1993) *Defining the Nonprofit Sector: India*, Johns Hopkins Comparative Nonprofit Sector Project Working Paper #12 (MD: Johns Hopkins University).

Sengupta, S. (1998) 'Role of Panchayat and Non-Governmental Organisations in Rural Development (Seen Through Rabindranath's Social Philosophy and Actions)' in All India Council for Mass Education and Development (ed.).

Sethi, H. (1998) 'Evolving Accountability of Voluntary Organisations' in Dantwala et al (eds.).

Shah, R.C. (2001) *Ancestral Voices* (West Malling: Temenos Academy).

Shah, R.C. (1997) 'The Voice of the Sacred in our Time' *Proceedings of the Conference The Voice of the Sacred in our Times* 20-21 January, New Delhi, The Temenos Academy and the Indira Gandhi Centre for the Arts.

Siememsma, F. (1998) 'Hopes, Tensions and Complexity: Indian students' reflections on the relationship of values to management education and future career options' in *Journal for Human Values,* Vol.4/#2 .

Sievers, B. (1997) 'Accounting for the Caprices of Madness; narrative fiction as a means of organisational transcendence' in *Proceedings of the Conference: Organising in a Multi-Voiced World* 4-6 June, Leuven: European Institute for Advanced Studies in Management (EIASM).

Sievers, B. (1995) 'Beyond the Surrogate of Motivation' in Smircich and Calas (eds.).

Sievers, B. (1994) *Work, Death and Life Itself* (Berlin: de Gruyter).

Sievers, B. (1990) 'The Diabolization of Death: some thoughts on the obsolescence of mortality in organisation theory and practice' in Hasssard and Pym (eds.).

Simons, K. (2000) *Life on the Edge* (Brighton: Pavilion).

Singer, W. (1997) *Creating Histories: oral narrative and the politics of history making* (New Delhi: Oxford University Press).

Singh, A. (1994a) *Report of the Task Forces* (New Delhi: VANI).

Singh, A. (ed.) (1994b) 'Nagarpalika (74th Amendment) Act, 1992: the role of voluntary organisations' *Proceedings of the National Workshop* 14-15 May, Mumbai, VANI.

Singh, R. (!997) *Women Reborn* (New Delhi: Penguin).

Sivakumar, Mr. (1997) 'Financial and Legal Aspects for Voluntary Organisations' in *Conference Report* organised by the Gandhigram Dindigal District, and the Centre for Worldwide Solidarity, Secunderabad, India.

Smart, N. (1997) *Dimensions of the Sacred* (London: Fontana).

Smircich, L. (1983a) 'Organisation as Shared Meanings' in Pondy et al (eds.).

Smircich, L. (1983b) 'Concepts of Culture and Organisational Analysis' in *Administrative Science Quarterly,* 28: 339-358.

Smircich, L. and Morgan, M. (1995) 'Leadership: the Management of Meaning' in

Smircich and Calas (eds.).

Smircich, L. and Callas, M. (eds.) 1995 *Critical Perspectives on Organisation and Management Thinking,* (Aldershot: Dartmouth).

Smith, K.S. and Simons, V.M. (1983) 'A Rumpelstilskin Organisation: metaphors on metaphors in field research' in *Administrative Science Quarterly,* 28: 377-392

Smith-Sreen, P. (1995) *Accountability in Development Organisations: experiences of women's organisations in India* (New Delhi: Sage).

Sontag, S. (1988) *AIDS and its Metaphors* (London: Penguin).

Sorge, A. (1983) 'Culture's Consequences: book review' in *Administrative Science Quarterly* 28: 625-629.

Spivak, G. (2003) 'Discussion: an afterward on the new subaltern' in Chatterjee and Jeganathan (eds.).

Spivak, G. (2000) 'The New Subaltern: a silent interview' in Chaturvedi (ed.).

Spivak, G.C. (1999) *Towards A History of the Vanishing Past: a critique of postcolonial reason* (Cambridge MA: Harvard University Press).

Spivak, G.C. (1996) 'Subaltern Studies: deconstructing historiography' in Landry and Maclean (eds.).

Spivak, G.C. (1988) 'Can the Subaltern Speak?' in Nelson and Grossberg (eds.).

Stone-Mediatore, S. (2003) *Reading Across borders: storytelling and knowledges of resistance* Basingstoke: Palgrave Macmillan).

Stone-Mediatore, S. (2000) 'Chandra Mohanty and the Revaluing of "Experience"' in Narayan and Harding (eds.).

Sugirtharaj, F. (1997) 'A People-Centred Vision From Asia', in *Development,* 40/4: 54- 57.

Sundar, P.(1997) 'Women and Philanthropy in India', in *Voluntas* 7/4: 412-417.

Surendra, L. (1996) 'Science, History and Responsibility' in Surendra et al (eds.).

Surendra, L., Schindler, K. and Ramaswamy, P. (eds.) (1996) *Stories They Tell: a dialogue among philosophers, scientists and environmentalists* (Madras: Earthworm).

Tandon, R. (undated) *Voluntary Organisations Yesterday and Today* (New Delhi: PRIA).

Tandon, R. (2003) 'Overcoming Disability: lessons from participatory research' in Schwabenland (ed.).

Tandon, R.(1993) *Forms of Organisations: square pegs in round holes* (New Delhi: PRIA).

Tandon, R. (1991a) *Holding Together: collaborations and partnerships in the real world* (New Delhi: PRIA).

Tandon, R. (1991b) *Management of Voluntary Organisations* (New Delhi: PRIA).

Tandon, R. (1989) *NGO Government Relations: a source of life or a kiss of death?* (New Delhi: PRIA).

Tandon, R. (1981) 'Dialogue as Inquiry and Intervention' in Reason and Rowan (eds.).

Tandon, R. and Mohanty, R. (2002) *Civil Society and Governance* (New Delhi: PRIA).

216   *Stories, Visions and Values in Voluntary Organisations*

Tandon, R., Chaudhary, A., Dhar, S., Pandey, R., Narula, N. and Kapoor, A. (1991) *Voluntary Development Organisations in India* (New Delhi: PRIA).

Tandon, R., Kanhere, V., Gothoskar, S. and Lugo, O. (no date) *How to Conduct Participatory Research Among Women* (Delhi: PRIA).

Thekaekara, M. and Thekaekara, S. (1994) *Across the Geographical Divide* (London: Centre for Innovation in Voluntary Action).

Thompson, J.P. (1981) *Critical Hermeneutics: a study in the thought of Paul Ricoeur and Jurgen Habermas* (Cambridge: Cambridge University Press).

Tomlinson, F. (2005) 'Marking Difference: placing the category "refugee" in diversity discourses' *Proceedings of the conference on Critical Management Studies* 1-3 July, Cambridge.

Tsoukas, H. (ed.) (1994) *New Thinking in Organisational Behaviour* (Oxford: Butterworth Heinemann).

Turner, B. (1992) 'The Symbolic Understanding of Organisations' in Reed and Hughes (eds.).

Turner, B. (1991) (ed). in *Organisational Symbolism* (Berlin: de Gruyter).

Usher, R. (1996) 'A Critique of the Neglected Epistemological Assumptions of Educational Research' in Scott and Usher (eds.).

Vaill, P.B. (1996) *Learning as a Way of Being: strategies for survival in a world of permanent white water* (San Francisco: Jossey Bass).

Vail, P.B. (1989) *Managing as a Performing Art* (San Francisco: Jossey Bass).

Vandenbroek, P. and Wouters, A. (1997) 'Harnessing the Power of Narrative: the dilemma of normative scenarios' *Proceedings of the Conference: Organising in a Multi-Voiced World* 4-6 June, Leuven: European Institute for Advanced Studies in Management (EIASM).

Van den Haar, D. and Hosking, D.M. (2004) 'Evaluating Appreciative Inquiry: a relational constructivist perspective, in *Human Relations* 57/8: 1017-1036.

Voluntary Action Network India (VANI) (1994-95, 1995-96, 1996-97) *Annual Reports* (New Delhi: VANI).

VANI (1998) 'Action Plan to Bring About a Collaborative Relationship Between Voluntary Organisations and the Government' *Proceedings of the Conference* 7-8 March, New Delhi, VANI.

Van Leeuwan, T.M. (1981) *The Surplus of Meaning: ontology and eschatology in the philosophy of Paul Ricoeur* (Amsterdam: Rodopi).

Varma, P.K. (1999) *The Great Indian Middle Class* (New Delhi: Penguin).

Viswananthan, G. (ed). (2004) *Power, Politics and Culture: interviews with Edward Said* (London: Bloomsbury).

Vittal, N. (2001) 'Ethics in Public Administration' in *Journal of Human Values* 7/1: 5-20 (New Delhi: Sage).

Vivekananda, S. (1993) *Swami Vivekananda's Addresses at the World's Parliament of Religions, Chicago, 1983* (Kolkata: Advaita Ashrama).

Vivekananda, S. (1997) *My India, The India Eternal* (Kolkata) The Ramakrishna Mission of Culture).

Von Franz, M.L. (1995) *Creation Myths* (Boston: Shambala).

Wallace, B. (2004) *Gender Revisited? meanings of sustainability from the perspective of community based social entrepreneurs* unpublished MA dissertation (London: University of East London).

Weber, M. (1958) *The Religions of India: the sociology of Hinduism and Buddhism* Gerth, H.H. and Martindale, D. (trans.) (Glencoe, IL: Free Press).

Weber, M (1958) *The Protestant Ethic and the Spirit of Capitalism* Parsons,T. (trans.) (NY: Schreibners & Sons).

Weick, K.E. (1995) *Sensemaking in Organisations* (Thousand Oaks: Sage).

Werner, K. (1994) *A Popular Dictionary of Hinduism* (Richmond: Curzon).

Westwood, R. and Linstead, S. (eds.) *The Language of Organization* (London: Sage).

Wierzbicka, A. (1998) 'German "Cultural Scripts": public signs as a key to social attitudes and cultural values' in *Discourse and Society* 9/2: 241-283.

Wilkins, A. (1983) 'Organisational Stories as Symbols Which Control the Organisation' in Pondy et al (eds.).

Wilkins, A.L. and Ouchi, W.G. (1983) 'Efficient Cultures: exploring the relationship between culture and organisational performance' in *Administrative Science Quarterly* 28: 468-481.

Wilkinson, R. (1996) *Unhealthy Societies: the afflictions of inequality* (London: Routledge).

Yeats, W.B.(1968) *Selected Poetry* (London: Papermac,Macmillan).

Yunus, M. (2003) *Banker to the Poor: the story of the Grameen Bank* (London: Aurum Press).

Zachariah, M. and Sooryamoorthy, R. (1994) *Science for Social Revolution? The Achievements and Dilemmas of a Development Movement; the Kerala Sastra Sahitya Parishad* (London: Zed Books).

Index